The Bukharan Crisis

CENTRAL EURASIA IN CONTEXT SERIES

Douglas Northrop, Editor

The Bukharan Crisis

A CONNECTED HISTORY OF 18TH-CENTURY CENTRAL ASIA

SCOTT C. LEVI

UNIVERSITY OF PITTSBURGH PRESS

Published by the University of Pittsburgh Press, Pittsburgh, Pa., 15260
Copyright © 2020, University of Pittsburgh Press
All rights reserved
Manufactured in the United States of America
Printed on acid-free paper
10 9 8 7 6 5 4 3 2 1

Cataloging-in-Publication data is available from the Library of Congress

ISBN 13: 978-0-8229-4597-0
ISBN 10: 0-8229-4597-5

Cover art: "Canonnier Persan," from *Moeurs, usages et costumes de tous les peuples du monde*, Auguste Wahlen. Brussels: La Librairie historique-artistique, 1843.
Cover design: Joel W. Coggins

To Karen, Madeleine, and Abigail

CONTENTS

ACKNOWLEDGMENTS
ix

NOTE ON GEOGRAPHIC TERMINOLOGY
xiii

INTRODUCTION
3

ONE
BUKHARA IN CRISIS
12

TWO
SILK ROADS, REAL AND IMAGINED
37

THREE
THE EARLY MODERN SILK ROAD
70

FOUR
THE CRISIS REVISITED
120

CONCLUSION
173

BIBLIOGRAPHY
181

INDEX
201

ACKNOWLEDGMENTS

This book emanates from a number of questions that remained unanswered after I completed work on my first book in 2002. At that time, my research on Indian merchants in Central Asia led me to conclude that Indian commercial firms centered in and around the city of Multan developed a network that extended into Central Asia in the mid-sixteenth century, grew dramatically in the seventeenth century, and remained in place even through the end of the nineteenth century. Turning attention to recent work in Chinese, Russian, and other related fields of history, I found additional scholarship that chipped away at the notion that early modern Central Asia sank into a lengthy period of isolation and decline as a product of the collapse of the so-called Silk Road trade (which itself is a problematic concept, for reasons addressed below). Clearly, that notion needed to be reconsidered.

At the same time, the Bukharan Khanate suffered a well-documented crisis in the first half of the eighteenth century. This crisis was severe, so much so that it culminated in the Bukharan Khanate's collapse in 1747. But if the evidence indicates that the causal factor behind this crisis was not economic isolation from the early modern globalizing world, what was it?

It was partly with that question in mind that I turned my attention to the history of Khoqand, a Central Asian state that began to emerge in the Ferghana Valley during the first half of the eighteenth century, at the very time that the Bukharan Khanate descended into crisis. In an effort to understand why it was that Khoqand came into being just as Bukhara fell, I made my way back to Tashkent to begin working in the Central Asian sources. In the United States, I explored ways to connect early modern Central Asia to larger discussions and debates in Eurasian and world history. What I had initially intended to constitute a few discreet discussions peppered throughout my book on Khoqand gradually expanded into a chapter, and then several chapters, and then this book.

In grappling with multiple fields of history and the ways that world historical processes influenced developments in early modern Central Asia, I have amassed a considerable number of debts. To recognize the institutions first, I am profoundly grateful to the National Endowment for the Humanities Division of Research Programs for the support that enabled me to spend the 2013–2014 academic year fully engaged in the discussions and debates that unfold in the pages to come. I am also deeply indebted to Samuel Jubé, Aspasia Nanaki, and the rest of the administrators and staff of the Institut d'Études Avancées de Nantes for hosting me, and my family, during the 2016–2017 academic year and providing an exceptionally stimulating environment in which to develop this project and bring it nearly to completion. The other residential fellows at the IÉA provided valuable insights, comments, critiques, and suggestions on my ideas. I would single out Lakshmi Subramanian for her interest in this manuscript, her feedback on an early draft, and her valued friendship. I am also grateful to the editors of *History Compass* for granting permission to revisit the article that I published in that journal and present it here in a revised and expanded format.

Over the years, a number of colleagues have offered me the opportunity to present my (often still quite rough) work in progress as I was thinking my way through the questions that I aimed to engage. I am grateful for those opportunities and for the valuable feedback and criticisms that I received. I thank Mark Elliot and the Inner Asia Forum at Harvard University; Peter Holquist, Siyen Fei, and the Pennsylvania University Department of History's Annenberg Seminar; James Millward and the Sawyer Seminar on Critical Silk Road Studies at Georgetown University; John Woods, Russell Zanca, and the Committee on Central Eurasian Studies at the University of Chicago; Abbas Amanat and the participants of the workshop titled "The Caspian in the History of Early Modern and Modern Eurasia," at Yale University; Robert Crews and the Stanford University Center for Russian, East European and Eurasian Studies; Ed Schatz and the Centre for European, Russian and Eurasian Studies at the University of Toronto; Nile Green, the UCLA Center for India and South Asia, and the UCLA Central Asia Initiative; and Matthew Romaniello at the University of Hawai'i at Manoa.

This manuscript has benefited from discussions with and the reviews of a number of colleagues and friends. I would like to express my deep gratitude to Adeeb Khalid, James Millward, Erika Monahan, and Hal Parker, who generously read and commented on the full manuscript at various stages of preparation. I am grateful to John Brooke for his guidance in navigating the fields of environmental history and climate science, and for his help preparing the chart that appears in chapter four. My conversations with Alisher

Khaliyarov have been very helpful in sharpening discussions on Central Asian economic history. Other colleagues who read drafts of parts of the manuscript include Greg Anderson, Wayne Lee, Geoffrey Parker, Thomas Welsford, and Ying Zhang. The manuscript has also benefited from discussions with Nick Breyfogle, Stephen Dale, Joe Guilmartin, Jane Hathaway, Nurten Kılıç-Schubel, Victor Lieberman, Alexander Morrison, Geoffrey Parker, Beatrice Penati, Eric Schluessel, Ron Sela, Gulchekhra Sultonova, and Ilya Vinkovetsky. I am deeply appreciative to the anonymous reviewers for their comments, criticisms, and helpful suggestions for ways to improve the manuscript. I thank Bill Nelson for his careful work in preparing the many maps that illustrate this volume. I also thank Douglas Northrop for his support for this project as well as Peter Kracht at the University of Pittsburgh Press for supervising the production of this book.

This publication has been made possible, in part, through support from the Center for Slavic and East European Studies at the Ohio State University through funding from the International and Foreign Language Education division of the U.S. Department of Education. I am also grateful to the Ohio State University Department of History and the College of Arts and Sciences for their additional support.

One hot summer afternoon on a family outing to Conner Prairie Interactive History Park in Fishers, Indiana, I had the good fortune to step into a model of an early nineteenth-century frontier trading outpost and meet Mr. Mitchell Meigs. At that time, I was in the midst of working my way through the historiography of the early modern Military Revolution, preparing the discussion that appears in chapter four. Mr. Meigs generously spent a substantial part of his afternoon instructing me in the fine details of flintlock muskets, and his lesson included giving me the opportunity to load, fire (three times!), and clean the 1816 British model that he had in his possession. I have learned much about early gunpowder weapons technologies and their impact on societies through books and museum exhibits, but there was no substitute for the instruction and hands-on experience that Mitchell Meigs gave me that day.

Most of all, I thank my wife, Dr. Karen Spierling, and our two fantastic daughters, Madeleine and Abigail. Time and again Karen has had to juggle the demands of her own career as a historian and the needs of our family as I have been too single-mindedly focused on advancing this project and bringing it to completion. I dedicate this volume to them.

NOTE ON GEOGRAPHIC TERMINOLOGY

The discussions in this volume focus on Central Asia, but they also take readers far afield. I have therefore worked to include maps that will provide readers a helpful orientation as the chapters take readers from the Mediterranean Sea to Beijing, and from Moscow even to the Deccan Plateau, in southern India. But especially as it relates to Central Asian history, geographic terminology can be unfamiliar and confusing, and so it is helpful first to introduce some of the terms that readers will encounter.

In contemporary scholarly literature, **Central Asia** is most commonly used to refer to the region that includes the modern nation-states of Uzbekistan, Kyrgyzstan, Tajikistan, Turkmenistan, and (in a historical context, southern) Kazakhstan. In the early modern era, this includes the territory of the Bukharan Khanate in **Mā'warā al-nahr** ("that which lies beyond the river"), the Arabic iteration of the earlier Greco-Latin **Transoxania**, as well as the later Khivan Khanate in the Khwarezmian oasis and the Khanate of Khoqand centered in the Ferghana Valley. Beyond the territories of the former Soviet republics, Central Asia is also usually considered to encompass northeastern Iran, northern Afghanistan, and, farther to the east, **Altishahr**. Often referred to in historical terms as Chinese or **Eastern Turkestan**, Altishahr (literally "Six Cities") is the famed location of Kashgar, Yarkand, and the other agricultural oases in the southern stretches of the modern Chinese province of **Xinjiang**. Collectively, the common feature among these areas is that they include the majority of the region's agricultural lands. But one should not lose sight of the fact that early modern Central Asia had abundant pastureland interspersed among its agricultural oases, and nomadic populations inhabited those areas even into the twentieth century.

Farther to the north, pastoral-nomadic peoples themselves were the dominant populations of **Inner Asia**, the term most often used to identify the vast open grasslands, or steppe, that stretches from the area north of the Black Sea (modern Ukraine) eastward to Mongolia, including much of Kazakhstan as well as **Jungaria** (also Zungaria and Dzungaria) in northern Xinjiang. In historical sources, this veritable ocean of grass is often referred to as the **Dasht-i Qipchaq**, or the Qipchaq Steppe, after the Qipchaq Turks, who were once its principal occupants. Stretching over a distance of seven time zones, Inner Asia is enormous in its size, much larger than Central Asia. But more expansive still is **Central Eurasia**, a term that references the full Eurasian interior and includes all of Central Asia and Inner Asia, as well as the Caucasus and the Tibetan Plateau.

Readers with an interest in Central Asia's historical geography will find great value in Yuri Bregel, *An Historical Atlas of Central Asia* (Leiden: E. J. Brill, 2003). I have used that resource extensively in the preparation of the maps for this volume.

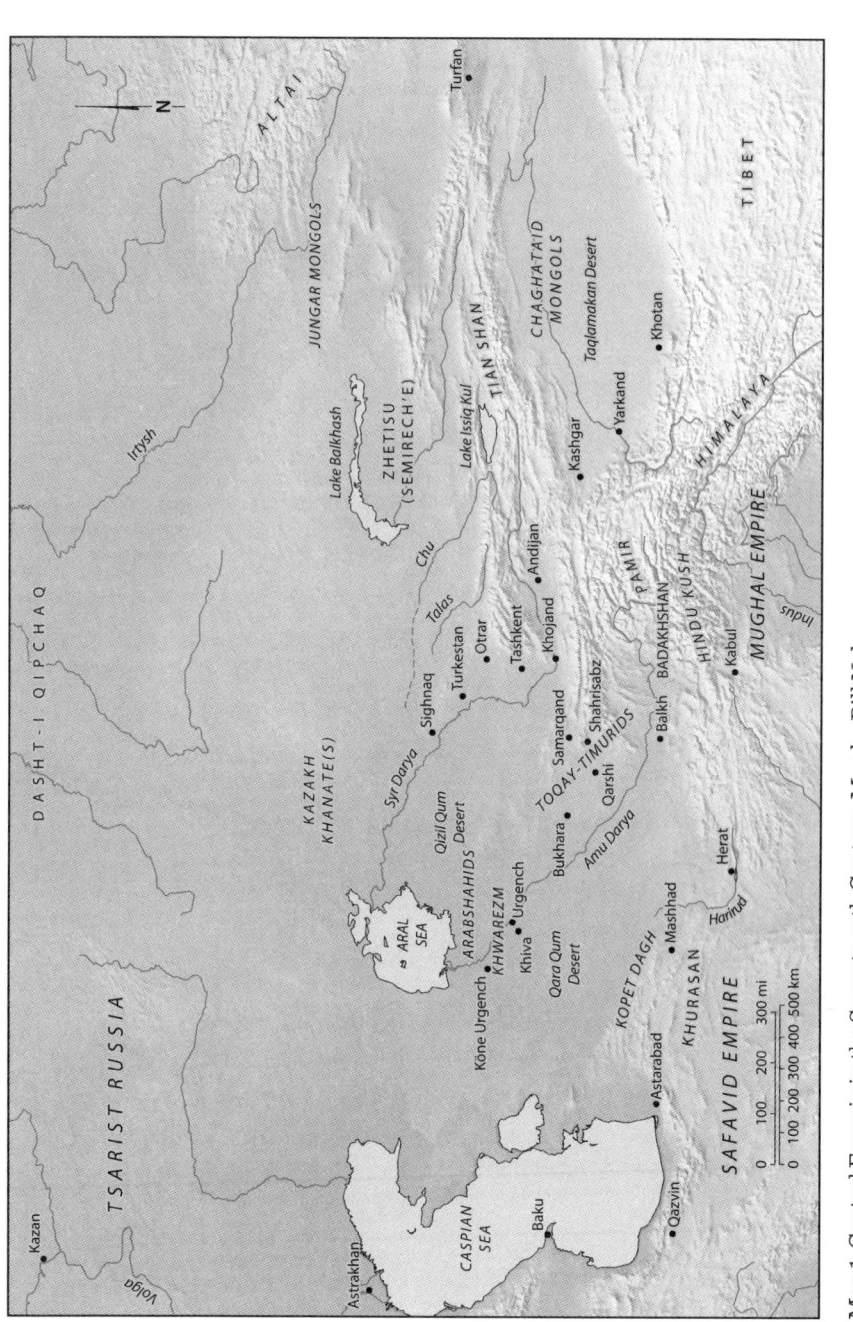

Map 1. Central Eurasia in the Seventeenth Century. Map by Bill Nelson.

The Bukharan Crisis

INTRODUCTION

This is a book about Central Asia's place in the early modern world. The discussions that follow reference a few original sources, but only a few. The central concerns here are historiographic, and so I have endeavored to pull back the lens to provide the reader a vantage point from which it is possible to appreciate a number of ways that the field of Central Asian history has changed in recent decades.

Studies of Central Asia that address the period between the sixteenth and nineteenth centuries have traditionally portrayed the region as passive, disengaged, and pushed to the margins of the rapidly globalizing early modern world. This interpretation is changing, but even today, efforts to explain the region's eighteenth-century crisis remain focused on the presumed collapse of Central Asia's historical role in overland Eurasian trade. Whether scholars have framed this in terms of the end of Central Asia's privileged position in the Silk Road trade or something else, they have generally assumed that economic isolation not only undermined the Bukharan Khanate but caused the region as a whole to suffer a civilizational decline. The chapters that follow aim to demonstrate that such notions, while highly resilient, are built upon erroneous understandings of Central Asian commercial history.

The resilience of these notions can be attributed to several factors. One is the relatively small amount of attention that scholars in the field have directed to questions of commercial history. In fact, there has yet to be a study that applies a sufficiently broad scope to determine even the key features of Central Asia's early modern commercial economy.[1] It is therefore not surprising to find that no researcher has yet stepped forward to compare Central Asia's early modern commercial economy with earlier periods. Without a deeply critical and evidence-based analysis of such questions, we are ill-prepared to understand how overland trade through Central Asia in the seventeenth and eighteenth centuries compared to the fourteenth and fifteenth centuries, or earlier periods. So, how is one even to measure economic decline? The discussions that follow do not fully fill these lacunae.[2] They do, however, demonstrate that Central Asia's mediatory role in transcontinental trade continued throughout the early modern era, and that in some measurable ways commercial activities actually increased.

That is not to say that early modern Central Asians did not suffer political and economic crises or that, in the first half of the eighteenth century, the Bukharan Khanate did not fall into decline. These points are well documented in the historical sources, they are presented quite clearly in the secondary literature, and they are also discussed below. However, this book argues that the concept of decline is a blunt instrument that cannot be applied with any precision to the region as a whole, that early modern Central Asia was far from isolated, and that the actual causal factors propelling the Bukharan crisis have remained obscure. In an effort to resolve that problem, chapter four of this study advances a new explanation for the weakening of the Bukharan Khanate in the seventeenth century, its fall into a state of deepening crisis during the early eighteenth century, and its utter collapse in the wake of the Persian invasions of the region in 1737 and 1740.

There was no single causal factor that precipitated these developments. The available evidence points to several factors, some interrelated and some independent, some of which unfolded over long periods of time while others shocked the region more abruptly, and all of which converged in the

---

1. Audrey Burton merits recognition for her exceptional contributions to this field, though she brings her study to an end at the turn of the eighteenth century. See Audrey Burton, *The Bukharans: A Dynastic, Diplomatic and Commercial History, 1550–1702* (New York: St. Martin's Press, 1997).
2. I aim to advance research into these question with a forthcoming collaborative project: Scott C. Levi, ed., *The Oxford Research Encyclopedia for Asian Commercial History*.

early eighteenth century to the great detriment of the Bukharan Khanate and those dependent upon it. In Central Asia, the first half of the eighteenth century was a harsh period of transition that confronted regional power holders with great uncertainties and a number of insurmountable challenges. At the same time, one must ask just how far this crisis extended. While this convergence of historical processes drove political decentralization and unleashed hardship and rebellion in some areas, new opportunities emerged elsewhere in the region. The history of early modern Central Asia was neither simple nor straightforward. History rarely is.

With that point in mind, this book presents a number of thematic discussions pertaining to Central Asia's early modern historical context. Chapter one, "Bukhara in Crisis," introduces the crisis that led to the ultimate collapse of Chinggisid rule in the Bukharan Khanate and surveys the ways that historians have endeavored to explain it. Chapter two, "Silk Roads, Real and Imagined," critically examines the Silk Road concept and illustrates a number of ways that shallow and romanticized interpretations of Central Asia's commercial history have misdirected researchers toward certain modes of thought and away from others. Extinguishing the specter of isolation, chapter three, "The Early Modern Silk Road," turns attention to the networks of commodity exchange, circulation of precious metals, merchant diasporas, and other structures that kept early modern Central Asians economically engaged with the large agrarian civilizations on the Eurasian periphery. This chapter draws on a number of recent studies to demonstrate that, far from falling into decline, commercial relationships that one could cast as a continuation of the fabled "Silk Road" exchange remained quite active throughout this period, and in some ways even expanded. Chapter four, "The Crisis Revisited," returns attention to the Bukharan crisis and endeavors to connect local events to a number of larger historical processes. While previous treatments of this subject have focused on describing the crisis, this chapter aims to identify the causal factors behind it, explaining why it occurred when it did and its uneven impact across the region.

This book takes stock of recent achievements in multiple historical fields, examines how that research collectively demonstrates that Central Asia remained a connected region throughout the early modern era, and identifies a number of ways that those connections shaped Central Asia's occasionally tumultuous historical trajectory. Put another way, it aims to demonstrate that a connected histories approach can provide valuable perspectives and insights into important questions pertaining to early modern Central Asian history that one cannot satisfactorily address by relying on local sources alone.[3] While scholars have long worked to connect Central Asia to other regional histories in some periods—the Mongol era represents an obvious example—there have been very few such efforts for the early modern era.

In the Central Asian context, I use *early modern* to refer to the roughly three and a half centuries between the end of Timurid rule (c. 1500) in Central Asia and the beginning of Russian imperial expansion into the region in the nineteenth century. In the past, some have categorized this as the "Uzbek Period" in Central Asian history. Such a label is not objectionable insofar as it draws attention to the dominant role that the Uzbek tribes came to play in Central Asian politics. However, I have a strong preference for *early modern* as it focuses attention on the ways that Central Asia was intertwined with larger Eurasian, and global, historical processes throughout these centuries.

Like all efforts at periodization, the concept of an "early modern period" is a device, an effort to identify common themes within a particular era and set them against distinctive themes that characterize the previous era (medieval) and the following one (modern). Its identification and application are complicated, not least because many of the processes that are considered to be the defining features of the early modern period remained obscure, even invisible, to those living at the time. Nobody in seventeenth-century England would have identified themselves as living in the early modern era, just as nobody in second-century Rome would have recognized themselves as living in antiquity. A further complication is that, for some time, the application of the early modern era as a discreet historical period within Europe, much less beyond it, encountered some resistance. In a 1998 essay on the subject, sociologist Jack Goldstone critiqued the term as "neither 'early,' nor 'modern'" and, insofar as it was designed to reference a period prefacing the emergence of the modern world, wholly inapplicable beyond Europe and poorly applicable within it.[4]

But even as Goldstone was drafting his critique, other scholars were refining their use of the term in ways that have made it more useful for European history, and more versatile beyond the European context. This

---

3. For a detailed source-based treatment highlighting the use of power and authority in Manghit state-building efforts beyond the capital in the period after the Bukharan crisis, see Andreas Wilde, *What is Beyond the River? Power, Authority and Social Order in Transoxania, 18th and 19th Centuries*, 3 vols. (Wien: Österreichischen Akademie der Wissenshchaften, 2016).
4. Jack Goldstone, "The Problem of the 'Early Modern' World," *Journal of the Economic and Social History of the Orient* 41, no. 3 (1998): 249.

has involved deemphasizing the need for the early modern period to serve as a springboard into a rigidly defined (and overtly Eurocentric) modernity on the one hand and highlighting the importance of increased mobility and tightening interconnections across regions on the other. In his work on connected histories, Sanjay Subrahmanyam provides one example of just this type of approach.[5] Victor Lieberman has since articulated another example, one that emphasizes parallel social, political, and other historical developments ("Strange Parallels") unfolding in apparent synchrony across great spaces.[6]

In recent years, there has been a blossoming of new works that use early modernity as a framework for global analysis. Jerry Bentley, a founder of the field of world history, studied the development of the early modern era as a distinct period in European history and then, from the 1980s, its subsequent expansion onto the global stage.[7] Bentley takes stock of Goldstone's critique, but surveying the notion's merits he finds that "the early modern era was a genuinely global age not so much because of any particular set of traits that supposedly characterized all or at least many lands, but rather because of historical processes that linked the world's peoples and societies in increasingly dense networks of interactions and exchange, even if those interactive processes produced very different results in different lands."[8] The historian of Mughal India, John Richards, provides an especially pertinent example from the perspective of environmental history in his study of the ways that four quite specific early modern dynamics led to dramatic environmental changes across the globe. Of these, the most relevant to recent discussions in Central Asian history is a significant increase in the use of land for agriculture spurred by global market trends.[9]

For his part, Goldstone himself has more recently adopted a decidedly different view of what constitutes the early modern world. This course

---

5. Sanjay Subrahmanyam, "Connected Histories: Notes Towards a Reconfiguration of Early Modern Eurasia," *Modern Asian Studies* 31, no. 3 (1997): 735–62.
6. Victor Lieberman, *Strange Parallels*, vol. 1, *Integration on the Mainland* (Cambridge: Cambridge University Press, 2003); vol. 2, *Mainland Mirrors: Europe, Japan, China, South Asia, and the Islands: Southeast Asia in Global Context, c. 800–1830* (Cambridge: Cambridge University Press, 2009).
7. Jerry H. Bentley, "Early Modern Europe and the Early Modern World," in *Between the Middle Ages and Modernity: Individual and Community in the Early Modern World*, ed. Charles H. Parker and Jerry H. Bentley (Lanham, MD: Rowman and Littlefield, 2007), 13–31.
8. Bentley, "Early Modern Europe," 20, 22.
9. John F. Richards, *Unending Frontier: An Environmental History of the Early Modern World* (Berkeley: University of California Press, 2003).

correction is at least partly in response to Lieberman, whose work, Goldstone finds, presents "an overwhelming case that the attributes of 'early modernity'—administrative centralization under a state bureaucracy, consolidation of national vernacular languages, the emergence of politicized ethnicity throughout the influence of more powerful states using those languages, extensive commercialization and the growth of urban centers, economic and population growth—were pan-Eurasian phenomena, and in no way made European states distinctive."[10] That said, what constitutes early modernity is necessarily, as Bentley suggests, "a messy affair," as the historical processes that linked distant regions affected disparate societies in different ways.[11] Some of the characteristics Goldstone identifies are relevant to discussions of Central Asia, while others are not. Nevertheless, exploring these linkages stands to offer new insights into historical developments throughout the early modern era.

Following in the footsteps of the late Joseph Fletcher, a Central Asianist and one of the earliest voices in the discussion of what constitutes early modern world history, I am intrigued by the "horizontal continuities" across the Eurasian space during this period, and the ways in which the early modern context informed historical developments in Central Asia.[12] By focusing on Eurasian connections rather than regional distinctiveness, Fletcher argued, historians would find that "in the seventeenth century, for example, Japan, Tibet, Iran, Asia Minor, and the Iberian peninsula, all seemingly cut off from one another, were responding to some of the same interrelated, or at least similar demographic, economic, and even social forces."[13] Fletcher went on to identify a set of seven features that he found applicable to the early modern world, and which represent a framework for global analysis. These are: (1) population growth, (2) a steady increase in the rate of transregional interactions, (3) a sustained pattern of urbanization, (4) the rise of larger and more powerful "urban commercial classes," (5) religious reformations, (6) peasant rebellions, and (7) a gradual decline in the nomadic way of life.[14]

---

10. Jack Goldstone, "New Patterns in Global History," *Cliodynamics: The Journal of Theoretical and Mathematical History* 1, no. 1 (2010): 97.
11. Bentley, "Early Modern Europe," 23.
12. Joseph Fletcher, "Integrative History: Parallels and Interconnections in the Early Modern Period, 1500–1800," *Journal of Turkish Studies* 9 (1985): 37–57. Fletcher's ideas are addressed in greater depth in chapter two.
13. Fletcher, "Integrative History," 38.
14. Fletcher, "Integrative History," 40–56.

I consider such lists to be works in progress and do not cling too tightly to them.[15] Looking back over the decades since Fletcher drafted his essay, which was very near the end of his life in 1984, one finds that subsequent research has proven some of his features to be more resilient than others. The chapters in this book emphasize certain aspects of this discussion—most notably a general trend in population growth (while accounting for certain important exceptions), an increase in transregional interactions, a general trend toward urbanization (again, noting certain exceptions), and the decline of nomadism, partly in response to advancements in military technologies. At the same time, today, one might be more inclined to attribute the proliferation of early modern peasant rebellions to recurrent famines caused by the global climate crisis of the seventeenth century, and not the emerging Marxist aspirations that one might have expected to encounter in the literature of the 1970s and 1980s. That is not to say that a general increase in peasant rebellions is not a feature of the early modern era. Rather, it is to suggest that efforts to identify the causal factors propelling such historical patterns—and even the patterns themselves—are destined to change as historical research continues to advance and reshape our understanding of the past.

At the same time, scholars working on Central Asian history both within the region and in the West have approached their research with a tendency to examine Central Asia between the sixteenth and nineteenth centuries either in relative isolation from larger Eurasian historical processes or vis-à-vis the region's relations with *one* of the neighboring agrarian empires on the Eurasian periphery, most often doing so from the perspective of the outside power. Scholarly studies of Central Asian states have used earlier states in the same geographic zone as their framework for comparison: drawing a linear (in Fletcher's model, "vertical") connection between the nineteenth-century Bukharan Amirate and the sixteenth-century Shibanid state, for example. Their conclusions have often supported Soviet-era interpretations that the Uzbek tribal dynasties were in essence feudal states led by tribal chieftains who exhibited little in terms of innovative abilities. This leaves unasked the larger question of whether the subjects of our research were sensitive to developments external to their homeland—and

---

15. John F. Richards identified six "distinct but complementary large-scale processes" as defining features of early modernity in "Early Modern India and World History," *Journal of World History* 3, no. 2 (1997): 198. See also the similar list presented in Bentley, "Early Modern Europe," 22–27. These overlap in some ways with those that Fletcher proposed, but not completely.

here I mean political, commercial, technological, intellectual, artistic, spiritual, and more—and if they were, to what extent. Such a rhetorical question should be an easy one to answer. The historical literature is rich with information that demonstrates not only an awareness of broader developments across Eurasia and the globe but a sustained thirst for just this type of knowledge. This was true even during the heart of the eighteenth-century Bukharan crisis.[16]

Prior to venturing into the thematic discussions below, there is one final point that merits attention. In examinations of the remarkable cultural exchanges that unfolded along the trans-Eurasian commercial and communication networks commonly referred to as the Silk Road, the framework for analysis most often emanates from the field of Chinese studies. I argue that there is much to be gained by shifting the gravitational center of analysis westward and exploring more fully the ways that Central Asians mediated the transmission of merchandise, knowledge, technology, and more among multiple Eurasian societies. This is relevant for studies of the Silk Road in the classical period, and it is equally relevant for the early modern era. It was during this period that the great Inner Asian nomadic empires came to an end; localized crises in the eighteenth century contributed to the end of more than five centuries of political legitimacy based on Chinggisid ancestry; political authority in the region became divided among multiple compact and competing tribal dynasties, and then by Chinese and Russian imperial powers; the outside world experienced a rapid and unprecedented degree of integration and technological advancement; and, I argue, Central Asians became even more deeply integrated into that outside world in new ways, though not always willingly and not always in ways that were to their advantage.

From the perspective of Central Asian history, understanding the ways that early modern Central Asian societies were linked to larger world historical processes is critical if we are to reach an improved understanding of such historical problems as: the causal factors behind the eighteenth-century crisis; why it occurred when it did, and in the ways that it did; its impacts beyond the governing administration; the ways that the Uzbek tribes and other groups within Central Asia responded to the crisis; and how their decisions influenced their historical trajectory as they moved out of crisis and into a new era. I examine these questions in an effort to shed new

---

16. For one brief but enlightening example, see Devin DeWeese, "Muslim Medical Culture in Modern Central Asia: A Brief Note on Manuscript Sources from the Sixteenth to Twentieth Centuries," *Central Asian Survey* 32, no. 1 (2013): 3–18.

light on ways that global political, economic, technological, and environmental developments influenced states and society in early modern Central Asia. No less important is that they provide a foundational framework from which researchers working in Russian, Chinese, and other fields of history can better understand Central Asians' agency in shaping historical events and processes far beyond their homeland, at the seemingly remote heart of the early modern Silk Road.

ONE

BUKHARA IN CRISIS

For almost 140 years, Samarqand had been the capital of our family. Then came the Uzbeks, a foreign foe, and it slipped from our hands.

Zahir al-Din Muhammad Babur

Zahir al-Din Muhammad Babur (1483–1530), the last Timurid prince to rule from the family's ancestral capital of Samarqand, wrote the lines in the epigraph to this chapter in reference to his defeat in the year 1500 at the hands of the Chinggisid ruler Muhammad Shibani Khan (1451–1510). Babur and his followers were able to recover Samarqand the following year, but their victory was short lived. Shibani Khan and his Uzbek forces returned soon thereafter, and Babur was left with no choice but to withdraw. Outmatched in Central Asia, Babur made his way southward, where he eventually established himself as ruler over Kabul. In 1526, he and his followers launched a campaign into north India, defeated the Lodi Afghan sultans of Delhi at the Battle of Panipat, and gave rise to a new Timurid state—the celebrated Mughal Empire in India (1526–1857).[1]

Babur's legacy in India is well known, but these events had lasting implications for Central Asian peoples as well. During his lifetime, historical

---

Epigraph: Zahir al-Din Muhammad Babur, *The Bábar-náma: Being the Autobiography of the Emperor Bábar, the Founder of the Moghul Dynasty in India*, facsimile of the Hyderabad manuscript, ed. Annette S. Beveridge, E. J. W. Gibb Memorial Series, 1 (London: Luzac and Co., 1971 [1905]), f. 85a.

1. For a full account, see the biography of Babur by Stephen F. Dale, *Babur: Timurid Prince and Mughal Emperor, 1483–1530* (Cambridge: Cambridge University Press, 2018).

sources indicate that Muhammad Shibani Khan was known alternatively as Shaybak (Wormwood), Shah Bakht, and Shahibeg. The name by which he came to be remembered is highly significant, though, as it signals his descent from Chinggis Khan (d. 1227) through his grandson Shiban, one of the many children born to Chinggis Khan's eldest son, Jochi. In the thirteenth-century context of the rise of the Mongol Empire, Jochi's questionable parentage had been an obstacle to legitimacy—he was born to Chinggis Khan's wife Börte some nine months after the rival Merkit had kidnapped her. As time passed, that association diminished in importance, and Jochi's descendants were accepted as the proper Chinggisid rulers of the Qipchaq Khanate, now more widely known as the Golden Horde.

Meanwhile, other historical processes unfolded in ways that would have a profound influence on life in the Golden Horde, and Central Eurasia more broadly. In the fourteenth century, the Islamic religion, long present in the region, began to take root among the Turkic subjects of the Jochid ruler Uzbek Khan (r. 1313–1341).[2] In the fifteenth century, these Turkic-Muslim "Uzbek" tribes were under the Chinggisid leadership of Abu'l Khayr Khan (1412–1468), and they came to occupy the southern steppe region that includes much of what is today Kazakhstan. In 1456, another nomadic steppe power, the non-Chinggisid Mongol Qalmaqs (also Oirats), confronted and defeated Abu'l Khayr Khan and his Uzbek followers. In the wake of that loss, two Chinggisid leaders, Janibeg and Giray (also Kiray, or Qaray), famously abandoned Abu'l Khayr Khan to set out on an independent path as vagabonds, or brigands (a status known as *qazaqlïq*). Their followers came to be known as the Kazakh-Uzbeks, then simply as the Kazakhs.[3] The Uzbek tribes were left in disarray, but several decades after the Kazakh separation they were once again united under the leadership of Abu'l Khayr Khan's grandson, Muhammad Shibani Khan. In the late 1490s, these Shibanid Uzbeks turned their attention southward to Transoxania.

Shibani Khan's Uzbek invasion would represent the final large-scale nomadic migration from the steppe into the sedentary zone. To be sure, nomadic incursions would continue in the sixteenth, seventeenth, and eigh-

---

2. See Devin DeWeese, *Islamization and Native Religion in the Golden Horde: Baba Tükles and Conversion to Islam in Historical and Epic Tradition* (University Park: Penn State University Press, 1994).
3. For an innovative study of the early history of the Kazakhs, see Joo-Yup Lee, *Qazaqlïq, or Ambitious Brigandage, and the Formation of the Qazaqs: State and Identity in Post-Mongol Central Eurasia* (Leiden: E. J. Brill, 2016). For a treatment of Babur's time as a refugee in light of this concept, see Dale, *Babur*, 23–51.

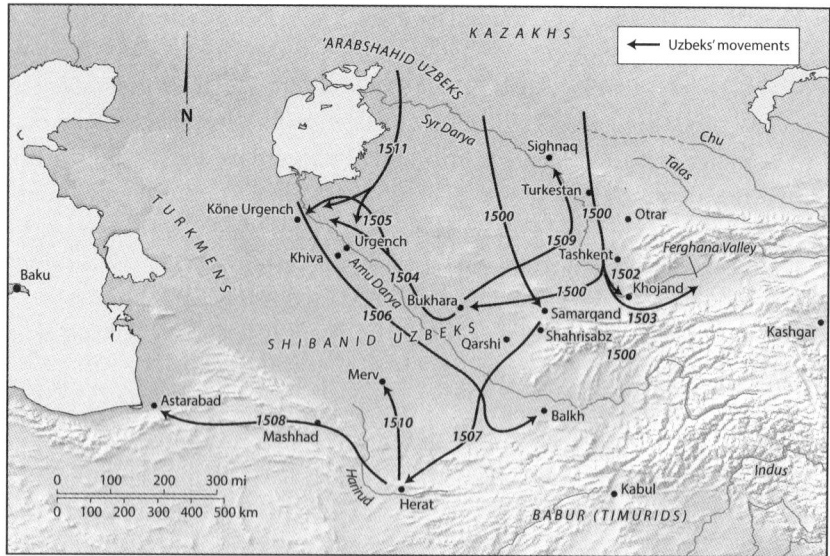

Map 2. The Uzbek Invasion of Transoxania. Map by Bill Nelson.

teenth centuries. Some of these would be exceptionally large and disruptive, and they are discussed below, but even the largest of these would pale in comparison to the Uzbek invasion. At the turn of the sixteenth century, Shibani Khan led between two hundred thousand and four hundred thousand Uzbeks southward from the steppe into the agricultural zone.[4] Unlike the earlier migrations of the Seljuk Turks of the tenth and eleventh centuries, or the other nomadic steppe peoples who moved southward into and then at least in part passed through Central Asia, the Uzbek tribes occupied the semiarid pastures that stretch between the agricultural oases of Transoxania and northern Afghanistan, and went no farther. Their descendants remain in the region today.

From the beginning of the sixteenth century, the Uzbeks were the dominant political force in the region. Following Muhammad Shibani Khan himself, the Uzbek tribes pushed the Timurids from their capital of Samarqand, then from the region as a whole. After 140 years of Timurid dynastic rule, the Uzbeks restored Chinggisid rule to the region. So began the Bukharan Khanate, an early modern Chinggisid state established by the Shibanids (1500–1599, also referred to as the Abu'l Khayrids), then ruled by another

---

4. The figures come from Bregel, who suggests that his estimate is conservative and the total number may have been higher: Yuri Bregel, "Turko-Mongol Influences in Central Asia," in *Turko-Persia in Historical Perspective,* ed. Robert L. Canfield (Cambridge: Cambridge University Press, 1991), 74 and note.

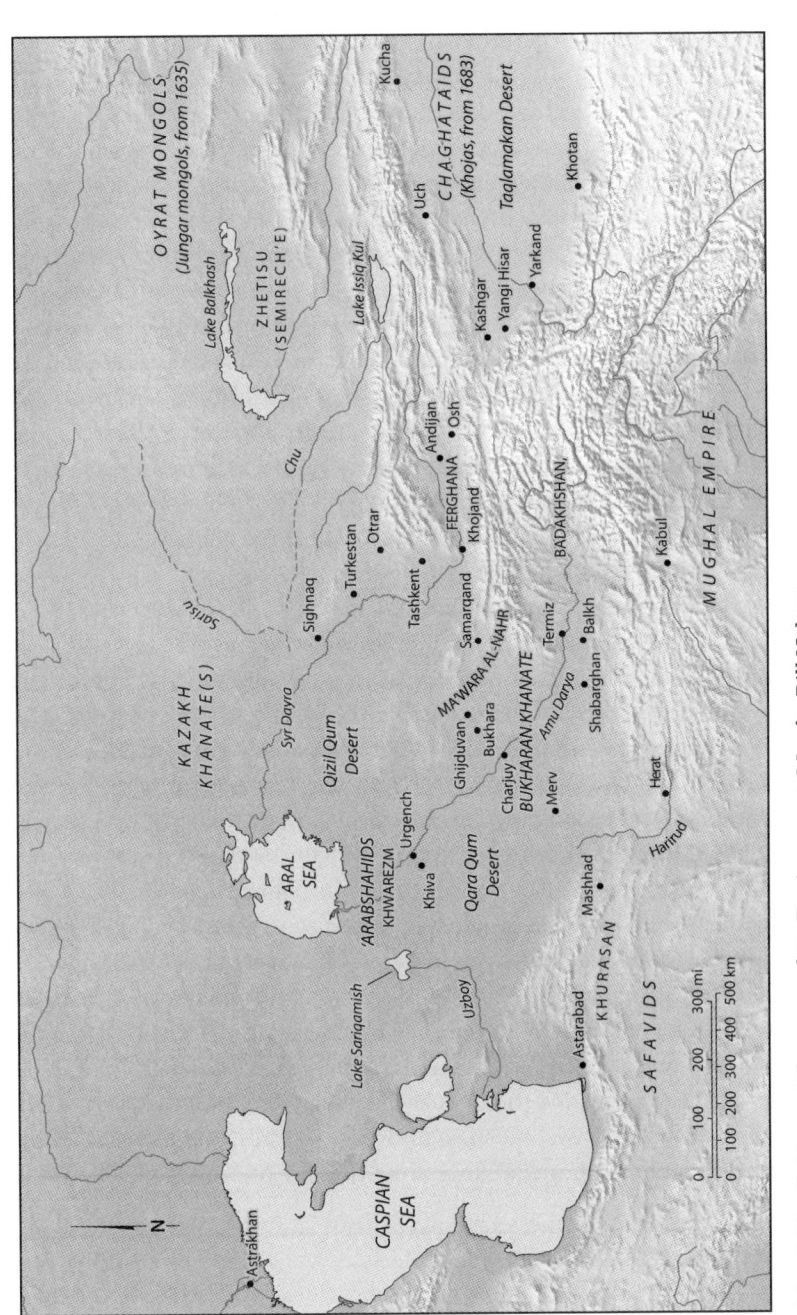

Map 3. The Bukharan Khanate and Its Environment. Map by Bill Nelson.

Jochid dynasty, the Toqay-Timurids (1599–1747/85). From about 1511, a different Shibanid lineage, the so-called 'Arabshahid Shibanids, established their own dynastic rule to the north in Khwarezm.

The Shibanids and their Toqay-Timurid successors governed the Bukharan Khanate following a number of principles deeply rooted in nomadic tradition.[5] Arguably the most important of these was what scholars have designated the appanage system, a method of governance that recognized the senior member of the ruling family as the greatest among equals but divided the state's territorial resources among the ruling family and made the exercise of power a corporate affair. Bukhara emerged as the seat of the senior member of the ruling family, but leading family members ruled over the khanate's other major urban centers of Tashkent, Samarqand, and Balkh, and they enjoyed positions that, while technically subordinate, occasionally reached near autonomy. This fundamentally decentralized system of governance and control over resources set the Bukharans apart from their Mughal, Safavid, and Ottoman neighbors, all of whom applied systems of governance that, while never as centralized as the official chronicles and certain bodies of scholarship would have one believe, aspired for considerably greater centralization than the appanage system would permit.

During the first decades of Shibanid rule in Transoxania, there was a contest of sorts between the leadership in Samarqand and Bukhara to determine which would claim primacy over the other as the dynastic capital. Bukhara emerged dominant, and the city's gradual elevation as a center of political authority brought urban growth and the development of a more active commercial economy. This began in earnest under the supervision of Shibani Khan's nephew, 'Ubaydullah (r. 1533–1539).

In the early years of the sixteenth century, the Sunni Muslim Uzbeks under the leadership of Shibani Khan were also in a pitted struggle against their Shi'a Muslim Safavid rivals in Persia, who were under the leadership of the young Shah Ismail (r. 1501–1524). Although the conflict was primarily a territorial struggle over the rights to Khurasan, it often manifest in religious terms, with the Safavids championing the rightful legitimacy of the family of the prophet and the Uzbeks vilifying them as Shi'a heretics. That confessional rivalry became especially tense in 1507–1508, after the Uzbeks occupied much of Khurasan, including the city of Mashhad, where they

---

5. The best summary of this point is found in R. D. McChesney, "The Chinggisid Restoration in Central Asia: 1500–1785," in *The Cambridge History of Inner Asia: The Chinggisid Age*, ed. Nicola di Cosmo, Allen J. Frank, and Peter B. Golden (Cambridge: Cambridge University Press, 2009), 277–302. For further elaboration, see Wilde's discussion, "Social Order in Uzbek-Dominated Transoxania," in Wilde, *What is Beyond the River*, 1:109–16.

Figure 1.1. Mir Arab Madrasa, Bukhara. Photograph licensed for public use under the Creative Commons: https://commons.wikimedia.org/wiki/File:Mir-i-Arab_Madrasa.jpg. The original color image is reproduced here in black and white.

looted the shrine of the eighth Imam.[6] Soon thereafter, the wheel of fortune began to turn against Shibani Khan. In 1509–1510, the Uzbek forces ventured into a disastrous conflict with the Kazakhs in the steppe. Later that year, Shah Ismail capitalized on the Uzbek defeat by leading his Qizilbash troops in an offensive to retake Khurasan. The Safavids quickly recovered Mashhad, and, as they made their way northward to Merv, Shibani Khan rushed to meet them on the battlefield. With insufficient time to gather reinforcements, the Uzbeks were defeated and Muhammad Shibani Khan died in battle. In celebrating his victory, Shah Ismail ordered that his vanquished foe's right arm be removed from his body and sent to the Timurid prince Babur to signal the impressive reach of the Safavid forces. He ordered that the skin be removed from Shibani Khan's severed head, stuffed with straw, and sent as a warning to the Ottoman Sultan Bayezid II (r. 1481–1512). As for the skull itself, Shah Ismail had it gilded and turned into a bejeweled drinking goblet. This, he kept for himself.[7]

In the power struggle that followed Shibani Khan's gruesome death at

---

6. Abbas Amanat, *Iran: A Modern History* (New Haven: Yale University Press, 2017), 50.
7. Amanat, *Iran*, 51.

BUKHARA IN CRISIS

Figure 1.2. Poi Kalan Masjid. Photograph licensed for public use under the Creative Commons: https://commons.wikimedia.org/wiki/File:View_of_Po-i-Kalyan.jpg. The original color image is reproduced here in black and white.

the Battle of Merv, 'Ubaydullah and his father, Mahmud Sultan, managed to retain governance over Bukhara. Much as Timur and his heirs had adorned Samarqand, Herat, and their other important possessions with grand imperial architectural projects, 'Ubaydullah began to do the same with Bukhara. Early on, he financed the construction of the Poi Kalan Masjid, a large new congregational mosque, and then financed the magnificent Mir-i Arab Madrasa, where he was interred after his death in 1540. During these years, Bukhara gradually rose to become the most powerful of the Shibanid appanages, and, from 1533, 'Ubaydullah was recognized as the senior member of the Shibanid ruling family. From that point onward, Bukhara enjoyed undisputed status as the capital city for both the Shibanid and Toqay-Timurid dynasties. For that reason, the state they ruled has come to be known as the Bukharan Khanate.

That is not to say that the Bukharan Khanate's ascent proceeded without significant obstacles. Indeed, with no clear line of succession in place, 'Ubaydullah Khan's death in 1540 set off a civil war among the Shibanid family, a lengthy struggle that clearly illustrates the precarious nature of the corporate sovereignty associated with the appanage system. In 1557, a young member of the Shibanid clan named 'Abdallah took control of Bukhara and four years later managed to have his father, Iskander (r. 1561–1583), recognized as the senior member of the family. While Iskander was the titular ruler, his political aspirations were modest. He left affairs of the state to his son, and when he died, 'Abdallah Khan II (r. 1583–1598) easily assumed his place on the throne. The nearly four decades during which 'Abdallah Khan served as ruler of Bukhara stand out as a period of exceptional political stability in the region. This period witnessed 'Abdallah Khan's subjugation of a number of rebellious Shibanid lineages, punctuated by decisive military victories over rivals in Samarqand in 1578 and Tashkent in 1582, a sustained effort to encourage transregional commercial relations, successful monetary reforms, territorial expansion into Badakhshan and Khurasan, and the completion of multiple major construction projects within the capital and in the provinces. In 1569, the Shibanid governor of Tashkent financed the construction of the still extant Kukeldash Madrasa, for example.

The Shibanid dynasty would not reap the rewards of these achievements. 'Abdallah Khan's death in 1598 set in motion yet another dynastic crisis. His son and successor, 'Abd al-Mumin, had earned a reputation for tyranny in his youth and upon his father's death began purging his uncles, cousins, and others who would stand in the way of his efforts to rule in Bukhara.[8] It seems likely that 'Abd al-Mumin's objective was to subvert the appanage system and perhaps even abolish the corporate structure through which executive authority was shared among the ruling family. Centralized control over the khanate would have put him on a similar footing to the other Islamic powers at the time and paved the way for him at least to match the Safavids in military strength. But the resistance he encountered was fierce, and the end result was rebellion. In 1599, just six months after 'Abd al-Mumin ascended the throne, he was executed by a group of his own *amirs* (military commanders).

With no sons of 'Abdallah Khan left alive and the other most capable candidates purged, the Uzbek amirs looked elsewhere for leadership. In a recent study of this fraught political transition, Thomas Welsford examines the overlapping systems of loyalties that led the Uzbek tribal leaders to elevate a Chinggisid from a different lineage to rule over the Bukharan Khanate. Some years earlier, in the wake of the Russian conquest of the Astrakhan Khanate in 1556, a Chinggisid named Yar Muhammad fled that state and sought refuge in Bukhara. 'Abdallah Khan welcomed this noble refugee, and the two consolidated their relationship by arranging for 'Abdallah

---

8. See the discussion in McChesney, "Chinggisid Restoration," 297–99.

Figure 1.3. Registan, Samarqand. Photograph by Ekrem Canli, licensed for public use under the Creative Commons: https://commons.wikimedia.org/wiki/File:Registan_square_Samarkand.jpg. The original color image is reproduced here in black and white.

Khan's sister to marry Yar Muhammad's son, Jani Muhammad. With both 'Abdallah Khan and his son 'Abd al-Mumin dead, in 1599 popular support began to shift in favor of these Chinggisids from Astrakhan.[9] Jani Muhammad's ancestry was also traced back to the Jochids of the Golden Horde, but through another of Jochi's sons, Toqay-Timur. For this reason, this second dynasty to rule the Bukharan Khanate is commonly referred to as the Toqay-Timurids and occasionally as the Astrakhanids (also Ashtarkhanids), or the Janids.

In terms of the Bukharan Khanate's state structures, during the Toqay-Timurid period more stayed the same than changed. The territorial holdings that were established during the Shibanid period remained relatively stable. Bukhara retained its status as the principal city and the seat of the senior member of the family, Balkh was the khanate's second most important city, and governance remained a corporate affair. Traditions associated with the Chinggisid *yasa* were applied in relation to certain military and political practices, but both dynasties generally adhered to the principles

---

9. Thomas Welsford, *Four Types of Loyalty in Early Modern Central Asia: The Tūqāy-Tīmūrid Takeover of Greater Mā warā al-Nahr, 1598–1605* (Leiden: E. J. Brill, 2013).

of the Hanafi *madhhab*, or legal school, that were widely accepted in the region to determine *shari'ah*, or Islamic law, and both dynasties endeavored to demonstrate their support for religious institutions. Under the Toqay-Timurids, the construction of monumental Islamic architecture continued, both in the capital city and elsewhere. Following an earthquake that destroyed a caravanserai in Samarqand, for example, the Toqay-Timurid leadership financed the construction of the Sherdar Madrasa and then the Tilakari Madrasa and Masjid. Respectively, these were built facing, and adjacent to, the fifteenth-century Ulugh Beg Madrasa. The three together constitute the Registan public square, which today remains Central Asia's most celebrated architectural monument.

Both Chinggisid dynasties also directed considerable support to Naqshbandiyya Sufi orders. In Bukhara, that was conducted largely through the mediation of the Juybari Sheikhs, a Sufi dynastic family that developed an extensive spiritual and economic presence in the region over the course of the sixteenth and seventeenth centuries, as well as exercised considerable political influence. The collaborative relationship between Sufi orders and the state had deeper historical roots in Central Asia. The Juybari Sheikhs were analogous to the Ahrari Sheikhs who rose to prominence in and around fifteenth-century Samarqand.[10] Both families were highly influential in regional and international politics, controlled extensive tracts of agricultural land, were heavily involved in manufacturing and regional commerce, and orchestrated networks that extended southward as far as the Deccan in India and northward into Russia.

Over the course of the sixteenth and seventeenth centuries, the Shibanid and Toqay-Timurid leadership endured multiple periods of intense internal conflict and wars against neighboring powers, including the Kazakhs, the Khivans, the Safavids, and even the Mughals. But these were interspersed among lengthy periods of relative stability, and they can in no way be said to have defined the political culture of the Bukharan Khanate. That began to change in the latter half of the seventeenth century, as the Uzbek amirs, those who had elevated the Toqay-Timurids to the throne, began to distance themselves from their Chinggisid leadership and increasingly assert their

---

10. For an introduction to the Central Asian Sufi dynasties, see especially R. D. McChesney, *Central Asia: Foundations of Change* (Princeton, NJ: Darwin Press, 1996), 71–115. For additional reading on the Ahraris, see Jo-Ann Gross and Asom Urunbaev, *The Letters of Khwajah 'Ubayd Allah Ahrar and His Associates* (Leiden: E. J. Brill, 2002). For the Juybaris, see Florian Schwarz, "Bukhara and Its Hinterland: The Oasis of Bukhara in the Sixteenth Century in Light of the Juybari Codex," in *Bukhara: The Myth and the Architecture*, ed. Attilio Petruccioli (Cambridge, MA: Aga Khan Program for Islamic Architecture, 1999), 79–92.

autonomy.[11] By the end of the seventeenth century, the Bukharan Khanate was on a decentralizing trajectory with unmistakable signs of a growing political crisis in the capital. This was a crisis from which the Chinggisid leadership would not recover.

THE CRISIS

In 1681, the sixty-seven-year-old ruler of the Bukharan Khanate, 'Abd al-'Aziz Khan (r. 1645–1681), suffered a humiliating defeat at the hands of the Khivan ruler Anusha Muhammad Khan (r. ca. 1662–1685). The Khivans had launched several successful campaigns against Bukharan territories, and despite multiple marriage alliances that aimed to secure peaceful relations, the two Chinggisid dynasties often sparred on the battlefield. But in 1681, Anusha Muhammad's forces actually managed to take possession of the capital city of Bukhara itself. The Bukharan troops who had been campaigning elsewhere quickly returned and recovered the city. But by this time, the aged 'Abd al-'Aziz Khan had grown tired of political leadership and within a few weeks he resolved to abdicate in favor of his younger brother, Subhan Quli Khan (r. 1681–1702), who had long coveted the throne from his de facto independent post in Balkh. Following in the footsteps of many Central Asian rulers who descended from the throne either willingly or unwillingly, 'Abd al-'Aziz Khan left Bukhara for Mecca, and he died two years later.

We will see below that the roots of the Bukharan crisis extend deeper than the 1680s, and that the Khivan campaigns against Bukhara were symptomatic of a larger problem. Numismatic evidence from 'Abd al-'Aziz Khan's reign, for example, indicates that the Bukharan currency had already become severely debased by that time.[12] We will direct closer attention to this evidence in chapter four. For now, it is sufficient to note that 'Abd al-'Aziz Khan was confronted with a fiscal crisis that was already undermining Toqay-Timurid authority and would soon become even more pronounced. At the same time, other evidence complicates this narrative. For example, despite the growing fiscal crisis, both 'Abd al-'Aziz and Subhan Quli managed to divert resources to the beautification of their realms and the construction of monumental architecture, some of which, including the 'Abd al-'Aziz Khan Madrasa in Bukhara, still exist today. But in political terms, 'Abd al-'Aziz Khan's abdication in 1681 can be said to mark the beginning of the end for the Bukharan Khanate.

---

11. McChesney, "Chinggisid Restoration," 301.
12. E. A. Davidovich, *Istoriia monetnogo dela Srednei Azii XVII–XVIII vv. (zolotiie i serebranie moneti Dzhanidov)* (Dushanbe: Akademiia Nauk Tadzhikskoi SSR, 1964), 92.

On the face of it, Subhan Quli Khan's ascension to the throne in Bukhara and the reunification of the khanate's two most important political centers should have signaled a consolidation of Toqay-Timurid authority. But even the reunification of the state was insufficient to overcome the centrifugal forces driving political decentralization, and the increasing recalcitrance of the Uzbek amirs continued to weaken his authority. At the very beginning of his reign, during the calendar years of 1683, 1684, and 1685, Subhan Quli successively appointed four of his sons to serve as heir apparent in Balkh. Subhan Quli Khan had spent decades ruling over Balkh, and one might therefore expect that he enjoyed strong relationships with the local Uzbek amirs. Nevertheless, Robert McChesney notes that all four of his sons were killed, "victims of amirid political infighting."[13]

At the beginning of the seventeenth century, the Uzbek amirs had elevated the Toqay-Timurid leadership to power in place of the Shibanids. Over the course of that century, they had gradually turned away from Bukhara to assert a greater degree of independence.[14] Now, at the end of the century, their efforts focused on consolidating control over the territories that the Bukharan leadership had earlier assigned to them, and that were now slipping out of Bukharan control.[15] Audrey Burton dates the last Bukharan effort to assert control beyond the Syr Darya to 1688, after which a number of formerly Bukharan territories, including the Ferghana Valley, were left effectively independent.[16] That is not to say that the growing state of crisis can be attributed to any singular action, or lack of initiative, on the part of Subhan Quli Khan himself. On the contrary, as we will see, the most important forces driving this crisis were beyond the ability of any single ruler to control.

After more than two decades on the throne in Bukhara, Subhan Quli Khan grew ill and died in 1702. He had initially intended for his grandson, Muhammad Muqim, to succeed him. Already in 1697, he formally announced as much and appointed Muhammad Muqim to serve as ruler of Balkh, the post traditionally assigned to the heir apparent.[17] But at the end of his life, for reasons that remain somewhat unclear, Subhan Quli Khan shifted his

---

13. See Robert McChesney's article in the *Encyclopaedia Iranica*, s.v. "Central Asia in the 10th–12th/16th–18th Centuries," 191.
14. Robert McChesney, "The Amīrs of Muslim Central Asia in the XVIIth Century," *Journal of the Economic and Social History of the Orient* 26 (1983): 33–70.
15. McChesney, "Chinggisid Restoration," 300–301. This process is examined in detail in Wilde, *What is Beyond the River*, 1:120–213.
16. Burton, *Bukharans*, 342.
17. Burton, *Bukharans*, 361.

favor to his son 'Ubaydullah, who, despite being Muhammad Muqim's uncle, was a year his junior.[18] Unlike his nephew, 'Ubaydullah Khan (r. 1702–1711) had been isolated from court life and could boast no practical experience in government. During his short and ill-fated term as khan, he again lost control over Balkh and proved to be completely incapable of overcoming the divisive interests of the Uzbek amirs. His heavy-handed efforts to achieve that goal only further alienated the amirs, and efforts to secure the financial resources necessary to force them into submission (another topic to which we will return below) led to a rebellion in Bukhara in 1708. Three years later, 'Ubaydullah Khan was assassinated. The Uzbek amirs had engineered the rise and fall of a weak khan, and they would do the same with 'Ubaydullah's brother and successor, Abu'l Fayz Khan (r. 1711–1747).

Despite the length of his reign, Abu'l Fayz Khan was no more successful in reasserting Bukharan authority over the Uzbek amirs than his brother or his father had been. In fact, despite several attempts to reverse the process, his administration deteriorated to such an extent that Abu'l Fayz Khan could barely be said to be ruler of anything more than the capital itself. Yuri Bregel summarizes that, under Abu'l Fayz Khan, "the central government lost all its authority, and the country practically disintegrated into a number of tribal principalities."[19] The later decades of his rule witnessed a deepening fiscal crisis, a spike in internal conflicts, rebellion, and multiple invasions from abroad. The central features of this crisis are now well rehearsed in the secondary literature, and a number of them are discussed in greater detail below.[20] What follows represents a brief overview.

In 1708, as 'Ubaydullah Khan suffered a rebellion in Bukhara, the Jungar Mongols launched a campaign westward into Kazakh territories.[21] They

---

18. Burton provides a thorough analysis of the circumstances that led Subhan Quli Khan to elevate 'Ubaydullah over Muhammad Muqim. She suggests that multiple factors were at play, not the least of which is that Subhan Quli had grown concerned that Muhammad Muqim had come under the influence of "low, vulgar men" and others who would lead him into trouble. Burton, *Bukharans*, 361–62.
19. Yuri Bregel, "Central Asia in the 12th–13th/18th–19th Centuries," *Encyclopaedia Iranica*, s.v., 193.
20. For a detailed treatment of the crisis, cf. Wolfgang Holzwarth, "Relations between Uzbek Central Asia, the Great Steppe and Iran, 1700–1750," in *Shifts and Drifts in Nomad-Sedentary Relations*, ed. Stefan Leder and Bernhard Streck (Wiesbaden: Dr. Ludwig Reichert Verlag, 2015), 179–216, and Ron Sela, *The Legendary Biographies of Tamerlane: Islam and Heroic Apocrypha in Central Asia* (Cambridge: Cambridge University Press, 2011), 117–40.
21. For a description of these events in the larger context of Kazakhs' political and commercial relations with their Central Asian neighbors to the south with useful references, see Zhuldyz

had done so before, and they would do so again in 1716, that time temporarily occupying both Turkestan and Tashkent. A few years later, in 1722, a number of Uzbek amirs under the leadership of Ibrahim Keneges in Shahrisabz launched a rebellion in which they claimed independence from Abu'l Fayz Khan in Bukhara and elevated Rajab Sultan, a Chinggisid from Khiva, as their new (puppet) khan in Samarqand. The following year, in 1723, the Jungars launched yet another much larger campaign into Kazakh territories. This displaced a substantial portion of the Kazakhs, many of whom took flight in what has become known as the Aqtaban Shubryndy, "The Barefooted Flight," an event that was so devastating that its memory has become part of the modern Kazakhs' national heritage.[22] In the event, hundreds of thousands of Kazakhs fled, and many of them made their way southward across the Syr Darya and into Bukharan territory. The Kazakh refugees settled in the areas around Samarqand and remained there for several years, during which time they destroyed crops, disrupted urban life, and exacerbated an already difficult situation.[23] Facing famine, the population of Samarqand fled the city, with a reported twelve thousand people seeking refuge as far away as India.[24]

Ibrahim Keneges sought to take advantage of this situation by establishing an alliance with the Kazakh invaders. Ibrahim had several times endeavored to throw off Abu'l Fayz Khan, but the campaigns against Bukhara that he and his Kazakh allies ran between 1723 and 1728 were especially damaging.[25] Assessing his own difficult circumstances, Abu'l Fayz Khan was left with little option but to pursue an alliance with the Jungars. The Bukharans had a history of active commercial engagement with the Buddhist Jungars that stretched back well into the seventeenth century.[26] But the establishment of this interconfessional military alliance against other Muslim pow-

---

Tulibayeva, "The Qazaqs and the Central Asian Principalities in the 18th and the First Half of the 19th Centuries," *Oriente Moderno* 96, no. 1 (2016): 25–45.

22. Michael Hancock-Parmer, "Running Until Our Feet Turn White: The Barefooted Flight and Kazakh National Identity," PhD diss., Indiana University, Bloomington, 2017.
23. For a detailed description of the Kazakh occupation, see Holzwarth, "Relations between Uzbek Central Asia," 193–98.
24. See the study by Timur K. Beisembiev, "Migration in the Qöqand Khanate in Eighteenth and Nineteenth Centuries," in *Migration in Central Asia: Its History and Current Problems*, ed. Hisao Komatsu, Chika Obiya, and John S. Schoeberlein (Osaka: Japan Center for Asian Studies, 2000), 35.
25. For a survey of Ibrahim's efforts to secure independence from Bukhara, see Wilde, *What is Beyond the River*, 1:238–52.
26. Onuma Takahiro, "The Development of the Junghars and the Role of Bukharan Merchants," *Journal of Central Eurasian Studies* 2 (2011): 83–100.

ers represented a situation that Wolfgang Holzwarth describes as "unparalleled in the history of Uzbek Central Asia."[27] As this was unfolding, between 1727 and 1730, the Kazakhs to the north managed to recover their steppe territories from the Jungars, and those who had occupied Transoxania were at last free to return home. They did so, pillaging Bukharan possessions and destroying crops as they withdrew into the steppe. Here again, Holzwarth aptly summarizes that "the Kazakhs had come as refugees and left as conquerors."[28] By this time, what little power there was in Bukhara had shifted from the Chinggisid Abu'l Fayz Khan to the hands of his *ataliq* (*atālīq*, most senior advisor at court) Muhammad Hakim Bey of the Uzbek Manghit tribe.

Events unfolding elsewhere further exacerbated this already deleterious situation. In 1722, a relatively small group of Afghan tribesmen who had rebelled against their Safavid governor in Qandahar ran a campaign into Iran and put the capital of Isfahan under siege. By that time, the Safavid state had deteriorated to such an extent that it was unable to muster an effective defense, and after seven months of siege the Afghans occupied the city.[29] Four years later, the Safavid commander Nadir Quli Beg of the Turkmen Afshar tribe forced the Afghans to withdraw and assumed control of the Safavid government. In 1736, he extinguished the Safavid dynasty and took the throne for himself, ruling as Nadir Shah (r. 1736–1747) of the Afsharid dynasty (1736–1796).

Nadir Shah went to work establishing a strong military state and he rapidly recovered territories that the Safavids had lost to Russia and the Ottomans in the north and west. In 1737, Nadir Shah's son led a sizable force across the Amu Darya to an easy victory against Abu'l Fayz Khan. In 1740, in the wake of his invasion of Mughal India, Nadir Shah himself led a second campaign into Central Asia, targeting both Bukhara and Khiva. He departed with little in terms of spoils—the region offered nothing to compare with the extraordinary amount of wealth he had taken from India the previous year. He did, however, force the Khivans to submit and confirmed the subordinate position of both Abu'l Fayz Khan and his Manghit ataliq, Muhammad Hakim Bey. Nadir Shah returned to Iran with the ataliq's son, Muhammad Rahim Bey, whom he placed in charge of a force of some ten thousand Central Asian cavalry soldiers.[30]

For the next several years, Muhammad Rahim accompanied Nadir Shah on his campaigns, and he remained a loyal companion. Learning of a rebel-

---

27. Holzwarth, "Relations between Uzbek Central Asia," 196.
28. Holzwarth, "Relations between Uzbek Central Asia," 197.
29. Amanat, *Iran*, 126–42.
30. Bregel, "Central Asia in the 12th–13th/18th–19th Centuries," 194.

lion that unfolded in Bukhara in the wake of Muhammad Hakim Bey's death in 1743, Nadir Shah dispatched Muhammad Rahim in order to restore the peace and assume his father's position. In 1747, when news reached Bukhara that Nadir Shah himself had been assassinated, Muhammad Rahim Bey had both Abu'l Fayz Khan and his twelve-year-old son executed, and he personally assumed executive authority over Bukhara, ruling from 1747 to 1758 as ataliq, amir, and khan.[31] The Manghit leadership maintained Chinggisid puppets until 1785, when Muhammad Rahim's cousin Shah Murad (r. 1785–1800) dismissed them and began to draw upon a different model of legitimacy.[32] But in all meaningful ways, the previous decades of crisis brought the Toqay-Timurid dynasty to a ruinous end in 1747.

THE SEARCH FOR CAUSATION

In 1999, I published a historiographical study of scholarship on Central Asia's so-called early modern decline.[33] My survey traced this notion to the Orientalist scholarship of the Russian imperial era. Moving forward, it identified a small degree of discord on the subject among some scholars working within the Soviet academy, primarily regarding the periodization of the decline—whether it should be applied to the entire early modern era, or just part of it—and its extent. But overall, I found that scholars exhibited a tendency to favor the early modern decline model even into the post-Soviet era.[34] In justifying such a position, this scholarship points to

---

31. Andreas Wilde notes that Muhammad Rahim ruled from 1747 to 1756 as *atālīq* and *Amīr Al-Umarā'*, or "commander-in-chief." In 1756, he assumed the title of *khān*. Later Bukharan amirs also adopted the title of khan as well, although the Manghit claim to Chinggisid ancestry passed through their maternal line. See the discussion in Andreas Wilde, "The Emirate of Bukhara," *Oxford Research Encyclopedia of Asian History*, October 2017, http://asianhistory.oxfordre.com/view/10.1093/acrefore/9780190277727.001.0001/acrefore-9780190277727-e-14.
32. Anke von Kügelgen, *Die Legitimierung der mittelasiatischen Mangitendynastie in den Werken ihrer Historiker* (Istanbul: Orient-Institut, 2002). Published in Russian translation as *Legitimatsiia Sredneaziatskoi dinastii Mangitov v proizvedeniiakh ikh istorikov (XVIII–XIX vv.)* (Almaty: Daĭk-Press, 2004).
33. Scott C. Levi, "India, Russia and the Eighteenth-Century Transformation of the Central Asian Caravan Trade," *Journal of the Economic and Social History of the Orient* 42, no. 4 (1999): 519–48. For further discussion, see Scott C. Levi, *The Indian Diaspora in Central Asia and Its Trade, 1550–1900* (Leiden: E. J. Brill, 2002), 21–84, and Scott C. Levi, ed., "Introduction," in *India and Central Asia: Commerce and Culture, 1500–1800* (Delhi: Oxford University Press, 2005), 1–36.
34. Eli Weinerman, "The Polemics between Moscow and Central Asians on the Decline of Central Asia and Tsarist Russia's Role in the History of the Region," *Slavonic and East European Review* 71, no. 3 (1993): 428–81. The work of Ol'ga Chekhovich stands as a notable exception to this rule; see Ol'ga Chekhovich, "O nekotorykh voprosakh istorii Srednei Azii XVIII–XIX

foreign invasion from the steppe and from Persia, deurbanization, a decline in international trade and diplomatic relations, internal conflict, and a deterioration in the cultural life and intellectual production of the region. With very few exceptions, scholars identified the causal factor driving this downward spiral in Central Asian civilization as the rise of the European maritime powers and their usurpation of the transcontinental caravan trade. Summarizing this position in the Marxist framework favored in the Soviet academy of the time, I found that, "whereas prior to the Europeans' dominance of the Indian Ocean trade Central Asia's role in transregional commerce is argued to have promoted the development of handicraft production and to have brought prosperity to the middle-class, the subsequent 'breakdown' in these trade relations is purported to have inflicted economic hardship upon handicraft producers and furthered class distinction."[35]

Into the 1990s, Western scholarship on Central Asian history lagged behind Soviet scholarship, and if it diverged from the Soviet narrative it was not by much. Writing in 1970, Bertold Spuler characterized Central Asia from the beginning of the sixteenth century as isolated and pushed from the center of the Silk Road to "the margin of world history." Echoing many before him, Spuler suggested that "the discovery of the sea-route to East Asia rendered the Silk Road increasingly superfluous [and] from the threshold of modern times Central Asian history becomes provincial history. This justifies us in giving no more than a rapid sketch of the following centuries."[36] Writing in the 1980s, the eminent historian of Central Asia Yuri Bregel attributed the "political and economic decline of Central Asia ... primarily to the decline of the international caravan trade in Asia and the growing isolation of Central Asia from the main routes of commercial and cultural exchange, parallel to the degradation of the Chingizid dynasties, the increasing role of nomads in the political life, and the growing independence of tribal chieftains, all of which combined to produce political anarchy." For Bregel, the European companies' rise to a dominant position in the Indian Ocean trade was the causal factor that underpinned Central Asia's decline. This continued until Central Asia's "rapid growth of trade with Russia" led

vekov," *Voprosy istorii* 3 (1956): 84–96. Additionally, one can point to a tradition of Central Asian scholarship that does not directly engage the decline paradigm but that advances contradictory conclusions. A number of examples are cited below and in the bibliography.

35. Levi, "India, Russia," 520.
36. Bertold Spuler, "Central Asia from the Sixteenth Century to the Russian Conquests," in *The Cambridge History of Islam*, vol. 1, *The Central Islamic Lands*, ed. P. M. Holt, Ann K. S. Lambton, and Bernard Lewis (Cambridge: Cambridge University Press, 1970), 470, 483.

to a "new economic and political revival."[37] Some also pointed to the (presumed) cultural backwardness of the Uzbeks and the confessional divide following the rise of the "Shia heresy" in Iran as two additional factors that contributed to Central Asia's decline and growing isolation from the outside world.[38] Others more generally characterized Central Asian society as having shifted from an "active phase" to a "passive phase."[39] More recently, some scholars have observed that these perspectives are supported by the authors of early modern Central Asian sources, and that these sources represent the foundations on which the Russian Orientalists themselves based their conclusions.[40]

In considering this final point, our discussion might benefit from a brief digression into Ottoman historiography. Thirty years ago, Douglas Howard authored an essay in which he sought to challenge scholarly interpretations of Ottoman declinist literature that, at the time, were widely accepted at face value. Focusing his attention on court literature produced during the 130 years between the death of Sultan Suleyman the Magnificent (r. 1520–1566) and the Austro-Ottoman Treaty of Karlowitz in 1699, Howard analyzes a specific genre of Ottoman political tracts that, one generation after the next, employed a declinist framework as a means to critique current administrative policies. Rather than reflecting any actual decline (which an uncritical observer might date from 1566 until the end of the First World War, or more than three and a half centuries), Howard found that this literary genre represented an effort on the part of scribal authors to intervene in "the contemporary intellectual debate . . . concerning the bases of Ottoman sovereignty and legitimacy."[41] In other words, it set a harsh critique of contemporary circumstances against a mythologized portrait of an earlier golden age stripped of all nuance for the purposes of advancing a particular political agenda.[42]

Another Ottomanist, Jane Hathaway, has more recently identified a

---

37. See Bregel, "Central Asia in the 12th–13th/18th–19th Centuries," 195.
38. Vartan Gregorian, *The Emergence of Modern Afghanistan* (Stanford: Stanford University Press, 1969), 20; Seymour Becker, *Russia's Protectorates in Central Asia: Bukhara and Khiva, 1865–1924* (Cambridge, MA: Harvard University Press, 1968), 4.
39. S. A. M. Adshead, *Central Asia in World History* (London: Macmillan, 1993), 177, 194.
40. Sela, *Legendary Biographies*, 119, 135–40.
41. Douglas A. Howard, "Ottoman Historiography and the Literature of 'Decline' of the Sixteenth and Seventeenth Centuries," *Journal of Asian History* 22, no. 1 (1988): 54.
42. Cemal Kafadar, "The Myth of the Golden Age: Ottoman Historical Consciousness in the Post-Süleymânic Era," in *Süleymân the Second and His Time*, ed. Halil Inalcik and Cemal Kafadar (Istanbul: Isis Press, 1993), 45–57.

number of problems generally associated with applying the notion of decline as a historical construct. While her argument is aimed specifically at early modern Ottoman historiography, several of her points also resonate with Central Asian history, and so they merit consideration here.[43] Looking into earlier historical studies, Hathaway notes that the tendency to rely on political treatises and literature produced for an elite audience provided very little insight into the social and political dynamics outside of the imperial capital. Such Ottoman sources say much about political culture in Istanbul and provide valuable insights into specific military and administrative achievements and failures, but they are a poor barometer for assessing the well-being of the larger society and are even less useful in determining whether that well-being has improved or deteriorated over time. Related to this is the need to maintain a clear distinction between two concepts that are all too often conflated: decentralization and decline. It was when Ottoman historians began to pay attention to social dynamism and circumstances outside of the imperial capital, as well as among women, eunuchs, and other groups underrepresented in the official sources, that they began to appreciate the ways in which a weakened center created problems for some and opportunities for others. This was especially so at the provincial level.[44]

These observations are pertinent to the Central Asian case, where many have applied the "Silk Road" framework as a golden age in Central Asian commercial history analogous to the Ottoman Empire during the sixteenth-century reign of Suleyman. Additionally, one can point to a real decline in the power of the Bukharan khans and a corresponding shift in authority to the hands of the provincial Uzbek amirs: a textbook case of decentralization. To be sure, these former provinces of the Bukharan Khanate were not immune to the disruptions of the times. The case of Samarqand and its surrounding areas serves as one obvious example of the traumas that non-elite peoples experienced during the eighteenth century. But this trauma was by no means uniform across the region. Some areas suffered dearly, others were hardly affected at all, and some of the provincial amirs were even able to use the Bukharan crisis to their advantage. From the beginning of the eighteenth century, the Uzbek

---

43. Jane Hathaway, "Rewriting Eighteenth-Century Ottoman History," *Mediterranean Historical Review* 19, no. 1 (2004): 29–53.
44. Dina Rizk Khoury, "The Ottoman Centre versus Provincial Power-Holders: An Analysis of the Historiography," in *Cambridge History of Turkey*, vol. 3, *The Later Ottoman Empire, 1603–1839*, ed. Suraiya N. Faroqhi (Cambridge: Cambridge University Press, 2006), 135–56.

Ming, for example, gradually usurped political authority in the Ferghana Valley, where they eventually established the Khanate of Khoqand. Meanwhile, the Keneges consolidated their power in and around Shahrisabz, and the Yuz did much the same in the vicinity of Khojand, Jizzakh, and Urateppe.[45]

Returning attention to historiographical concerns, the collapse of the Soviet Union in 1991 brought new attention to Central Asian history. As new ideas began to circulate, researchers began to formulate an array of new questions. Recognizing this, the article aimed to provide a sense of the direction that the field appeared to be moving in the 1990s by surveying the contributions of a number of scholars, including Audrey Burton, Robert McChesney, Morris Rossabi, Jos Gommans, Stephen Dale, and Muzaffar Alam. Burton's work is based on an extensive survey of published and unpublished Persian- and Russian-language chronicles and other sources, which she used to develop an impressively detailed study of the Bukharan Khanate's foreign diplomacy and commercial economy from the mid-sixteenth century to the turn of the eighteenth century.[46] Among his many contributions, McChesney exposed a number of critical problems with the early modern decline thesis in general, challenging the long-standing thesis that confessional differences represented a "barrier" that divided early modern Central Asians and Persians. Additionally, he found that the market prices for commodities such as tobacco and cotton in Central Asia fluctuated in harmony with global trends.[47]

Meanwhile, Rossabi argued that, at least in terms of a northern trade route passing between China and Russia, overland Eurasian trade persisted throughout the early modern era.[48] Gommans turned his attention to the magnitude of the Central Asian horse trade and its critical importance for both Indian military markets and the economy of the emerging Durrani Afghan state.[49] Dale presented a pathbreaking study of Indian merchant activities in the commercial markets of early modern Iran, Russia, and Cen-

---

45. McChesney, "Chinggisid Restoration," 300–301. McChesney observes that, unlike the Ming, the Manghit and Qongrat tribes focused their efforts in the established centers of "khanly" power, Bukhara and Khiva, respectively.
46. Burton, *Bukharans*.
47. McChesney, *Central Asia*, 41–43; Robert McChesney, "'Barrier to Heterodoxy'?: Rethinking the Ties between Iran and Central Asia in the 17th Century," in *Safavid Persia: The History and Politics of an Islamic Society*, ed. Charles Melville (London: I. B. Tauris, 1996), 231–67.
48. Morris Rossabi, "The 'Decline' of the Central Asian Caravan Trade," in *The Rise of Merchant Empires*, ed. J. Tracy (Cambridge: Cambridge University Press, 1990), 351–70.
49. Jos Gommans, *The Rise of the Indo-Afghan Empire, c. 1710–1780* (Leiden: E. J. Brill, 1995).

tral Asia.[50] Alam contributed an analysis of Mughal and Uzbek diplomatic relations and official efforts to promote trade between their two realms. Challenging the received wisdom, Alam was the first to argue explicitly that the early modern overland and maritime trade routes worked in harmony with each other, rather than in competition.[51] The article then presents information I extracted from a handful of primary sources in an effort to demonstrate that, in some areas, the commercial economy of early modern Central Asia was actually quite vibrant. I concluded that the emerging evidence suggests that "the eighteenth century in Central Asia was a period of marked transition and, just as it must be acknowledged that in certain areas, at specific times, historical processes and events wrought socio-economic trauma to segments of the population, there were concomitant historical processes which encouraged growth in different areas and new directions."[52]

Two decades later, a body of new research engaging Central Asia's commercial history has emerged from the fields of Chinese, Russian, and South Asian history, as well as from Central Asian history itself. At the same time, the field of world history has become a more highly regarded forum for historical research that crosses traditional boundaries to explore transregional linkages. Surveyed in chapter three, these more recent achievements build upon the earlier interventions to present a clearer image of Central Asia's commercial history and its economic integration with the early modern globalizing world. These studies appear to have had an impact. Revisiting this theme in his 2009 study of the "Uzbek states" of Bukhara, Khiva, and Khoqand that rose in the wake of the Bukharan crisis and collapse, Bregel takes a step back from his earlier position. Here, he addresses the crisis but does not advance a theory as to what caused it.[53]

Others continue to advocate for an interpretation that attributes the Bukharan crisis, or even a general early modern Central Asian decline, to economic isolation. Christopher Beckwith is one example, and his work

---

50. Stephen F. Dale, *Indian Merchants and Eurasian Trade, 1600–1750* (Cambridge: Cambridge University Press, 1994).
51. Muzaffar Alam, "Trade, State Policy and Regional Change: Aspects of Mughal-Uzbek Commercial Relations, c. 1550–1750," *Journal of the Economic and Social History of the Orient* 37, no. 3 (August 1994): 202–27.
52. Levi, "India, Russia," 542.
53. Yuri Bregel, "The New Uzbek States: Bukhara Khiva and Khoqand: c. 1750–1886," in *The Cambridge History of Inner Asia: The Chinggisid Age*, ed. Nicola di Cosmo, Allen J. Frank, and Peter B. Golden (Cambridge: Cambridge University Press, 2009), 392–411.

in this area is addressed in chapter two.⁵⁴ Ron Sela, a student of Bregel's, presents another example. In his 2011 study of the *Tīmūr-nāma*, or *Book of Timur*, an eighteenth-century Central Asian literary genre that elevates Timur (1336–1405) to mythical proportions, Sela finds efforts to challenge the decline thesis to be "premature," "simply erroneous," and informed by a Saidian postcolonial agenda.⁵⁵ The bulk of Sela's book surveys the *Tīmūr-nāma* literature and argues that it emerged in response to the Central Asian crisis. His treatment of the crisis itself is restricted to his final chapter, which points to a deterioration in trade connections, deurbanization in several important locations, a fiscal crisis evidenced in the steady debasement of coinage, multiple nomadic invasions, weak and corrupt leadership, and political fragmentation exacerbated by the inherently decentralized nature of the Bukharan state.⁵⁶ These features are by now familiar. They are well established in the Soviet-era and Russian imperial literature, and also, as Sela rightly notes, the literature of eighteenth-century Central Asia itself.⁵⁷ But the features that Sela highlights are best characterized as *symptoms* that illustrate the severity of the Bukharan crisis. They are not the *causal factors* that drove it. Ultimately, Sela offers the general observation that "there appears to be no one particular factor that caused or dominated the crisis."⁵⁸ His rather truculent intervention describes the Bukharan crisis and identifies one way Central Asians responded to it, but it does not bring us closer to understanding what caused it.

Paolo Sartori has more recently weighed in on this debate as well.⁵⁹ Basing his conclusions on a body of nineteenth-century Khwarezmian governmental records, Sartori identifies a substantial amount of short-range

---

54. Christopher I. Beckwith, *Empires of the Silk Road: A History of Central Eurasia from the Bronze Age to the Present* (Princeton: Princeton University Press, 2009), 241–42, 262. A slightly more nuanced interpretation with some interesting observations is found in the recent synthetic survey of Central Asian economic history by Stephan Barisitz, *Central Asia and the Silk Road: Economic Rise and Decline over Several Millennia* (Vienna: Springer, 2017), 151.
55. Sela, *Legendary Biographies*, 6, 121. I take issue with Sela's dismissal of this scholarly trend and present a response in Scott C. Levi, "Early Modern Central Asia in World History," *History Compass* 10, no. 11 (2012): 866–78.
56. Sela, *Legendary Biographies*, 117–40.
57. Sela, *Legendary Biographies*, 119. In supporting his position, Sela erroneously, and bewilderingly, claims that scholars who have argued against the decline thesis "have relied on no eighteenth-century sources to support their claims."
58. Sela, *Legendary Biographies*, 118 and note 4.
59. Paolo Sartori, "Introduction: On Khvārazmian Connectivity: Two or Three Things That I Know about It," *Journal of Persianate Studies* 9 (2016): 133–57.

connections at the level of Khwarezmian regional history. But he finds no evidence in his sources to suggest any significant transregional connections. Extrapolating from this, he concludes that Central Asia in this period was in all meaningful ways isolated from larger global processes. Sartori expresses his support for a connected histories methodology in principle, but he remains dismissive of efforts to identify external connections for Central Asia in the eighteenth and early nineteenth centuries.[60] Sartori then goes on to discourage further research on themes that challenge the notion of Central Asia's early modern isolation, arguing that an "approach that accords greater relevance to global connections" carries with it "serious risks" and "potentially poses more problems than what it claims to solve."[61]

Sartori's intervention makes a number of important points, not the least of which are that studies that claim to apply a global framework often do so to mask shallow research, and the field of Central Asian history needs more, not fewer, scholars trained to carry out careful and rigorous research in locally produced sources. Sartori is also right to point out that the currents of globalization moved much more quickly by ships than by the camels that one is more likely to encounter in these local sources. The question of scale is an important one. Bukhara, arguably the most cosmopolitan urban center in eighteenth-century Central Asia, was no Bombay, or Macau, by an order of magnitude.[62] At the same time, I argue that it is wholly inappropriate to place Bukhara and the other Central Asian polities at the other end of the spectrum. Just as early modern Central Asia was no "hot spot" of global interconnectivity, it also was not isolated from the outside world and immune from globalization and other external forces. Approaching it as if it were masks other sins and does the region's history a serious disservice. We will return to this question in chapters three and four.

In essence, I argue that there is much to learn from exploring the many connections that linked Central Asian states and societies with those in China, Russia, India, and beyond. I do not claim that such a perspective should replace carefully produced microhistories based on deep research into locally produced sources.[63] But I do argue that Central Asia was inte-

---

60. Sartori, "Introduction: On Khvārazmian Connectivity," 134–35.
61. Sartori, "Introduction: On Khvārazmian Connectivity," 140.
62. Sartori, "Introduction: On Khvārazmian Connectivity," 134.
63. For an insightful critique of the "global turn" that both champions the merits of microhistory and demonstrates its potential to serve global history, see Francesca Trivellato, "Is There a Future for Italian Microhistory in the Age of Global History?" *California Italian Studies* 2, no. 1 (2011), https://escholarship.org/uc/item/0z94n9hq. Sebouh Aslanian has also produced a number of masterful global microhistories, principally on the overseas Armenian merchant

grated in larger early modern processes—even as the Bukharan state fell into decline during the first half of the eighteenth century—and that research in local sources can be made more meaningful through efforts to understand those local histories in a broader historical context.[64]

BUKHARA IN CRISIS

At the turn of the sixteenth century, the Chinggisid ruler Muhammad Shibani Khan led several hundred thousand Uzbeks southward from the steppe into the agricultural zone of Transoxania. Shibani Khan and his Uzbek followers rapidly established themselves as the dominant political force in the region. After some 140 years of Timurid rule in the ancestral capital of Samarqand, the Uzbek conquests represented a Chinggisid restoration in the region and an elevation of certain nomadic principles of governance. This included the appanage system, a fundamentally decentralized method of governance that shared authority and resources among the leading members of the ruling family. Those individuals who controlled the appanages of Tashkent, Samarqand, and Balkh were technically subordinate to the senior member of the family in Bukhara. But the extent to which they placed that loyalty over their own independence was, in practice, a matter of perpetual negotiation. The level of centralized control over the appanages fluctuated and at times appears to have disappeared almost completely. But from the 1530s, Bukhara enjoyed an undisputed position as the principal center of power and seat of the senior member of the ruling family.

The crisis that would ultimately lead to the collapse of the Bukharan Khanate took shape gradually and began to grow severe in the late seventeenth century. Over the course of that century, the Uzbek amirs turned away from their Chinggisid leadership. From the abdication of 'Abd al-'Aziz Khan in 1681, their resistance to Bukharan authority intensified, and they focused their energies on consolidating their own territorial claims. This

communities. See especially Sebouh Aslanian, "Une vie sur plusieurs continents: Microhistoire globale d'un agent arménien de la Compagnie des Indes orientales (1666–1688)," *Annales: Histoire, Science Sociales* 73 no. 1 (2018/2019): 19–56, and Sebouh Aslanian, "From Autonomous to Interactive Histories: World History's Challenge to Armenian Studies," in *An Armenian Mediterranean: Worlds and Worlds in Motion*, ed. Kathryn Babayan and Michael Pifer (London: Palgrave, 2018), 83–132.

64. For an example of such a study, see Scott C. Levi, *The Rise and Fall of Khoqand, 1709–1876: Central Asia in the Global Age* (Pittsburgh: University of Pittsburgh Press, 2017). See especially the preface, "On Connecting Histories," ix–xii, as well as Paolo Sartori's generous blurb on the back cover.

left the Bukharan khans in a terminally weakened position and rendered them incapable of restoring their control over the very local powers upon which they relied. Repeated efforts to achieve that goal only further repelled the amirs. This situation was exacerbated by a growing fiscal crisis that became critical in the eighteenth century, by weakened leadership, and by successive invasions from the steppe and from Persia. In 1747, the Uzbek Manghit tribal leadership killed Abu'l Fayz Khan, the final Toqay-Timurid ruler in Bukhara, and effectively usurped regal authority for themselves.

The previous discussion has pointed to a long scholarly tradition of attributing the Bukharan crisis to a collapse of Central Asia's commercial economy, believed to have stemmed from a shift in Eurasian trade from overland to maritime routes, and a more recent body of literature that calls that tradition into question. This received wisdom is largely based upon a number of flawed assumptions deeply embedded in common understandings of the Silk Road. The next chapter locates the roots of these assumptions in the early Orientalist scholarship on the region and surveys a number of ways that more recent scholarship continues to perpetuate them.

Looking ahead, readers will find that the commercial economy of early modern Central Asia remained quite active and that, even during the heart of the eighteenth-century crisis, the region was anything but isolated. But that still leaves unanswered the question: What caused the Bukharan crisis? It is from that particular phenomenon that the now familiar evidence of Central Asia's so-called decline has been drawn and then misapplied to the region as a whole for the entire early modern era. Identifying an answer to this problem will help determine not only what brought the Bukharan Khanate to an end but also the extent of the crisis in both temporal and geographic terms, as well as its impact beyond just the Bukharan state and those dependent upon it. We will return to that question in chapter four.

TWO

SILK ROADS, REAL AND IMAGINED

Scholars have studied the cultural exchanges that unfolded along the network of Central Asian routes of commerce and communication popularly known as the Silk Road for well over a century, since even before Sir Aurel Stein, Sven Hedin, Paul Pelliot, and other scholar-adventurers first led expeditions into Xinjiang (Altishahr to the local population).[1] Their collective work has done much to illuminate the trans-Eurasian transmission of scientific knowledge and technologies, religions, languages and literary traditions, artistic motifs, fine silks and other merchandise, and much more. At the same time, considerably less attention has been directed to the Silk Road traders themselves, the actual individuals and merchant groups whose labors are credited (often mistakenly so) for having propelled these cultural exchanges.

The primary objective of this chapter is to identify a number of false assumptions long embedded within the Silk Road paradigm. Paramount among these is the notion that Central Asia's economic prosperity rested wholly upon the region's ability to mediate China's westward trade.

---

1. For the importance of the term *Altishahr* as opposed to *Xinjiang* in the local context, see Rian Thum, *The Sacred Routes of Uyghur History* (Cambridge, MA: Harvard University Press, 2014), 2–7.

Although the concept of the Silk Road was derived in the West, its history is most often presented from the Chinese perspective, with Central Asian traders playing the role of cultural intermediaries and functioning as subsidiary agents and middlemen cargo carriers whose principal economic activity involved moving Chinese goods to the Mediterranean and, to a lesser extent, linking the latitudinal caravan routes with India. Too often, scholars working in various subfields of what might be termed "Silk Road Studies" have uncritically accepted and propagated this perspective, and in a number of important ways this has resulted in a Sinocentric distortion of Central Asian history.

This oversimplified notion is a legacy of Orientalist scholarship produced more than a century ago, and the discussion here addresses its origins, examines its resilience, and illustrates a number of ways that it continues to misinform scholarship in the field. This is especially so for the early modern era, when many have assumed that Central Asians lost their privileged mediatory position in Eurasian trade and, as a result, became isolated from the outside world. As a commercial phenomenon, readers will find that even today the Silk Road concept remains poorly defined, overly malleable, and often misused.

Dissatisfaction with the frequent misapplication of the Silk Road concept has led some scholars to advocate for the term's wholesale dismissal. But considering the growing popularity of the Silk Road, the likelihood of achieving that goal seems doubtful at best. For that reason, this chapter applies a perspective deliberately rooted in Central Eurasia. Here, the Silk Road is conceived of as a pulsating network of overlapping commercial structures orchestrated by multiple competing and collaborating groups—sedentary and nomadic alike—that linked Central Asia with its neighbors on the Eurasian periphery. One aim in applying this approach is to help reclaim early modern Central Asian history from the "back of beyond" and to encourage new efforts to situate the region in scholarly discussions of early modern world history. Doing so stands to enhance our understanding of the many ways that larger Eurasian historical processes influenced developments within the region. It also promises to shed new light on the motivations of Central Asian peoples and the methods they used to influence their larger and more powerful neighbors in the periods leading up to, and following, Chinese and Russian colonial expansion into the region.

MAPPING THE SILK ROADS

Transregional trade is as old as civilization itself, but the long-standing narrative of the Silk Road suggests that it emerged only in the second century BCE, after the Chinese Han dynasty (206 BCE–220 CE) secured a decisive victory over the neighboring Xiongnu nomadic confederation in 133 BCE. Like the earlier Qin dynasty (221–206/7 BCE), the Han had long engaged in "silk diplomacy" with their nomadic neighbors, gifting large quantities of silk in an effort to maintain a tenuous peace and delivering even more in exchange for horses bred in the vast steppe beyond their frontier. But following the Han victory, the Chinese armies expanded their territory far to the west, annexing the Gansu (or Hexi) corridor, a narrow strip of fertile land between the Gobi Desert and the Qilan Mountains, and reaching even as far as the desert oases of modern Xinjiang. Han rulers extended the Great Wall, built fortifications, and assigned military garrisons to protect merchants, pilgrims, and other travelers who made their way along the caravan routes. The Han dispatched envoys to establish diplomatic contacts with neighboring rulers, and they made a sustained effort to secure their frontier and promote the overland caravan trade to the west.[2] The Han succeeded, and, according to the standard historical narrative, apart from a few temporary interruptions, the Silk Road trade that they inaugurated continued for more than sixteen hundred years.

In Europe, trade with China through Central Asia was associated with luxurious wealth and exotica long before Marco Polo returned from his travels to the Yuan court at the end of the thirteenth century. But the scholarly image of Central Asia as a center for Silk Road commerce dates only to 1877, when the German geographer Baron Ferdinand von Richthofen (1833–1905) first coined the term *Seidenstrasse* (Silk Route or Road) in reference to China's overland caravan trade through Central Asia. It did not take long before mention of the Silk Road conjured romanticized images of dusty, dark-skinned merchants with thick beards, turban-wrapped heads, and razor-sharp sabers strapped to their sides. Leading long caravans of ornately decorated camels heavily laden with packs full of fine silks, spices, porcelains, and other luxury goods, these intrepid, nameless figures were imagined traversing rugged mountain passes and a vast rolling landscape of grassy steppe, skirting deserts as they made their way from city to city the full distance from China to the Mediterranean. Exchanging their silks for gold and silver, the traders would then lead their camels back to the East and repeat the process over again.[3]

2. See, for example, Xinru Liu, *The Silk Road in World History* (Oxford: Oxford University Press, 2010), 1–19.
3. See my critique of the romanticized Silk Road in Scott C. Levi, "Objects in Motion," in *A Companion to World History*, ed. Douglas Northrop (Chichester, West Sussex: Wiley-Blackwell, 2012), 322–26.

Scholars have exploited a wealth of historical documents and artifacts in a continuing effort to illustrate the ways in which Central Eurasian peoples were involved in the trans-Eurasian transmission of scientific knowledge, languages, artistic motifs, and, of course, religious traditions. One can point to a rich body of literature studying the impact that the Silk Road travelers' slow and steady interactions had on the trajectory of historical developments across Eurasia.[4] It is only recently, however, that scholars have begun to interrogate the long-distance caravan trade model believed to have propelled the Silk Road exchange, exposing it as a dramatic oversimplification. Prior to turning to this new body of literature, it is first useful to direct some attention to the ways in which such romanticized notions of the Silk Road came into being, and their stubborn persistence in Central Asian historiography today.

"We are heir to two Silk Roads," observes Tamara Chin, "not the ancient and the modern, but the invented and reinvented."[5] In recent years, Tamara Chin has joined Daniel Waugh, Valerie Hansen, Étienne de la Vaissière, Khodadad Rezakhani, and other researchers in revisiting Richthofen's work to determine his original intent in coining the term *Seidenstrasse* and the multiple ways in which the term has gradually taken on a meaning quite different from his original purpose.[6] According to Waugh, Richthofen deliberately used the term in the singular ("Silk Road") to refer to the route (highlighted on his original map in orange and enhanced in black on Map 4) that the agent of a first-century Phoenician silk merchant traveled, as presented in the second-century geography by Marinus of Tyre and repeated slightly later by Ptolemy (c. 90–168).[7] Elsewhere in his study, Richthofen uses the plural, "Seidenstrassen" ("Silk Roads"), and Waugh observes that

---

4. There are many accessible historical surveys. In addition to those studies referenced elsewhere in this discussion, see especially Luce Boulnois, *Silk Road: Monks, Warriors and Merchants on the Silk Road*, trans. Helen Loveday (Hong Kong: Odyssey, 2005); Frances Wood, *The Silk Road: Two Thousand Years in the Heart of Asia* (Berkeley: University of California Press, 2004); Xinru Liu and Lynda Norene Shaffer, *Connections across Eurasia: Transportation, Communication, and Cultural Exchange on the Silk Roads* (New York: McGraw-Hill, 2007); Richard C. Foltz, *Religions of the Silk Road: Overland Trade and Cultural Exchange from Antiquity to the Fifteenth Century* (New York: St. Martin's Press, 1999); and Susan Whitfield, *Life Along the Silk Road* (Berkeley: University of California Press, 2001).
5. Tamara Chin, "The Invention of the Silk Road, 1877," *Critical Inquiry* 40, no. 1 (2013): 194.
6. Daniel Waugh, "Richthofen's 'Silk Roads': Toward the Archeology of a Concept," *Silk Road* 5, no. 1 (2007): 1–10; Chin, "Invention of the Silk Road," 194–219; Khodadad Rezakhani, "The Road That Never Was: The Silk Road and Trans-Eurasian Exchange," *Comparative Studies of South Asia, Africa and the Middle East* 30, no. 3 (2010): 420–33.
7. Waugh, "Richthofen's 'Silk Roads,'" 4–6.

Map 4. Richthofen's "Die Seidenstrasse." This is a black-and-white rendering of the color map printed in Ferdinand von Richthofen, *China: Ergebnisse eigener reisen und darauf gegründeter studien*, vol. 1 (Berlin: D. Reimer, 1877), plate facing page 500.

here, too, he does so in a limited sense, in reference "only to the Han period, in discussing the relationship between political expansion and trade on the one hand and geographical knowledge on the other."[8] In later years, others would appropriate the term as shorthand for all transcontinental trade passing through Central Asia. But for Richthofen, whether singular or plural, the Silk Road was by definition a Han phenomenon.

There remains considerable variation in the ways in which scholars understand just what constituted the Silk Road trade. Both Chin and Waugh emphasize that, for his part, Richthofen was careful to recognize that caravan traders followed many different routes, and that, while Chinese silk was an especially important article of trade greatly valued by nomadic peoples, traders dealt in a wide variety of merchandise. Both also carefully deconstruct Richthofen's research methodology and expose a number of problems with his focus on Chinese and Greek sources, along with other aspects of his analysis. Waugh, for example, observes that Richthofen overstates the importance of silk and points to a number of ways more recent scholarship has altered the perception of the Silk Road trade. Not the least of these is a greater appreciation for the impressive magnitude of China's overland trade with Central Asia both prior to the Han period, which Richthofen presented as "episodic" and inconsequential, and after the Han period.[9]

Adding further clarification to this point, Vaissière has observed that "a trickle of Chinese silk" may have passed along the Central Asian caravan routes prior to the Han period, but at that time silk itself was a relatively unimportant commodity in Eurasian trade.[10] Rather, Vaissière finds that archeological and textual evidence strongly suggests that trade across the region included a much wider variety of merchandise and that, for example, precious stones such as lapis lazuli that originated in Central Asia were traded widely from India to Mesopotamia and beyond already in the fourth millennium BCE. In addition to silk, the Sogdian traders of antiquity also dealt in "musk, slaves, precious metals and stones, furs, silverware, amber, relics, paper, spices, brass, curcuma, sal ammoniac, medicinal plants, candy sugar and perfumes, etc."[11] Such a perspective leads to a quite different understanding of just what constituted overland Eurasian trade in antiquity. But this is a recent revelation.

---

8. Waugh, "Richthofen's 'Silk Roads,'" 5.
9. Waugh, "Richthofen's 'Silk Roads,'" 5.
10. Étienne de la Vaissière, "Trans-Asian Trade, or the Silk Road Deconstructed (Antiquity, Middle Ages)," in *The Cambridge History of Capitalism*, ed. Larry Neal and Jeffrey G. Williamson (Cambridge: Cambridge University Press, 2014), 102.
11. Vaissière, "Trans-Asian Trade," 104.

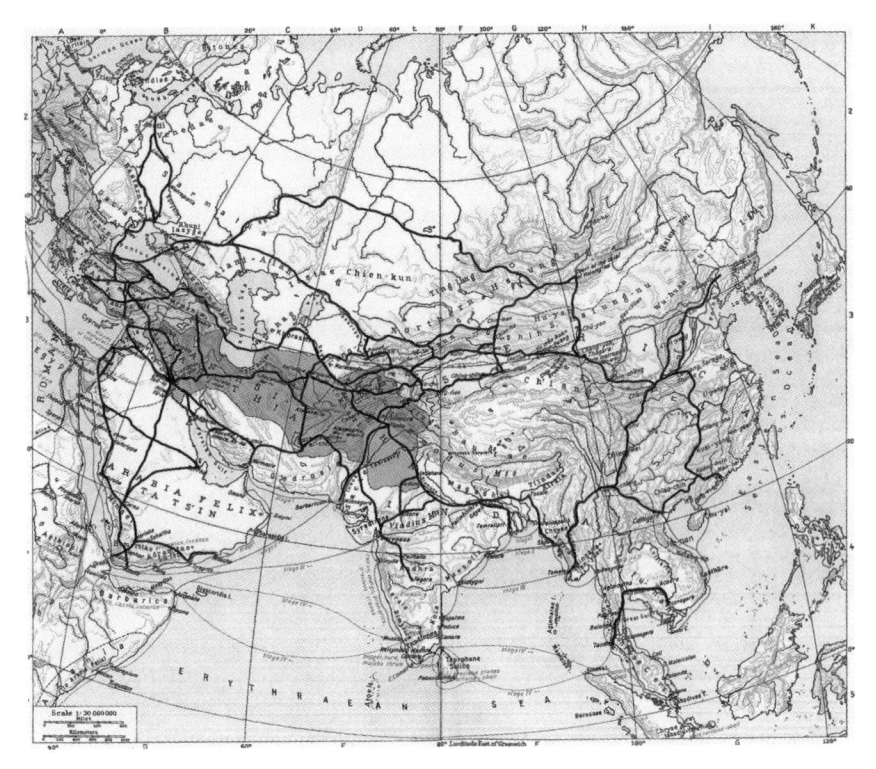

Map 5. Herrmann's "Asia ca. 100 A. D." This is a black-and-white rendering of Herrmann's color map. See Albert Herrmann, *Historical and Commercial Atlas of China* (Cambridge, MA: Harvard University Press, 1935), 26–27. To enhance clarity, I have highlighted in black the main overland Asian trade routes, which appear in red in Herrmann's original.

Returning attention to the nineteenth century, it did not take long for Richthofen's original concept of the Silk Road to be transformed into something quite different from what he had originally intended. Already in 1896, David-Léon Cahun had applied the term as a general way to refer to the trade routes linking the Roman and Chinese empires.[12] Just a few years later, the German geographer Albert Herrmann used the term as a way to connect his own work on Chinese trade routes with the work of other European researchers investigating the trade eastward from Syria. In 1915, Herrmann published an essay, "The Silk Roads from China to the Roman Empire."[13] He then spent the later years of his career researching Chinese maps and

---

12. David-Léon Cahun, *Introduction à l'histoire de l'Asie: Turcs et Mongols, des origins à 1405* (Paris: A. Colin, 1896), 43–44.
13. Waugh, "Richthofen's 'Silk Roads,'" 6.

ancient sources to identify other principal branches of the Seidenstrassen, the "Silk Roads," the result of which is presented in Map 5.

A short time later, in 1936, Richthofen's student, the Swedish scholar Sven Hedin, published the book *Sidenvägen*, which was released in German translation the same year and in English translation two years later as *The Silk Road*.[14] At the time, Hedin was embroiled in a competition with another celebrated scholar-adventurer, the Hungarian-born British archeologist Sir Aurel Stein. Both Hedin and Stein authored multiple volumes romanticizing their archeological escapades in the deserts of Chinese Turkestan, and both wove travel adventures into their scholarly narratives in a deliberate effort to reach popular audiences in both Europe and North America.[15] It is in this context that Hedin in particular can be credited, or perhaps reproached, for fully exploiting romanticized notions of the Silk Road concept as a means to market his work to the general public.

In terms of visual representations of the Silk Road, one could assemble a bewildering array of maps that aim to illustrate the trunk roads and secondary routes traversed by Central Asian caravan traders throughout the ages. Most of these shed the nuance of Herrmann's work in favor of adding only slight variations to Richthofen's original map, which itself appears more like a North American interstate highway than an unpaved route crossing mountains, deserts, steppe, and wilderness with little security and few amenities. The most significant of these modifications is the identification of secondary routes that venture off from the main trunk road: one set that skirts the north and south rims of the Tarim Basin to connect the oasis towns of northwest China; a route that passes northward across the steppe toward the Black Sea; and another "interstate off-ramp" to a route that passes through the Hindu Kush to connect traffic along the main latitudinal road passing through Samarqand with markets in India.

More recently, some scholars have sought to modify our visual understanding of the Silk Road even more thoroughly by emphasizing (as did Richthofen) that the commercial network spanning the Eurasian interior was actually comprised of many different roads, and different kinds of roads, and that a wide variety of factors relating to ecology, security, and the political vicissitudes of the time informed travelers' decisions to prefer one

---

14. Sven Anders Hedin, *Sidenvägen: En bilfärd genom Centralasien* (Stockholm: Bonniers, 1936); German edition, *Die Siedenstrasse* (Leipzig: F. A. Brockhaus, 1936); English edition, *The Silk Road* (New York: E. P. Dutton, 1938).
15. See Peter Hopkirk, *Foreign Devils on the Silk Road: The Search for the Lost Treasures of Central Asia* (London: John Murray, 1980).

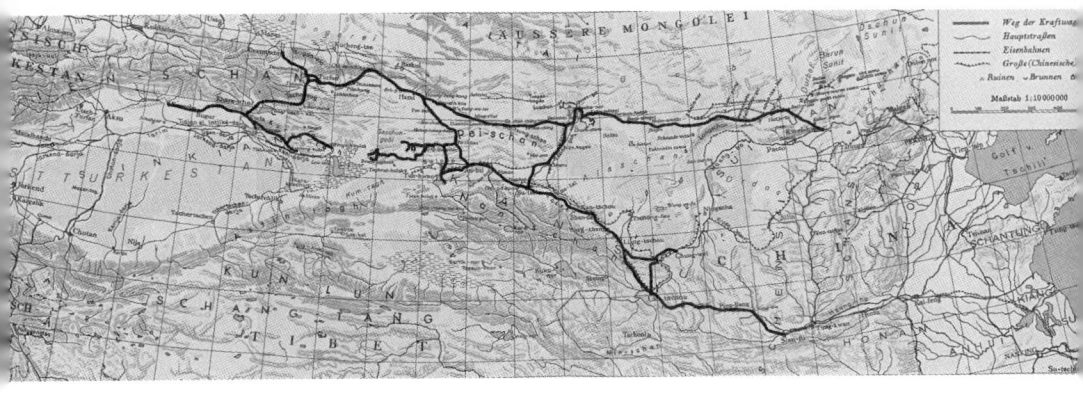

Map 6. Sven Hedin's "The Silk Road." This represents a black-and-white rendering of the foldout "Karte zu Sven Hedin, Die Seidenstrasse," found at the back of Hedin, *Die Siedenstrasse*. To enhance clarity, I have highlighted in black the caravan routes that appear in red in Heden's original.

route over another.[16] In identifying just the most important routes, these maps use varying levels of detail to suggest that overland trade through both sedentary zones and the open steppe connected virtually every Eurasian urban center in a pulsing web of commercial exchange. David Christian stretches the concept to its maximum elasticity, arguing that "the many trans-ecological exchanges mediated by the Silk Roads linked all regions of the Afro-Eurasian landmass, from its agrarian civilizations to its many stateless communities of woodland foragers and steppe pastoralists, into a single system of exchanges that is several millennia old."[17] Christian is not alone in his inclusivity. Others have no less vehemently argued in favor of conceptualizing premodern overland trade as a vast series of regional networks linked into a grand world system that, while changing over time, first developed some five thousand years ago, nearly as far back in history as human settlements themselves.[18]

This is a positive trend insofar as these scholars seek to move beyond the simplistic interstate highway model and better explain how overland trade traversing Central Asia linked the region with its neighbors and facilitated all varieties of transcontinental interactions. At the same time, some

---

16. Peter Golden is careful to articulate such a view in his survey text, *Central Asia in World History* (Oxford: Oxford University Press, 2011), 17.
17. David Christian, "Silk Roads or Steppe Roads? The Silk Roads in World History," *Journal of World History* 11, no. 1 (2000): 1.
18. One well-known advocate for this view is Andre Gunder Frank, *ReOrient: Global Economy in the Asian Age* (Berkeley: University of California Press, 1998).

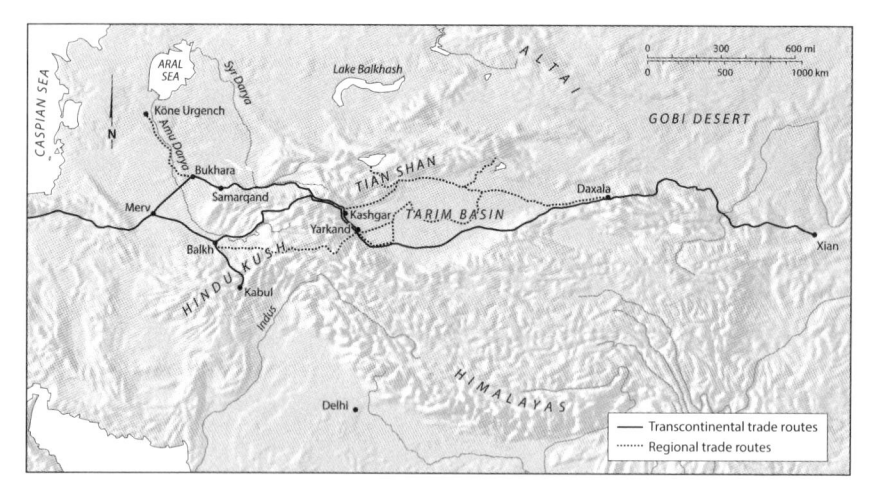

Map 7. Central Asia on the Early Silk Road. Map by Bill Nelson. Based on Rafis Abazov, *The Palgrave Concise Historical Atlas of Central Asia* (New York: Palgrave Macmillan, 2008), Map 13.

have gone further and applied the Silk Road concept in ways that are so broad as to be devoid of any analytical value.[19] Beginning his study of the Sogdian merchant diaspora of antiquity, Vassière cautions: "The concept of 'the Silk Road' has given rise to an abundant historiography concerning the commercial, religious and artistic contacts between the Hellenized, then Muslim, Near East and East Asia. The strength of the image has led to a wide diffusion of the theme. Even so, no historical object that might be named 'the Silk Road' has ever been defined with precision. Though certainly a necessary step in historiographical thinking, this idea does not rest upon any clear historical concept, and mixes commercial, diplomatic and religious features in an approach dominated by historical geography."[20] Considering such problems, it is perhaps to be expected that some have argued in favor of wholly dismissing the Silk Road as "a meaningless neologism which bears little relationship to the realities on the ground in early Eurasia."[21]

---

19. For example, the Silk Road concept is misappropriated and twisted into an analogy for all transregional interconnectivity throughout world history in Peter Frankopan, *The Silk Roads: A New History of the World* (New York: Alfred A. Knopf, 2016).
20. See Étienne de la Vaissière, *Histoire des marchands Sogdiens* (Paris: Collège France, Institute des Hautes Études Chinois, 2004). For the quote, see the English translation, Étienne de la Vaissière, *Sogdian Traders: A History*, trans. James Ward (Leiden: E. J. Brill, 2005), 1.
21. Warwick Ball, "Following the Mythical Road," *Geographical Magazine* 70, no. 3 (1998): 18–23. Cited in Waugh, "Richthofen's 'Silk Roads,'" 7. More recently, others have observed that the Silk Road concept makes no meaningful contribution to the study of trans-Eurasian com-

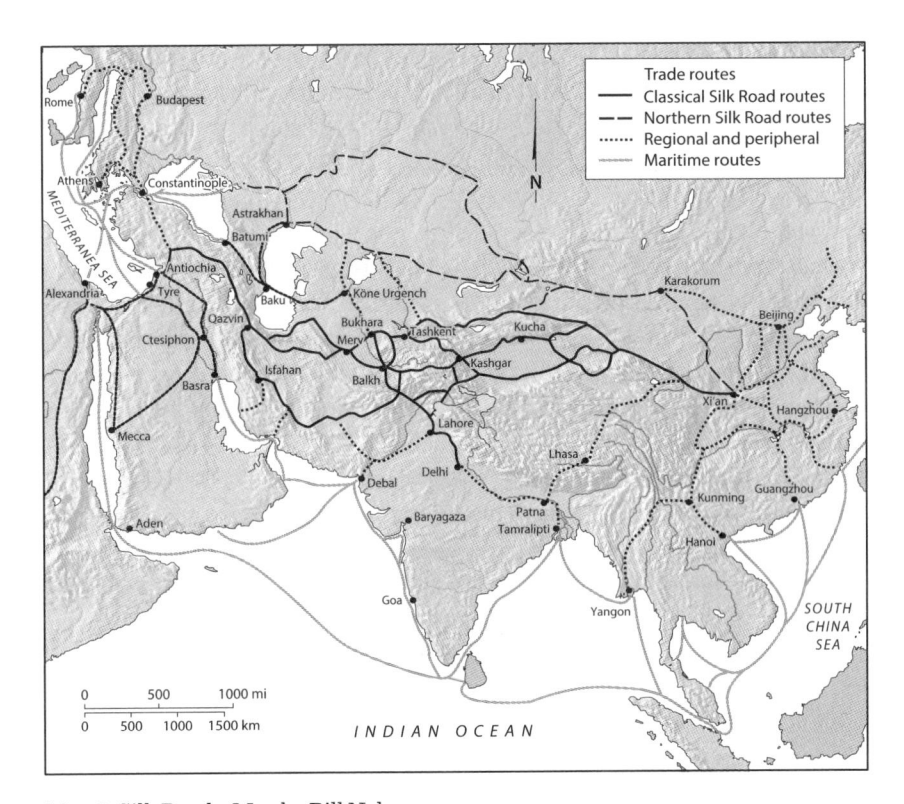

Map 8. Silk Roads. Map by Bill Nelson.

If such a critique misses the mark, it is not by much. But considering the growing popularity of the Silk Road both in the public imagination and academic discourse, achieving that goal seems unlikely. Rather than dismissing the concept completely, one potentially productive approach would be to enhance our understanding of it by directing serious attention to Asian commercial history, and in particular to the ways that commerce drove cultural exchanges. While some have taken inclusivity to the extreme, others have taken a more measured approach by recognizing, for example, that the vast majority of trade was local in nature, that merchandise passed through many hands as it moved from one locality to the next, and that long-distance caravan traders functioned as agents of an "archaic globalization," insofar as they linked many local economies across great distances.[22] This last

   mercial and cultural interactions during the period of late antiquity. See Johannes Preiser-Kapeller, *Jenseits von Rom und Karl dem Grossen: Aspekte der globalen Verflechtung in der langen Spätantike, 300–800 n. Chr.* (Vienna: Mandelbaum Verlag, 2018).
22. C. A. Bayly, "'Archaic' and 'Modern' Globalization in the Eurasian-African Arena," in *Globalization in World History*, ed. A. G. Hopkins (London: Pimlico Press, 2009), 47–93.

notion is best suited to the Central Asian case, where one might argue that the Silk Road represents the full range of commercial, cultural, technological, linguistic, literary, spiritual, and other human exchanges that unfolded at the heart of Asia, with a multiplicity of Central Asian regional actors and groups—both sedentary and nomadic—connecting the many peoples and civilizations of the Eurasian periphery.

Theoretically, that is a compelling image. But directing our attention to the actual commercial dynamics of the trade that passed along these routes, one finds that even the most current scholarship presents wildly differing interpretations of the roles that Central Asians played in overland Eurasian commerce. To a great extent, this can be attributed to the fact that, with only a few notable exceptions, scholarly inquiry into the Silk Road has had little to do with commercial history. In an essay that Richard Frye, the eminent historian of classical Persia and Central Asia, wrote near the end of his career, he lamented that some years earlier he had identified a number of important questions pertaining to Sogdian Central Asia that had not yet been satisfactorily answered. Frye lists his questions as follows: "Why did Khotan and Kucha become great Buddhist centers, whereas Kashgar and Turfan apparently did not? Is there a parallel in West Turkestan where the absence of Buddhist remains in Sogdiana contrasts with the great centers of Buddhism in Northern and Southern Bactria? What was the nature of Iranian Buddhism? What was the extent of Kushan rule in East Turkestan? What was the extent of Sasanian rule in the East and what kind was it?" Thus, despite titling his essay "The Merchant World of the Sogdians," not one of his questions has anything to do with matters pertaining to Sogdian trade.[23]

There are a number of reasons for this, not the least of which is that—in contrast to the early modern European maritime powers—the secretive nature of most premodern merchants and merchant groups resulted in a paucity of surviving commercial records, and this has made it difficult to access and analyze the complex commercial structures of Silk Road trade. A small number of exceptional studies aside, there have been few efforts to alter the assumption that the individuals believed to have propelled the Silk Road exchange, the traders themselves, were essentially long-distance peddlers whose business consisted of transporting luxury goods between

---

23. Richard N. Frye, "The Merchant World of the Sogdians," in *Nomads, Traders and Holy Men Along China's Silk Road*, ed. Annette L. Juliano and Judith A. Lerner (Turnhout, Belgium: Brepols, 2002), 71–72.

East and West, and who profited solely by buying cheap, transporting far, and selling dear.[24] I argue that this model is antiquated, that it fails to accurately characterize the commercial mechanics involved in overland trade, and that it continues to mislead scholarly inquiry into many of the actual historical factors that propelled trans-Eurasian cultural exchanges. Most important to the discussion at hand is that it leaves scholars in a poor position to understand the ways in which commercial structures linked societies in the vast Central Eurasian hinterland with their neighbors on the Eurasian periphery, as well as the ways that these structures transformed over the *longue durée*.

One unintended result of the failure of Silk Road studies to dig beneath the veneer of the peddler paradigm is that it has perpetuated the assumption that profits derived from mediating the West's overland caravan trade in luxury goods with China (and, to a lesser extent, India) was the prime economic engine for Central Asia itself. Central Asia's economic relationship with China was indeed very important, and this topic is further explored in greater detail in chapter three. However, in addition to ignoring the region's own agricultural and pastoral productivity, this narrative suggests that Central Asian states could prosper only so long as their traders could shuttle Asian luxuries to European consumers. Focusing on the early modern era, there is a long scholarly tradition of reifying, in one way or another, the notion that, whether conceptualized as the Silk Road or something else, Central Asia's role in overland Eurasian trade diminished from 1498 onward, as European maritime powers entered and then established a dominant position in the Indian Ocean commercial arena. According to this line of thought, as Portuguese and then Dutch and English maritime powers usurped the movement of merchandise from Asia to Europe, Central Asian societies grew isolated, they experienced economic decline, their states diminished in power, and the formerly great cities of the Silk Road gradually deteriorated into sand and dust.

THE ORIENTALIST LEGACY

That narrative is an old one, so much so that one might even suggest that it is written into the genetic code of the field. The celebrated Russian Orientalist Vasilii Vladimirovich Bartold (1869–1930) can be credited with having enshrined the theory that the rising European presence in the In-

---

24. A useful synthetic overview of some earlier works on Central Eurasian commercial history from prehistory to the colonial era can be found in Barisitz, *Central Asia and the Silk Road*.

dian Ocean cast Central Asia into decline.[25] Considered by many to be the founding father of the modern study of Central Asian history, Bartold was a brilliant and prolific scholar.[26] He was a master of Central Asian Arabic, Persian, and Turkic manuscripts, and, given that the region became incorporated into the Russian Empire during the course of his lifetime, he enjoyed unfettered access to Central Asian sources. Even now, a century after he wrote some of his greatest work, Bartold continues to influence many of the questions that historians of Central Asia ask, and how we ask them. Bartold's methodology was to establish a deep mastery of the sources that are the foundation for Central Asian history, critically analyze them, and then assemble his own work based on the knowledge he had retrieved. As the first scholar to direct attention to many of these texts, he authored the catalog entries that summarize their contents and, when possible, provide the textual chain of transmission through which the authors drew their information. Based upon his painstaking work with the manuscript sources, at barely thirty years old Bartold was able to propel the field forward by assembling what was, and arguably remains, the most comprehensive scholarly study of Central Asian history from the rise of Islam to the Mongol invasions.[27]

One cannot help but hold Bartold's work in high esteem—it brings together a wealth of information drawn from primary sources in a number of languages, and his richly documented and extensive body of work remains a valuable resource for researchers in the field. Still, one must recognize the ways in which his own historical context influenced the conclusions of his research. To be more specific, Bartold was a disciple of Victor Rosen, a renowned Russian adherent to the German positivist tradition. This school of thought holds the central premise that, like the physical world, human societies operate according to universal natural laws and that scholars can determine these laws through their analysis of empirical evidence drawn from primary source research. In an article examining Bartold's professional life and extoling his impressive scholarly legacy, Yuri Bregel observed that Bartold enthusiastically embraced this training, declaring: "As I came

---

25. Several parts of this discussion appeared in an earlier form in Levi, "Early Modern Central Asia," 866–78. I am grateful to the editors for permission to revisit that essay and present portions of it here in an expanded and updated format.
26. Yuri Bregel, "Barthold and Modern Oriental Studies," *International Journal of Middle East Studies* 12, no. 3 (1980): 385–403.
27. Available in English as V. V. Bartold, *Turkestan Down to the Mongol Invasion*, trans. T. Minorsky, ed. C. E. Bosworth (London: Luzac and Co., 1928 [1898–1900]).

from the school of Baron Rosen, so shall I sink into the grave."[28] He further asserted that he strictly adhered to a scientific methodology, the aim of which was to approach Central Asian history by "applying the same laws of historical evolution which had been established for the history of Europe."[29]

This scientific methodology was a key feature of the Rosen school, as it was intended to set Rosen and his disciples apart from the less rigorous work produced by nonacademic researchers employed by the government, military, and theological seminaries. In her recent study of Russian Orientalists, Vera Tolz notes that Rosen and his disciples were highly critical of this lay scholarship, which they found to be generally inadequate and "exhibiting Christian, Eurocentric, and racial biases."[30] Bartold in particular had little patience for his contemporaries whose work was tainted by an underlying prejudice against Muslim societies and the Islamic religion.[31]

As a whole, Tolz provides a selective, occasionally contradictory, and deeply apologetic analysis of fin de siècle Russian Orientalist scholarship, with a focus on Rosen's disciples and the larger political implications of their work. Her study illustrates a number of ways in which the Rosen school represents a demonstrable step forward in the Russian academy. But one might take issue with several aspects of her argument, not the least of which is her thesis that, through their influence on the work of Arab scholars in the 1960s, the Russian Orientalists can be credited with having laid the foundation for the modern field of postcolonial studies.[32] For Tolz, the Russian Orientalists (or "Orientologists") are exempt from the Saidian critique as their work emanated from a worldview that was categorically distinct from the work of their Western colleagues. In Tolz's view, the Russian Orientalists "were fully aware that the concepts of 'East' and 'West,' 'Europe' and 'Asia' were politically, culturally, and socially constructed. They wrote extensively about the origins of various definitions of Europe and Asia and, in the process, questioned and rejected the East-

---

28. Bregel, "Barthold and Modern Oriental Studies," 386.
29. Bregel, "Barthold and Modern Oriental Studies," 386.
30. See Vera Tolz, *Russia's Own Orient: The Politics of Identity and Oriental Studies in the Late Imperial and Early Soviet Periods* (Oxford: Oxford University Press, 2011), 12. For alternate perspectives, see the collection of essays in Michael David-Fox, Peter Holquist, and Alexander Martin, eds., *Orientalism and Empire in Russia* (Bloomington, IN: Slavica, 2006). See also Alexander Morrison, "'Applied Orientalism' in British India and Tsarist Turkestan," *Comparative Studies in History and Society* 51, no. 3 (2009): 619–47.
31. Tolz, *Russia's Own Orient*, 14.
32. Tolz, *Russia's Own Orient*, 19.

West dichotomy as a figment of the European imagination. The rejection of this dichotomy was central to their world view and strongly affected their perceptions of Russia itself."[33] The Russian Orientalists did not, therefore, envision Russian imperial expansion in the Caucasus and Central Asia as a victory of West over East, or Europe over Asia. Rather, in Tolz's understanding, Bartold and his colleagues viewed the Russian Empire as a grand Eurasian symbiosis.[34] The degree to which this is an accurate assessment of Russian Orientalist scholarship is a question that demands further analysis.

One might recall that the "laws of historical evolution" that Rosen and his disciples sought to employ were the same ones that had been advanced by such early social scientists as Lewis Henry Morgan (d. 1881) and Herbert Spencer (d. 1903). A concern of primary importance in the scholarly world of the late nineteenth century was to determine cultural hierarchy, and for social scientists of the time the highest elements of that hierarchy clearly rested in the West. Morgan, the American anthropologist, argued in favor of a unilineal theory of social evolution in which Western societies were the most evolved, followed by other, less developed societies that had failed to keep up in technological innovation. The English philosopher Spencer is famous for having coined the phrase "survival of the fittest," which other social scientists applied to human societies as social Darwinism.

Rather than approaching his subject with an appreciation for the constructed nature of the East-West dichotomy, Bartold himself was deeply influenced by these theories. As Bregel notes, Bartold "viewed the evolution of mankind as a gradual rapprochement of various societies through the expansion of culture from more advanced peoples to less advanced."[35] Even Tolz (contradicting herself) recognizes that Bartold found European scholarly traditions to be inherently superior, hoping that "Russians and 'natives' (*tuzemtsy*) would work together . . . , so that the Russians would learn from the 'natives' about various aspects of local life, whereas the 'natives' would 'gradually acquire the key scientific methods developed by European [scholars].'"[36] Such statements provide valuable insights in the mission of Russian scholarship at the time, and they add an important nuance to Tolz's conclusions.

As they aimed to discover universal truths about human societies, there is no overlooking the fact that these social science theorists were also shap-

---

33. Tolz, *Russia's Own Orient*, 21.
34. Tolz, *Russia's Own Orient*, 58.
35. Bregel, "Barthold and Modern Oriental Studies," 387.
36. Tolz, *Russia's Own Orient*, 29.

ing scholarly discussions in the particular context of their time. This was the late nineteenth century, when European powers—Russia included—were deeply engaged in the great "Race for Empire." However they justified their conclusions, and here I would be inclined to agree with Tolz, Bartold and the other Rosen disciples were acutely aware that "knowledge is power" and that the scholarship they produced had very real political implications.[37] Like their colleagues in Western Europe, the theories the Russian Orientalists advanced endeavored to address, explain, and, in some cases, justify the colonial enterprise.

To frame that in more specific terms, the Russian Orientalists viewed Central Asia's early modern decline as having paved the way for the nineteenth-century Russian colonization of the region. Following the same "laws of historical evolution" that dominated European history, Bartold unapologetically viewed Russian imperial expansion in the region as a benevolent and modernizing force for an isolated and backward civilization.[38] In his own words, he considered the eighteenth century to have been "a period of political, economical and cultural decadence for all of Muslim Asia."[39] And referring specifically to Central Asia, he found that "in the nineteenth century, when Europe had definitely assumed cultural leadership, Turkestan stood lowest of all Muslim lands, being as it was the part of Muslim Asia farthest removed from Europe."[40]

The fact that Bartold adhered to a social science theory bound to a nineteenth-century European imperial context does not necessarily mean that his conclusions are wrong. However, considering the context in which Bartold wrote, and given how influential he and his work remain in the field, it seems reasonable to suggest that they do warrant further investigation. Many scholarly treatments of early modern Central Asia continue to dismiss the region as inconsequential in the Eurasian arena. Following in the footsteps of Bartold, many of these studies attribute this turn of fate to the rise of European maritime interests in the Indian Ocean and the corresponding collapse of the Silk Road trade.

---

37. Tolz, *Russia's Own Orient*, 20. This theme is explored in great detail in Denis V. Volkov, *Russia's Turn to Persia: Orientalism in Diplomacy and Intelligence* (Cambridge: Cambridge University Press, 2018).
38. Tolz, *Russia's Own Orient*, 21.
39. V. V. Bartold, *Four Studies on the History of Central Asia*, vol. 1, *A Short History of Turkestan*, trans. V. and T. Minorsky (Leiden: E. J. Brill, 1956), 65.
40. Bartold, *Four Studies*, 66. Southeast Asia is geographically farther from Europe, but, apparently because it was Dutch colonial territory, Bartold perceived of Central Asia as having been the "part of Muslim Asia farthest removed from Europe."

IMAGINING THE SILK ROAD

Our present interests rest in the early modern era, and so there is no need to survey the full historiography of the Silk Road. But I do aim to demonstrate that erroneous assumptions about Central Asia's role in overland Eurasian trade have long been embedded in the historiography, and that this has led to wildly differing interpretations of Central Asian economic history. In and of itself, this is unacceptable. But the impact of this historiographical defect is amplified many times over as scholars look to the region's economic history to support a multitude of scholarly arguments relating to other aspects of the region's social and political history.

In an effort to illustrate this point, our discussion will next contrast the divergent interpretations of Central Asian commercial history found in the recent work of Christopher Beckwith, S. Frederick Starr, and Valerie Hansen. I have chosen to focus attention on these studies for a number of reasons: they are all authored by senior figures in the field, they are all relatively recent, they all aim to reach a broad audience, and they all advance arguments that engage with Central Asia's historic role in overland Eurasian trade, albeit in strikingly different ways.

In 2009, Christopher Beckwith published his magisterial survey of five thousand years of Central Eurasian history, *Empires of the Silk Road: A History of Central Eurasia from the Bronze Age to the Present*. His primary objective with this study was to overturn shallow and flawed stereotypes of Central Eurasian nomads as predatory barbarians whose only contribution to the history of the world was toppling sedentary empires when they became too weak to defend themselves. This is an admirable goal, especially when one considers, as Beckwith rightly notes, that so much of Central Eurasian history has been written from the perspective of the nomads' sedentary neighbors, and even much of the scholarship that does focus on the region tends to be based on research in heavily biased sedentary sources. Another aim is to demonstrate how, by nurturing the Silk Road exchange and facilitating trans-Eurasian cultural interactions, from antiquity until the early modern era the Central Eurasian nomadic empires functioned as a critical linchpin at the heart of Eurasian history.[41] Trade was important, but for Beckwith, "the Silk Road was not in essence a commercial transportation network at all. It was the entire Central Eurasian economy, or

---

41. Beckwith prefers the term *Central Eurasia*, a more inclusive geographical designation that includes Central Asia, as well as Tibet, the Caucasus, and much of central Siberia. Beckwith, *Empires of the Silk Road*, xix.

socio-economic-political-cultural system."[42] Beckwith exhibits no interest in exploring the activities of caravan traders. For him, it was the Central Eurasian nomads who mediated the cultural and technological exchanges among the agrarian civilizations on the Eurasian periphery. Without the Silk Road, there would be no progress, and without nomads there would be no Silk Road.

Charting the arc of Central Eurasian history, Beckwith finds that from the time of the ancient Scythians, Central Eurasians flourished—economically, culturally, and politically—at the center of the great Silk Road system of commerce and communication. The nomads who drove this system effectively linked the Eurasian periphery, but incursions from shortsighted peripheral powers (e.g., China and Rome) periodically disrupted this equilibrium. This led to the collapse of the nomadic states, which caused the disruption of overland trade, economic crisis, and the subsequent collapse of the peripheral states. This was then followed by the emergence of a new nomadic power in Central Eurasia and the stabilization of the Eurasian socioeconomic and political system, until that, too, was upset by another incursion from the periphery, and so on.

Echoing Bartold, Beckwith locates the permanent break in this cycle in the sixteenth century with the rise of Portuguese commercial activity in the Indian Ocean and the European establishment of a maritime littoral system that brought the continental Silk Road to an end. According to Beckwith, "the closing of the borders, severe restrictions of international trade, and elimination of all significant Central Eurasian polities destroyed the economy of Central Eurasia.... The direct result was the severe impoverishment of Central Eurasia—especially its center, Central Asia—and its rapid plunge backward into darkness in technology and every other aspect of culture."[43] He concludes that in the early modern era, "Central Eurasia suffered from the most severe, long-lasting economic depression in world history. It declined into oblivion, while the coastal regions of Eurasia, nurtured by the commercially minded European navies, prospered as they never had before."[44]

Not since René Grousset's classic study *L'Empire des steppes* was published in 1939 has there been a historical work of such grand scope that keeps the lens focused squarely on Central Eurasia, and Central Eurasians.[45] But

---

42. Beckwith, *Empires of the Silk Road*, 264.
43. Beckwith, *Empires of the Silk Road*, 241–42.
44. Beckwith, *Empires of the Silk Road*, 262.
45. René Grousset, *L'Empire des steppes: Atilla, Gengis-Khan, Tamerlan* (Paris: Payot, 1939).

despite some admirable goals, Beckwith fails to engage with commercial history in any meaningful way, preferring instead to construct a theoretical framework on the shaky foundation of assumption and speculation. This undermines a number of his key arguments, the most important of which for our purpose are his conclusions regarding the flourishing nature of the Silk Road up to the sixteenth century and the supposedly devastating Central Eurasian economic and cultural decline following the rise of European trade in the Indian Ocean.[46]

S. Frederick Starr's 2013 publication *Lost Enlightenment: Central Asia's Golden Age from the Arab Conquests to Tamerlane* also directly engages Central Asia's historical role at the crossroads of Eurasian trade routes.[47] But where Beckwith is concerned principally with championing the historical importance of nomadic groups, Starr's attention remains fixed on the sedentary zone. Nomadic peoples are superfluous to Starr's efforts to document medieval Central Asia's great period of cultural and scholarly efflorescence, which lasted from 800 to 1200. Over these four centuries, Starr argues, Central Asia became bound by both faith and political institutions to the 'Abbasid Caliphate in Baghdad, and Central Asians led the world in scientific discovery and scholarly achievement.

Starr's narrative weaves one remarkable Central Asian achievement after another. The end result is a synthetic survey of early Islamic (pre-Mongol) Central Asia that endeavors to highlight the magnificently "enlightened" environment of the time, and the seemingly endless line of Central Asian luminaries that emerged within it: Ibn Sina (Avicenna), al-Khwarezmi, al-Biruni, al-Bukhari, al-Farabi, al-Kashgari, and many more.[48] These scholars engaged with and advanced the classical achievements of Greece on the one hand, and they helped lay the foundations for the much more famous and well-studied early modern European Scientific Revolution and Enlightenment on the other.

Starr attributes this enlightened environment to Central Asia's prosperity, and he links that prosperity to several factors. These include the early development of irrigation agriculture in the oasis zones and the region's thriving commercial economy, which itself stemmed from its geographical position at the heart of Asia and the willingness and ability of Central

---

46. For further elaboration, see my review of this book in *American Historical Review* 115, no. 2 (2010): 512–13.
47. S. Frederick Starr, *Lost Enlightenment: Central Asia's Golden Age from the Arab Conquest to Tamerlane* (Princeton: Princeton University Press, 2013).
48. Despite the fact that these individuals wrote their principal works in Arabic and are known by Arabic-sounding names, they were all from Central Asia.

Asians to capitalize on that position by promoting long-distance Eurasian trade.[49] For Starr, the Central Asian "Enlightenment" was directly linked to the prosperity of the Silk Road trade.

Unlike Beckwith, Starr directs some attention to Central Asia's commercial infrastructure. For example, he observes that the Bactrian camels (the larger two-humped variety, as opposed to the smaller one-humped dromedaries) that constituted the backbone of Central Asian commerce were able to carry loads of some five hundred pounds each. From that, he extrapolates that Central Asian caravan traders moving merchandise strapped to the backs of one thousand such camels could transport roughly five hundred thousand pounds of merchandise: equivalent to ten of our modern cargo containers, or "a ten- or twelve-car freight train."[50] He further reasons that since the traders who orchestrated these caravans would naturally have been predisposed to focus on more expensive luxury items, as doing so offered greater profit, Silk Road merchants engaged in what must have been an extraordinarily valuable trade. His discussion does provide a useful critique of the ways in which overly simplified interpretations of Richthofen's Silk Road have done a very poor job of describing such factors as: the diversity of merchandise that the camels transported, the importance of India to the so-called Silk Road trade, and the tendency of scholars to emphasize Chinese merchandise at the expense of all else, including silks, paper, and other merchandise produced within Central Asia itself.[51]

In late antiquity, this vibrant commercial economy drew Buddhists from India, Nestorian Christians from Syria, and other groups from outside of Central Asia to the region, and during the centuries prior to the Arab conquests, it propelled Sogdian merchants outward as far as their caravans could take them. Within Central Asia, regions specialized in the production of high-quality steel blades, jewelry, pottery, silks, musical instruments, excellent quality paper, and more, for use locally and for export. Starr hyperbolically summarizes: "The presence from early times of all these merchants—most of them locally based—assured that Central Asian cities would become the major center of banking and finance for trade between China, India, and the Middle East. . . . Numerous service industries arose as well, including hostels or caravanserais, bazaars, and storage facilities. These enabled the cities to become the main inter-

---

49. Starr, *Lost Enlightenment*, 37–40.
50. Starr, *Lost Enlightenment*, 41. In constructing this example, Starr fails to consider the logistics involved in moving a caravan of one thousand camels across an arid zone without starving the animals.
51. Starr, *Lost Enlightenment*, 40–48.

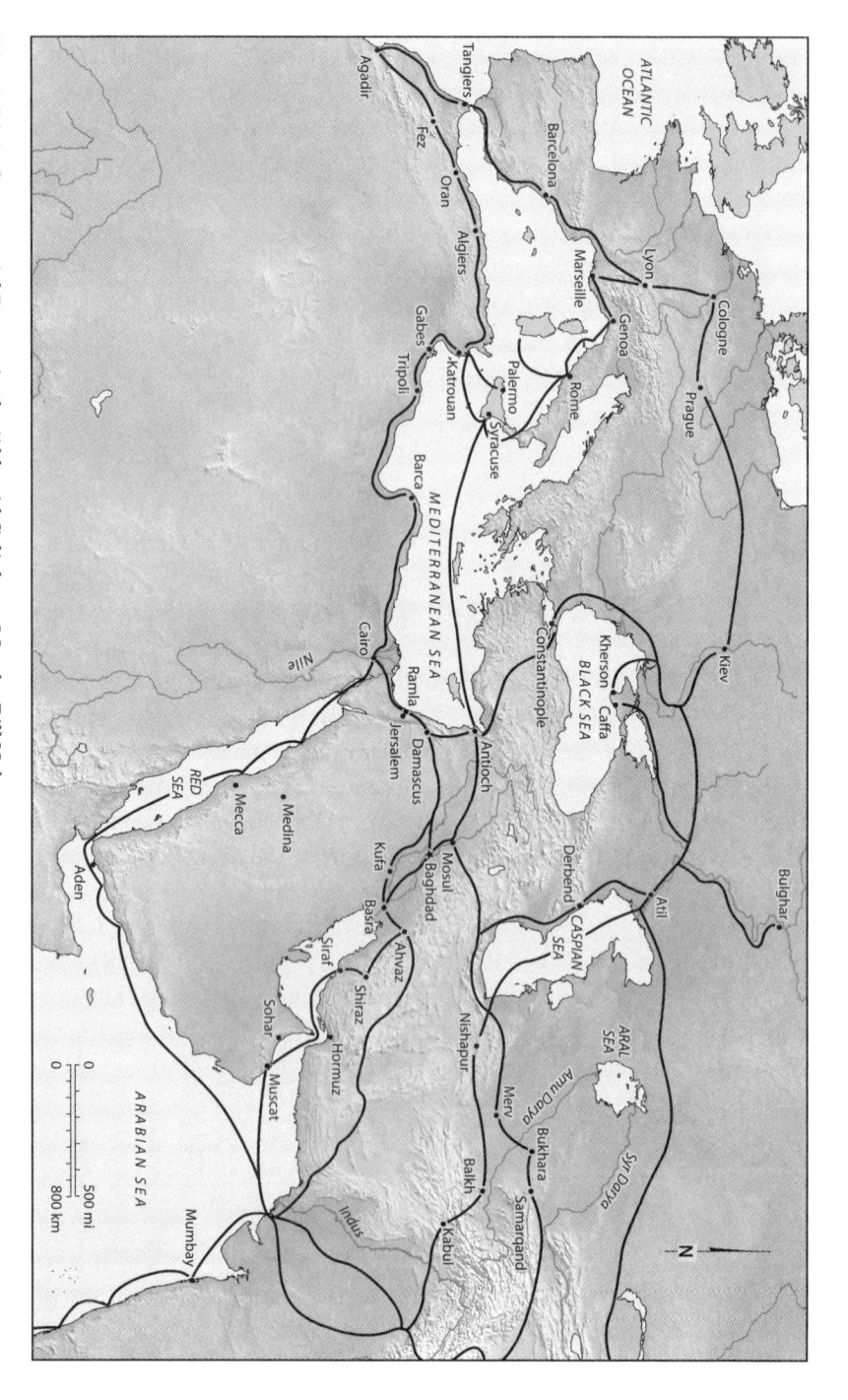

Map 9. Main Commercial Routes in the 'Abbasid Caliphate. Map by Bill Nelson.

national entrepôts on the entire Eurasian continent, the gathering place of all."[52]

In the eighth century, Central Asians leveraged this economic vitality to give rise to a magnificent scholarly efflorescence. Following the Tang defeat at the Battle of Talas in 751 and subsequent withdrawal from the entire region after the An Lushan rebellion in 755, Central Asians became politically and, increasingly, culturally bound to the 'Abbasid capital of Baghdad. Within decades, the 'Abbasid caliphs sought to transform their new capital into a center for scholarly exchange and production, and from the outset Central Asians led the way.[53] Starr attributes this to a number of cultural factors, which include Central Asians' penchant for travel as well as an open-mindedness that stemmed from their long history of exposure to many different modes of thought.

A century later, with Baghdad embroiled in conflict and the scholarly environment substantially less supportive, Central Asians found refuge back home. Thus, until the end of the tenth century, the most brilliant scholars of the era flourished in Central Asia itself under the patronage of the Muslim Samanid rulers in Bukhara (819–1005), whose own prosperity Starr suggests was a product of the low taxes and security they provided to international traders in their realm. Even after Samanid authority waned and then collapsed at the turn of the millennium, the region's most famous scholars found an equally supportive environment under the Muslim Turkic dynasties—Qarakhanids, Seljuks, and others—that succeeded them. And so it remained up to the cataclysmic trauma unleashed by the thirteenth-century Mongol conquests. Looking back, Starr claims that for roughly four hundred years Central Asia flourished as "the world's greatest entrepôt of trade and its most prosperous cities. A rich heritage from the past, worldly cultural contacts in the present, and affluence sufficient to support a bevy of thinkers and artists—all this created a nearly ideal environment for study and reflection.... By any measure, this was one of humanity's great ages of thought and creativity, a true Age of Enlightenment."[54]

In determining what propelled this Enlightenment, Starr identifies a climate of religious pluralism, a cultural openness, and a source of abun-

---

52. Starr, *Lost Enlightenment*, 44.
53. Starr, *Lost Enlightenment*, 158.
54. Starr, *Lost Enlightenment*, 515. Again, in advancing his claim regarding Central Asia's extraordinary commercial importance, Starr does not permit a lack of supporting evidence to get in his way.

dant wealth drawn from mediating the overland Eurasian caravan trade. In terms of what precipitated its end, the final chapter of his study critically surveys multiple theories and dismisses a number of them. Starr takes issue, for example, with Richard Frye's widely accepted argument that the end of the scholarly efflorescence in medieval Central Asia stemmed from the weakening power of the *dihqans*, the Persian landed aristocracy who served as the scholars' primary patrons, during and after the Samanid collapse.[55] Foremost among those theories that Starr considers to have merit are a cultural move away from open-mindedness in favor of restrictive Islamic theological traditions and a severe economic downturn, which, in his view, began centuries before the Portuguese first entered the Indian Ocean. In particular, Starr points to the failure of Central Asians "to provide security along the old trade routes; worse, they greedily raised tariffs to the point that transporters began searching for alternate routes.... It is fair to say that unwise policies on the part of the Central Asians killed the already ailing golden goose of free trade, and that Vasco da Gama merely dealt with the consequences."[56]

Like many scholars before them, Beckwith and Starr both envision the overland caravan trade as substantial in its magnitude and a defining feature of the Central Asian economy, providing stability for regional states and societies. Both attribute the region's prosperity to the ability of its merchants to mediate overland trade, and both argue that this ability came to an abrupt end, although they attribute that end to different causal factors unfolding centuries apart. While Beckwith places the decline squarely on the shoulders of early modern European merchants in the Indian Ocean, Starr locates it several centuries earlier, identifying the end of "free trade" in the region and the resulting economic decline as one of several factors that brought an end to Central Asia's Age of Enlightenment.

On close analysis, one finds that Starr's agenda with this book is driven more by a neoliberal economic policy objective than by academic inquiry.[57] In effect, Starr has manipulated a scholarly subject in order to advocate for free-market trade. But even those most eager for the post-Soviet Cen-

---

55. Starr, *Lost Enlightenment*, 527–28 and note 12.
56. Starr, *Lost Enlightenment*, 526–28.
57. Starr's policy objectives are evidenced by the publisher's decision to elicit dust jacket quotes in support of the book from Francis Fukuyama and Henry Kissinger, neither of whom would be in a particularly good position to assess the book's scholarly merits. These merits are accurately summarized in Devin DeWeese's review of the book, which appeared in *Journal of Interdisciplinary History* 45, no. 4 (2015): 611–13.

tral Asian states to open their markets to the West will find no evidence to support his assertion that the Samanids, or any other Central Asian state, embraced free trade economic policies. His study also ignores the quite substantial body of scholarly work and primary sources readily available in the English language that demonstrate the importance that the Mongol rulers attached to promoting long-distance trade across their empire, including Central Asia, during the thirteenth and fourteenth centuries.[58] In one recent study of this very subject, Virgil Ciocîltan examines the Mongols' sustained efforts to protect traders and keep taxes low (but not eliminate them entirely) precisely so that their overland routes could successfully compete with maritime transport and flourish. Ciocîltan argues convincingly that "the unprecedented amount of transcontinental trade in the Chinggisid era is clear proof that the khans' efforts were successful."[59] These efforts brought economic benefits and recovery to many peoples, including Central Asians, who had several decades earlier suffered as victims of the Mongol conquests.

The most rigorous of the three recent studies addressed here is Valerie Hansen's 2012 publication, *The Silk Road: A New History*.[60] While Beckwith and Starr both advance their own particular visions of Central Asian commercial history as a means to support other theses and agendas, Hansen's study is focused more directly on the question of what constituted the ancient Silk Road itself. She organizes her study around each of seven oasis cities situated along trade routes that extend westward from Chang'an (Xi'an), the capital of Han China, to Samarqand. She analyzes the diverse populations that inhabited each of these cities, their relations with each other and with distant colleagues and family members, and the commercial exchanges that very slowly moved merchandise from one oasis to the next.

---

58. For a general synthesis of scholarship on this topic, see the chapter "Pax Mongolica and Trade," in Timothy May, *The Mongol Conquests in World History* (London: Reaktion Books, 2012), 104–29. For a discussion of the larger Eurasian ramifications of Mongol efforts at promoting trade, see the classic study by Janet Abu Lughod, *Before European Hegemony: The World System A.D. 1250–1350* (New York: Oxford University Press, 1991). For an excellent scholarly study focusing on textiles, see Thomas T. Allsen, *Commodity and Exchange in the Mongol Empire: A Cultural History of Islamic Textiles* (Cambridge: Cambridge University Press, 2002).
59. Virgil Ciocîltan, *The Mongols and the Black Sea Trade in the Thirteenth and Fourteenth Centuries*, trans. Samuel Willcocks (Leiden: E. J. Brill, 2012), 12, 21.
60. Valerie Hansen, *The Silk Road: A New History* (Oxford: Oxford University Press, 2012).

Hansen's study delves deeply into scholarship on the Silk Road in multiple languages, and she makes good use of the remarkable documents and artifacts that Stein, Hedin, and others unearthed from the Tarim Basin oases, now located at museums across the globe, and other more recent discoveries made by Chinese archeologists. She exploits a wide variety of religious treatises, legal records, commercial contracts, personal correspondences, and cultural artifacts to present a descriptive analysis of the everyday lived experiences and cultural environments of the peoples who inhabited a number of seemingly remote Central Asian oasis towns. Her study also highlights the critical roles that imperial powers and various other types of peoples played in trans-Eurasian cultural exchanges, including refugees and other migrant populations. Her richly detailed study provides a firm foundation for future work on the subject.

From the outset, Hansen exposes a number of romanticized myths and exaggerations associated with popular and scholarly understandings of what constituted the Silk Road. She observes that Chinese merchants engaged in commercial interactions with traders in the western oases, in what is today Xinjiang, already during the Shang dynasty (1766–1045 BCE), more than one thousand years before the Han victory over the Xiongnu in 133 BCE. Contrary to Richthofen's map and later notions of a vibrant network driven by several main trunk roads, she also presents the Silk Road as a network of local roads—nothing grander than unmarked paths—that crossed wilderness, steppe, and desert to connect one oasis town to the next. Missing are the caravans of one thousand or more Bactrian camels loaded with half a million pounds of luxury goods. Most of the inhabitants of these towns were illiterate peasant farmers, not cosmopolitan traders, and Hansen draws valuable attention to the roles that all sorts of travelers played in the cultural exchanges along the so-called Silk Road: itinerant monks, craftsmen, and refugees are the principal agents, not merchants. What trade did pass along these treacherous dirt paths was primarily a small-scale transit trade. Silk played an important role for a time as it was produced in China in large quantities and used both for gifts in "silk diplomacy" with nomadic powers and as currency to pay the Chinese troops garrisoned in the distant provinces. But her research confirms that other merchandise, such as paper, spices, glass, and metals, outweighed silk in commercial importance.

Hansen advances an understanding of Silk Road trade that contrasts sharply with those encountered elsewhere. Beckwith and Starr, for example, both argue that there was a profound magnitude of commercial traffic that passed along the Silk Road. Neither provides evidence to support their assertions, but in both studies the amount of trade is presumed to have been so substantial that when it came to an end (whether circa 1200 or 1500), it resulted in economic depression and civilizational decline. Hansen, on the contrary, is thoroughly dismissive of the magnitude of the trade itself. Again, for Hansen the importance of the Silk Road was not the commercial exchange: it was the exceedingly slow exchange in religious traditions, philosophical ideas and scientific knowledge, languages, artistic styles, musical traditions, foods and culinary traditions, and, to a much lesser extent, merchandise. In correcting the exaggerations that permeate the Silk Road literature, she summarizes: "The Silk Road was one of the least traveled routes in human history and possibly not worth studying—if tonnage carried, traffic, or the number of travelers at any time were the sole measure of a given route's significance."[61]

Hansen makes a number of references to the famous eight Sogdian letters that more than a century ago Sir Aurel Stein's expedition unearthed in a mailbag buried in the sand some fifty-six miles outside of Dunhuang.[62] The letters, which were probably headed for Samarqand, are exceptional in that they were actually written by merchants, and they include a rare insight into the commercial interactions of the Sogdian diaspora. According to Hansen, "the letters, which date to 313 or 314, mention specific commodities: wool and linen, musk, the lead-based cosmetic ceruse, pepper, silver and possibly silk. The quantities are not large, ranging from 3.3 pounds (1.5 kg) to 88 pounds (40 kg), all consonant with small-scale trade managed by caravaneers."[63] This suggests only a modest exchange, nothing that would approach even a small fraction of the magnitude presumed by Starr.

Hansen's study is one of the few to apply documentary evidence to give shape to a discussion that has long remained too vague, and her conclusions regarding the importance of state actors and nonmerchants in cultural exchanges are on point. Still, stepping back and approaching Hansen's analysis from another perspective, one might suggest that her wholesale dismissal of the Silk Road as a commercial network represents an overcorrection. It seems reasonable to suggest, for example, that this single mailbag represents a microscopic view of a much larger, albeit very poorly documented, exchange that included many such merchants of multiple backgrounds and many such shipments of diverse cargo. It remains unknown whether other mailbags accompanied this particular caravan, how big (or small) that caravan was, and how many other caravans made their way along

---

61. Hansen, *Silk Road*, 235.
62. Hansen, *Silk Road*, 116–20.
63. Hansen, *Silk Road*, 239.

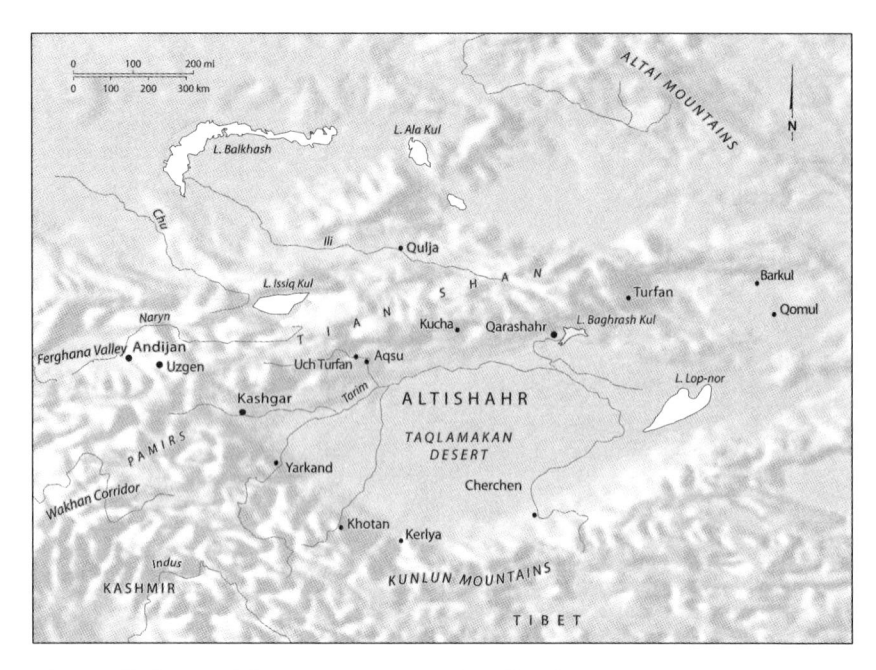

Map 10. Xinjiang and the Tarim Basin. Map by Bill Nelson.

this particular route, or other routes leading to Central Asian cities, in the weeks, months, and years before and after this one.

To be sure, even if one were to adopt the most optimistic perspective, it still seems highly unlikely that a caravan of one thousand Bactrian camels each carrying five hundred pounds of luxury goods made its way from Dunhuang to Samarqand in the environment that Hansen details. Something approaching that level of exchange seems more possible, however, if the range of analysis is extended to the totality of commercial exchanges over a full year. It seems more likely still if we expand its scope from the seven oases of Hansen's study—six of which are in an arid and sparsely populated region of western China—to the full Eurasian interior, including the urban centers, agricultural oases, and, especially, the steppe.

Here at last we get to the point. Recasting the Silk Road trade in such a way requires a shift in terms of one's conceptual center of gravity, setting aside the long-established latitudinal "Sinocentric" perspective, in which Central Asian commercial markets are envisioned as a projection of China's westward trade, in favor of a multivectored network more firmly situated in Central Asia. While such a proposition may make some scholars of the Silk Road uncomfortable, there are compelling reasons for doing so. Central Asia is, after all, the location where many of these celebrated cultural exchanges took place. It is true, of course, that the Silk Road was much more than a commercial phenomenon, and that merchants themselves were only one of several groups involved in the mediation of these cultural exchanges. But from the perspective of commercial history, approaching the Silk Road from the vantage point of China obscures the fact that the Eurasian interior was home to multiple merchant diaspora communities, caravan traders, state actors, soldiers, nomadic producers, and nomadic mediatory traders, as well as the stereotypical small-scale local peddler, all of whom participated in overlapping networks of exchange. And while nomadic communities are notoriously difficult to locate in documentary sources, it is especially important to appreciate the roles that they played in Eurasian commercial history.[64] Jeff Eden has recently illustrated this very point in his study of the Central Asian slave trade in the eighteenth and nineteenth centuries. Eden finds that the trade in slaves during this period "thrived," but that it was highly diffuse, largely external to urban markets, and often managed by nomadic groups whose poorly documented commercial activities beyond urban centers remain stubbornly invisible in the historical record.[65]

TOWARD AN INTEGRATIVE HISTORY OF EARLY MODERN CENTRAL ASIA

In essence, I am advocating for a more integrative approach to Central Asian history. I am not the first to advance such an argument.[66] Taking stock of the field in the early 1980s, Joseph Fletcher (1934–1984) observed an unfortunate tendency among historians at the time to focus on "political and diplomatic history, and, more recently, institutional history." In his view, such a narrow approach had been "not much help" in shedding light on the historical interconnectedness of non-Western societies. Exploring

---

64. For the classic introduction to this subject, see Anatoly M. Khazanov, *Nomads and the Outside World* (Cambridge: Cambridge University Press, 1984). See also Thomas Barfield, *The Nomadic Alternative* (Englewood Cliffs, NJ: Prentice-Hall, 1993); Thomas Barfield, "Steppe Empires, China, and the Silk Route: Nomads as a Force in International Trade and Politics," in *Nomads in the Sedentary World*, ed. Anatoly M. Khazanov and André Wink (Richmond, Surrey: Curzon, 2001), 234–49.
65. Jeff Eden, *Slavery and Empire in Central Asia* (Cambridge: Cambridge University Press, 2018), 57. See also Jeff Eden, "Beyond the Bazaars: Geographies of the Slave Trade in Central Asia," *Modern Asian Studies* 51, no. 4 (2017): 919–55. For the movement of many thousands of Indian slaves to Central Asian markets, see also Scott C. Levi, "Hindus Beyond the Hindu Kush: Indians in the Central Asian Slave Trade," *Journal of the Royal Asiatic Society* 3d ser., 12, no. 3 (2002): 277–88.
66. A similar perspective is advanced in James A. Millward, *The Silk Road: A Very Short Introduction* (Oxford: Oxford University Press, 2013). For insight into recent literature on the Silk

the benefits of both deeply researched "vertical" and contemporaneous but spatially vast "horizontal" continuities, Fletcher found it unfortunate that few scholars of Asian history had attempted to reach beyond the boundaries of their own specific geographic fields to produce anything other than narrowly focused vertical microhistories. For those working in non-Western fields in the United States, this was exacerbated by the imposition of the area studies paradigm, "in which historians talk to social scientists within their geographic specialty area but have little contact with other historians working on unrelated societies."[67] This rendered many historians in non-Western fields blind to larger processes unfolding beyond the periphery of their proverbial backyard, and poorly equipped to employ an approach that would enable them even to recognize the horizontal continuities that may represent the very causal factors propelling their own research questions.

In the decades since Fletcher wrote his essay, this paradigm has begun to shift for scholars working in Central Asian history. To some extent, this is a product of the collapse of the Soviet Union and the independence of the five former Soviet Central Asian republics. In the early 1990s, this brought a new wave of interest to the region, as researchers with more varied historical training were able to gain easier access to Central Asian archives and library collections. Meanwhile, many scholars working within Central Asia have begun to engage discussions and debates unfolding beyond the post-Soviet space. Collectively, these scholars' work in the primary sources produced both in the region and beyond, their engagement with a broader body of secondary literature, and the originality of the questions that they have brought to their work has helped to reshape our understanding of Central Asian history and its place in the early modern world.

Other factors propelling this trend are the growing appreciation for world history as a research field and a disciplinary trend favoring transnational or, for those of us who work on earlier periods, transregional history. To be sure, Fletcher's model of "integrated history" has its limits, and while some have elected to approach their historical subjects with a broader lens, there remains a firm appreciation for the merits of deeply researched microhistories.[68] This is as it should be, and the friction that arises among

---

Road, see the review of both Hansen's and Millward's books by Nile Green, "Winding between Myth and Politics: The Silk Road," *Los Angeles Review of Books*, June 13, 2014. https://lareviewofbooks.org/review/winding-myth-politics-silk-road.

67. Fletcher, "Integrative History," 39.
68. Referencing Marc Gaborieau, Alexandre Papas critiques Fletcher's model as seductive ("séduisante") but limited in its application. Alexandre Papas, *Soufisme et politique entre*

scholars who favor differing methodologies and interpretations can be helpful in moving a field forward. More importantly, and here I return to a point made in the previous chapter, I would emphasize the great potential to be found in putting those microhistories into conversation with scholars working on similar themes in other contexts. This follows in the constructive spirit of Sanjay Subrahmanyam's effort in the South Asian field "to implement a programme of... 'connected history,' reworking the history of South Asia into a larger Eurasian space of conjunctural movements."[69] Echoing Fletcher, Subrahmanyam cautions that "area studies can very rapidly become parochialism," and he points to the methodological merits of investigating historical connections across space rather than approaching an area in geographic isolation from the world around it, or privileging a region's unique nature through a comparative approach.[70] Or, as argued even more forcefully by Donald Davis:

> Connecting histories means more than finding connections between places and histories in Asia. It also means understanding how transformations in Asia have affected and were influenced by Africa, South America, Europe, and beyond. The notion that the world has ever been anything but connected has been largely exploded, thanks to the work of archaeologists for the ancient world, philologists for the classical periods, and world historians for the medieval and early modern global systems.... Insularity is a rare exception in human existence and in cultural evolution. Mobility and flows between areas and over long periods of time have been at the core of both change and stability in Asian history.[71]

I encourage readers to hold that thought closely as the discussion moves forward in the following chapters.

Chine, Tibet et Turkestan: Étude sur les Khwajas Naqshbandis du Turkestan orientale (Paris: Jean Maisonneuve, 2005), 16 and note.

69. Sanjay Subrahmanyam, *From the Tagus to the Ganges: Explorations in Connected History* (Delhi: Oxford University Press, 2012), ix–x. For a discussion of the methodological merits of connected history, see Subrahmanyam, "Connected Histories." Setting aside Subrahmanyam's overly dismissive position toward other methods of conducting integrative analyses, his essay lays out a useful methodology and makes a number of important points regarding the institutional hurdles to conducting connected history. See Subrahmanyam, "Connected Histories," 760–62. To examine his work in practice, see *From the Tagus to the Ganges* as well as its companion volume, *Mughals and Franks: Explorations in Connected History* (Delhi: Oxford University Press, 2012).

70. Subrahmanyam, "Connected Histories," 742.

71. Donald R. Davis, "Three Principles for an Asian Humanities: Care First... Learn From... Connect Histories," *Journal of Asian Studies* 74, no. 1 (2015): 61.

IMAGINING SILK ROADS

In 1877, the German historical geographer Ferdinand von Richthofen first advanced the notion of the Silk Road as a Eurasian trade route, or network of routes, that linked China with the Mediterranean. Like all such tropes, it gained popularity because it served a purpose—in this case, as an efficient way to reference the trans-Eurasian commercial arteries that facilitated cross-cultural exchanges in the Eurasian heartlands. More recent work has found this to be an oversimplification that fails to capture the means by which these cultural exchanges took place. The previous discussion has also argued that the Silk Road's value as a conceptual framework has been severely limited by its poorly defined and malleable nature.

In the area of commercial history, there are a number of reasons why the Silk Road has remained so difficult to define. Historians are at the mercy of our sources, and documentary sources on premodern overland Eurasian trade are sparse. That partly explains why overly generalized, romanticized mythologies regarding the Silk Road trade have proven to be so resilient. This chapter has identified a number of these mythologies, and it has illustrated how a lack of serious attention to Central Asian commercial history has enabled scholars to mold it and reshape it almost at will in order to support any of a number of often contradictory historical theories and interpretations.

This chapter has also endeavored to locate the origins of these mythologies in the Orientalist scholarship of more than a century ago. Bartold and his colleagues significantly advanced the study of Central Asian history by applying a rigorous and scholarly methodology to their work. Their techniques included a deep mastery of the Central Asian sources, and also the application of theoretical frameworks that were innovative for their time. But drawing upon notions of social hierarchies devised at least partly in response to colonial expansion during the Age of Empire, early scholars of Central Asian history perceived and portrayed Central Asian merchants as simple caravan traders whose commercial activities were limited to shuttling luxury merchandise (e.g., silk) between China and the Mediterranean. When the European companies entered the Indian Ocean commercial arena and began transporting large quantities of Asian spices, silks, porcelains, and other merchandise to European markets, it seemed only logical that the more advanced maritime traders outpaced the lumbering camel caravans, undermining the Silk Road trade and sending Central Asia into isolation and decline. I maintain that this notion poorly characterizes premodern Asian trade, and that it has produced a distorted image of early modern Central Asian history.

It is with good reason that some have argued that the concept of the Silk Road should be wholly dismissed as "a meaningless neologism." Nevertheless, the term remains exceedingly popular, and it seems unlikely that the goal of eliminating it from either the popular or scholarly vocabulary will be achieved in the near or distant future. It therefore seems reasonable to take steps to ensure that the concept is applied with greater precision and rigor, that it incorporates a more accurate understanding of Central Asian commercial history, and that the analytical center for Silk Road studies be shifted westward to Central Asia, where the great Silk Road exchanges unfolded.

In terms of early modern history, doing so stands to highlight the multiple ways that Central Asians were linked to changing Eurasian and global historical process, as well as Central Asians' agency in the period leading up to, and following, Chinese and Russian colonial expansion in the region. This approach moves beyond portraying caravan traders as simply mediators in China's westward trade. In its place, one finds a much richer understanding of early modern Central Asian trade as a dynamic complex of overlapping networks orchestrated by local and long-distance traders, merchant diasporas, state actors, soldiers, pilgrims, and, of course, nomadic producers and mediatory traders.

THREE

THE EARLY MODERN SILK ROAD

One need not look far to find references in travel literature, journalism, popular histories, and even contemporary scholarship that identify one or another city in Iran, Afghanistan, Central Asia, and China as "once great and prosperous," as it had been "an important stop along the historic Silk Road" before that trade route fell into decline. The previous chapter located the origin of the Silk Road concept in the Orientalist scholarship of the late nineteenth century. It explained how our understanding of that concept transformed over the following decades from referencing one quite specific aspect of Eurasian commercial history, the movement of luxury goods from China to the Mediterranean, into a shorthand for all Central Asian trade. It also argued that the assumption that Central Asia's commercial economy existed primarily to connect European markets with those in China and, to a lesser extent, India, has distorted Central Asian history in several key ways. Poorly defined and malleable, this understanding of the Silk Road trade has been too easily twisted and reshaped to support a multitude of arguments pertaining to Central Asian societies, the region's historical connection with the more populous agrarian societies on the Eurasian periphery, and Central Asia's changing place in the early modern world. The discussion also advocated for the merits of a broadly integrative historical methodology that aims to place local and regional histories within a world historical context.

This chapter employs such an approach to examine early modern Central Asia's commercial integration with its Eurasian neighbors. This is an enormous task and a single chapter can draw attention only to a few of the many interconnections that persisted throughout this period, or emerged during it. Nevertheless, a number of the studies referenced in this chapter demonstrate that, as the early modern global economy grew more substantial and expansive, state interests and commercial groups centered in India, China, and Russia all expanded their reach into the vast Central Asian hinterland.

More exciting is that Central Asians themselves were anything but passive in these exchanges. Looking back in time, one recalls Central Asia's classical Sogdian traders of antiquity, who for several centuries orchestrated an extensive merchant diaspora that stretched northward into the pastoral-nomadic steppe, eastward to Mongolia and China, westward to the Caucasus and the Mediterranean, and southward into India. A thousand years later, in the early modern era, at least two Central Asian commercial groups were engaged in similar activities, seeking out and exploiting emerging opportunities in distant foreign markets.

Of course, many things had changed as that millennium passed. Over the centuries, the relative importance of the commercial arteries that constituted these various overlapping exchange networks expanded and contracted, and some fell into disuse while new ones emerged. There were also changes in the merchandise traded. Luxury goods were outweighed by bulkier merchandise, and Chinese silk itself long ago became much less important as an article of trade. By the sixteenth century, merchants favored cotton textiles, horses and other livestock, medicinal herbs, chemicals, manufactured goods, precious metals, and more.

Like silk, horses and specie were long-standing staples in Central Asian trade. But the increased trade in cotton textiles, tea (from the eighteenth century), and other bulk goods suggests a growing commodification unfolding in early modern Central Asia that was linked to the commercial patterns of the maritime arena. Considered as a whole, the available evidence upends the notion that early modern Central Asia was in any way isolated from globalizing trends. Instead, as the commercial tempo increased, Central Asians became even more closely integrated in commercial patterns of the outside world.[1]

---

1. This supports Millward's argument that over the course of the early modern era, one finds "closer connections, expanded mutual knowledge, and increased trade between Russia, India, Persia, Central Asia, and China." Millward, *Silk Road*, 38. A similar argument is advanced in Matthew P. Romaniello, "Transregional Trade in Early Modern Eurasia," *Oxford Research*

EARLY MODERN EURASIAN TRADE NETWORKS

In 1492, Christopher Columbus sailed westward for Asia, intending to circumvent the Ottoman Empire and become the first person to establish a direct line of trade between European and Chinese markets. It is said that Columbus sailed with a copy of *The Book of Marco Polo* in hand. Whether or not that is apocryphal, copies of the book had circulated throughout much of Europe for nearly two centuries, and one can be reasonably certain that Columbus drew inspiration from Polo's account of the fantastic wealth and power of Qubilai Khan's Yuan China. Of course, Columbus never reached China, and he died before he even realized that the peoples he encountered on his voyages were not Asian. But his four journeys across the Atlantic (1492, 1493, 1498, and 1502) enabled the Spanish crown to extend its control into the Americas and develop a colonial enterprise that would prove far more profitable than Columbus could have imagined.

As Columbus was preparing to set off on his final voyage, on the other side of the world an army of Uzbek nomads under the leadership of Muhammad Shibani Khan forced Zahir al-Din Muhammad Babur, the last Timurid ruler in the ancestral capital of Samarqand, to flee his Central Asian homeland. With a small band of followers, Babur made his way into what is today Afghanistan, where he eventually managed to secure a position as ruler in Kabul. Babur describes the commercial economy of Kabul circa 1504 as follows:

> On the land route between Hindustan and Khurasan are two trading depots, Kabul and Kandahar. Caravans come to Kabul from Fergana, Turkistan, Samarkand, Bukhara, Balkh, Hissar, and Badakhshan. From Khurasan, they go to Kandahar. As the entrepôt between Hindustan and Khurasan, this province is an excellent mercantile center. Merchants who go to Cathay and Anatolia do no greater business. Every year seven, eight, or ten thousand horses come to Kabul. From Hindustan, caravans of ten, fifteen, twenty thousand pack animals bring slaves, textiles, rock sugar, refined sugar, and spices. Many Kabul merchants would not be satisfied with a 300 to 400 percent profit. Goods from Khurasan, Iraq, Anatolia, and China can be found in Kabul, which is the principal depot for Hindustan.[2]

Encyclopedia of Asian History, October 2017, http://oxfordre.com/asianhistory/view/10.1093/acrefore/9780190277727.001.0001/acrefore-9780190277727-e-296.

2. Zahir al-Din Muhammad Babur, *The Baburnama: Memoirs of Babur, Prince and Emperor*, trans. Wheeler M. Thackston (New York: Modern Library, 2002), 153. In reference to the large number of pack animals passing through Kabul, the word that Thackston reads as *oyluq* and

At the time Babur made this observation, the Portuguese had reached Calicut but had yet to take Goa and establish themselves as a major power in the Indian Ocean, the Lodi Afghan dynasty still ruled the Delhi Sultanate in north India, and Babur was more than two decades from defeating the Lodi armies at the Battle of Panipat (1526) and establishing his own dynastic rule in north India. While Babur was pleased with Kabul's stature as a commercial center that prospered by mediating India's trade with Central Asia and Iran at that time, several factors indicative of the early modern era would soon increase that trade many times over. These include the dramatic increase in the circulation of precious metals across the globe, sustained population growth brought about by the introduction of new foods, technological innovations and their dissemination across the globe, a rise in the commercialization and spread of plantation-style farming for the production of cash crops, and a general trend toward urbanization.

In the years following Columbus's initial voyage, Spanish ships carried thousands upon thousands of conquistadors and missionaries to the Americas. These adventurers encountered new peoples and unfamiliar crops, but failing to find the exotic spices and silks they were pursuing, they instead focused their efforts on extracting precious metals. The Spaniards used their firearms, iron swords, and horses to great tactical advantage. Benefiting from strategic alliances and the highly contagious diseases that the Spaniards carried with them from Europe and spread among the indigenous populations, they rapidly toppled the Aztec and Inca Empires. They focused attention on gathering as much of the gold and silver that was in circulation as they could get their hands on, and then establishing a colonial system that involved using indigenous populations to mine more from the ground. Many died from disease. Many of those who survived were forced to work as laborers on mining settlements across Mexico, Peru, and Bolivia, where, already in 1545, the Spanish enjoyed control over the largest silver mine in the world, the Cerro Rico ("Rich Mountain") at Potosí. Between 1545 and 1823, the silver output from Potosí *alone* totaled some 22,695 metric tons, an amount equal to approximately 60 percent of the estimated value of the entire European silver stock in the year 1500.[3]

>   translates as caravans of "pack animals," Beveridge reads as *awīluq* and translates as "heads-of-houses." Zahir al-Din Muhammad Babur, *The Baburnama: Memoirs of Babur*, ed. and trans. Annette Beveridge (London: Luzac and Co., 1921), 202. A close analysis of the context of the passage suggests that Thackston's translation is likely to be correct. I am grateful to Eric Schluessel for his help in unpacking this Chaghatay mystery.
> 3. Kendall W. Brown, *A History of Mining in Latin America: From the Colonial Era to the Present* (Albuquerque: University of New Mexico Press, 2012), 17. For a detailed history of the Cerro

Figure 3.1. First European Image of the Cerro Rico, 1553. Pedro Cieza de León, *La Crónica Del Perú* (Sevilla: Martín Montesdoca, 1553), 260 (public domain).

Despite the disparity in their relative values, mining for silver proved far more profitable than mining for gold, and silver exports from the Americas far exceeded gold both in quantity and total value. Spanish colonial records indicate that, over the course of the seventeenth century, on average each year more than 150 tons of silver was shipped from the Americas, through Europe, to Asian markets. From 1571, Spanish ships annually transported another 50 tons (and perhaps as much as 135 tons) of American silver westward across the Pacific, where it entered the Chinese economy through the Philippines.[4] This pattern increased over time. Even considering the tens of thousands of tons of silver injected into the global economy throughout the sixteenth and seventeenth centuries, more American silver was mined in the eighteenth century than in the sixteenth and seventeenth centuries combined.[5] Pointing to the high value of silver in Ming China and

---

Ricco, see Kris Lane, *Potosí: The Silver City That Changed the World* (Berkeley: University of California Press, 2019).

4. Dennis O. Flynn and Arturo Giráldez, "Born with a 'Silver Spoon': The Origins of World Trade in 1571," *Journal of World History* 6, no. 2 (1995): 203–4.
5. Dennis O. Flynn and Arturo Giráldez, "Cycles of Silver: Global Economic Unity through the Mid-Eighteenth Century," *Journal of World History* 13, no. 2 (2000): 391–428; Frank, *ReOrient*,

its greater purchasing power there than in Europe, historians have long emphasized the role that East Asian markets played in absorbing American silver.[6]

INDIA AND THE INDIAN OCEAN

At the same time, scholars of Indian history have similarly stressed that silver also had an inflated purchasing power in Indian markets. This is generally attributed to several factors, including a dearth of precious metal deposits in the otherwise rich Indian soil, which created a persistent demand for specie in order to monetize the expanding regional economies; the growing European demand for Indian cotton textiles, spices, and other agricultural goods; and the European merchants' access to American silver, which they used to offset their substantial trade deficit with Indian markets.[7] This final point is corroborated by a number of contemporary accounts. For example, in the mid-seventeenth century, the French merchant François Bernier found that "gold and silver, after circulating in every other quarter of the globe, come at length to be swallowed up, lost in some measure, in *Hindoustan*."[8] Writing at the beginning of the eighteenth century, Niccolao Manucci, an Italian physician who spent much of his adult life at the Mughal court of Aurangzeb (r. 1658–1707), elaborated:

> It ought to be remembered that the whole of the merchandise which is exported from the Mogul kingdom comes from four kinds of plants—that is to say, the shrub that produces the cotton from which a large quantity of cloth, coarse and fine, is made. These cotton goods are exported to Europe, Persia, Arabia, and other quarters of the world. The second is the plant which produces indigo. The third is the one from which comes opium, of which a large amount is used on the Java coast. The fourth is the mulberry-tree, on which their silk-worms are fed, and, as it may be said,

---

143. For a chart illustrating American silver production in millions of kilograms per decade, see Brown, *History of Mining in Latin America*, 30. For additional data, see John J. TePaske, *A New World of Gold and Silver*, ed. Kendall W. Brown (Leiden: E. J. Brill, 2010), 113.
6. Flynn and Giráldez, "Born with a 'Silver Spoon,'" 206–9. Circa 1600, the value of silver compared to gold was roughly twice as high in Canton as it was in European markets. Brown, *History of Mining in Latin America*, 13.
7. See: Om Prakash, "Precious-Metal Flows into India in the Early Modern Period," and Sushil Chaudhury, "The Inflow of Silver to Bengal in Global Perspective, 1650–1757," in *Global Connections and Monetary History, 1470–1800*, ed. Dennis O. Flynn, Arturo Giráldez and Richard von Glahn (Aldershot: Ashgate, 2003), 149–68.
8. François Bernier, *Travels in the Mogul Empire, AD 1656–1668*, trans. Irving Brock and ed. Archibald Constable (Westminster: Constable and Co., 1891), 202.

that commodity (silk) is grown on those trees. For the export of all this merchandise, European and other traders bring much silver to India.[9]

From the first half of the sixteenth century, the Spanish, Portuguese, and other Europeans pumped American silver into the global economy in exchange for Asian cotton textiles, spices, and other merchandise. In India, this increase in European demand created a more active and competitive commercial environment, spurring production and creating a variety of new opportunities for Indian business communities. Until relatively recently, scholars assumed that these business communities fully directed their attention to the maritime arena. But on closer inspection, one finds that, rather than the maritime routes competing with overland routes, the two modes of transport complemented each other.[10] As European activity in the Indian Ocean increased, Indian overland trade with Central Asia increased alongside it, linking Central Asia more closely to the Indian Ocean economy than ever before.[11] I have studied early modern Central Asia's commercial relations with India extensively and have presented my conclusions in multiple publications. I will limit the discussion here to a few key elements of that research.

Near the end of his 1973 study arguing that the technologically advanced Dutch and English East India Companies enjoyed a competitive advantage over Asian peddlers in the movement of Asian merchandise, Niels Steensgaard references seventeenth-century Dutch East India Company (V.O.C., or the Vereenigde Oost-Indische Compagnie, founded in 1602) records bemoaning their failure to overtake the caravan trade. In 1639, V.O.C. officials expressed profound disappointment that the company had failed to meet its objectives and that, despite efforts to profit by importing Indian textiles to Persia, caravan traders still transported to Persia some 25,000 to 30,000 camel loads of Indian cotton textiles each year.[12] Considering that dromedaries are known to have commonly carried some 400 pounds and

---

9. Niccolao Manucci, *Storia do Mogor, or Mogul India, 1653–1708*, 4 vols., trans. W. Irvine (London: J. Murray, 1907–1908), 2:418.
10. Again, see Alam, "Trade, State Policy and Regional Change," 202–27.
11. Levi, *Indian Diaspora*. See also Dale, *Indian Merchants and Eurasian Trade, 1600–1750*; Claude Markovits, *The Global World of Indian Merchants, 1750–1947: Traders of Sind from Bukhara to Panama* (Cambridge: Cambridge University Press, 2000). For an updated and distilled discussion of the early modern Indian caravan trade with Central Asia, see Scott C. Levi, *Caravans: Indian Merchants on the Silk Road* (Gurgaon: Penguin, 2015).
12. Niels Steensgaard, *The Asian Trade Revolution of the Seventeenth Century: The East India Companies and the Decline of the Caravan Trade* (Chicago: University of Chicago Press, 1974), 410–11.

that 32.5 yards of cloth weighed 5 pounds, such a number of camels could easily have transported more than 70 million yards of cloth.[13]

This figure may at first seem unbelievably large, but it becomes more reasonable when one considers that it takes roughly five yards of cloth to make a single outfit of clothing, that the Safavid Empire at the time was home to between seven and ten million people, that a significant proportion of this cloth would have been further exported to other markets, and that India was the largest producer of cotton cloth in the world at the time.[14] In his recent study of the cotton industry, Sven Beckert observes that even when China's cotton industry boomed as its population doubled to some four hundred million people in the eighteenth century, it was still only second to India.[15] Back in the mid-seventeenth century, the French monk Raphaël du Mans was so struck by the magnitude of India's overland trade through Persia that he compared the Safavid Empire to a great caravanserai with two doors: silver entered through one in the west and exited through another in the east, flowing into India, "where all the money in the Universe is unloaded as if into an abyss."[16] Setting aside the monk's hyperbole, it seems reasonable to conclude that the seventeenth-century Persian overland trade in Indian textiles was significant, and it represented only a small fraction of the early modern Eurasian caravan trade.

Alongside a sustained increase in transnational commercial activity, the support and encouragement of the state was another factor contributing to the development and maintenance of India's overland trade with its neighbors to the north and west from the middle of the sixteenth century to the colonial era.[17] Mughal, Safavid, and Uzbek rulers all supported these efforts, and they collaborated with one another in a number of ways, even during times of war. In addition to welcoming foreign subjects into their respective

---

13. The calculations and additional citations can be found in Levi, *Indian Diaspora*, 78–79 and note 263.
14. Rudi Matthee estimates the population of Safavid Iran to have been some seven or eight million people. Rudi Matthee, "The Safavid Economy as Part of the World Economy," in *Iran and the World in the Safavid Age*, ed. Willem Floor and Edmund Herzig (London: I. B. Tauris, 2012), 33. Stephen Dale suggests that the Safavid population at the time of Shah Abbas I was as high as ten million people. Stephen F. Dale, *The Muslim Empires of the Ottomans, Safavids, and Mughals* (Cambridge: Cambridge University Press, 2010), 107.
15. Beckert observes that the 1.5 billion pounds of cotton that China produced in 1750 is roughly equal to the amount of cotton that the United States produced a century later, on the eve of the Civil War. Sven Beckert, *Empire of Cotton: A Global History* (New York: Vintage Books, 2014), 14.
16. Raphaël du Mans, *Estat de la Perse en 1660* (Paris: Ernest Leroux, 1890), 192.
17. See the discussion "Merchants and the State" in Levi, *Caravans*, 10–26.

territories and offering safe and predictable environments for them to conduct their trade, their administrators shared information regarding commercial matters and financed substantial capital investment projects.[18] The rulers constructed bazaars, bridges, and caravanserais; planted trees for shade along important roads; and established fortresses at key locations to improve security for travelers.[19] These efforts bore fruit. In the *'Ain-i Akbari*, Emperor Akbar's vizier, Abu'l Fazl (d. 1602), boasts that Indian travelers to Kabul could choose from no fewer than five routes, and there were seven routes to select from if they should wish to travel onward to Central Asia from there.[20]

Toward the end of Akbar's reign, state efforts to promote trade with Central Asia were bolstered by the regular exchange of diplomatic embassies. This was a dramatic change from the earlier policies of Akbar's grandfather, Babur, who held the Uzbeks in contempt for ejecting him from the region, and his father, Humayun (d. 1556), who, while in exile in Iran (1540–1555), sought Safavid assistance to support his efforts to retake Samarqand. Setting aside ancestral conflicts, Emperor Akbar (r. 1556–1605) and 'Abdallah Khan II (r. 1583–1598) started anew and exchanged embassies for more than twenty-five years, beginning in 1572 when 'Abdallah was de facto ruler, though technically subordinate to his father, Iskander (d. 1583).[21] For his part, 'Abdallah had several objectives in establishing closer diplomatic relations with Akbar, not the least of which was his desire to convince Akbar to join him in war against his Safavid neighbors. Another theme that consistently runs throughout this diplomatic correspondence is that both rulers emphasized the importance of working together to promote caravan traffic and protect the traders who passed between their two realms. Akbar and 'Abdallah both strategically appointed ambassadors who would be in the best position to advance their common goals.[22]

At the same time, the Shibanid khans and Safavid shahs also worked

---

18. For additional detail, see Scott C. Levi, "Commercial Linkages with Central Asia and Iran," in *Oxford Handbook of the Mughal World*, ed. Richard M. Eaton and Ramya Sreenivasan (Oxford: Oxford University Press, forthcoming).
19. For Safavid Iran, see the detailed chapter titled "The Role of the Government in the Economy" in Willem Floor, *The Economy of Safavid Persia* (Wiesbaden: Dr. Ludwig Reichert, 2001), 27–64.
20. Abul Fazl Allami, *The Ain-i Akbari*, 3 vols., trans. H. Blochmann, 2nd ed. (Delhi, 1997), 2:405.
21. A selection from this correspondence is available in English translation in Mansura Haidar, ed., *Mukātabāt-i-'Allāmī (Inshā'i Abu'l Fazl), Daftar 1* (New Delhi: Munshiram Manoharlal, 1998). See also Levi, "Commercial Linkages."
22. See Gulchekhra Sultonova and Scott C. Levi, "Indo-Bukharan Diplomatic Relations, 1572–1598: The Role of the Actors," in *Insights and Commentaries: South and Central Asia*, ed. Anita

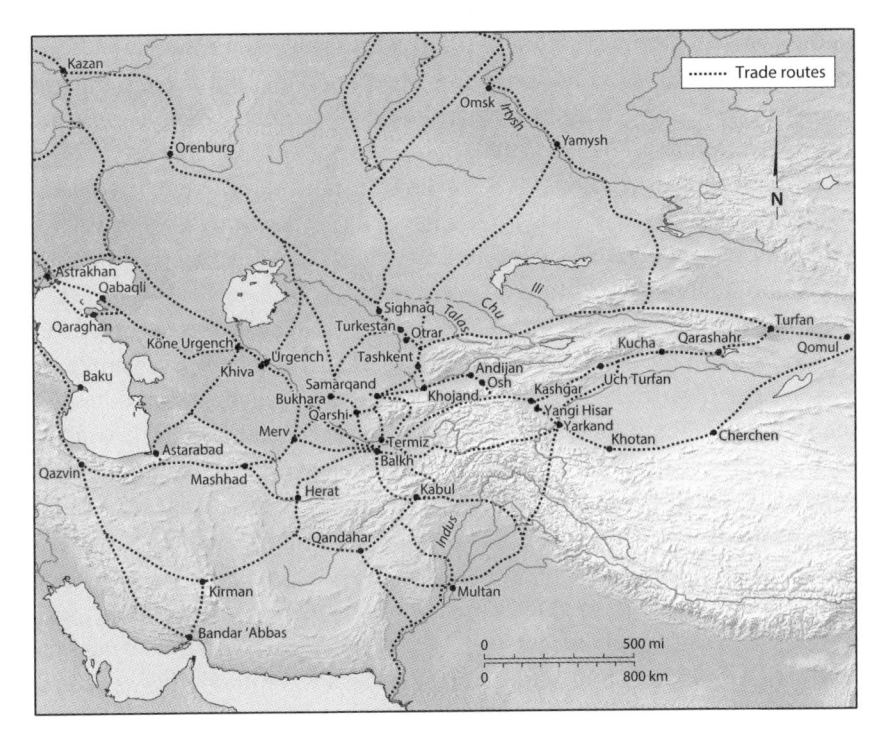

Map 11. Trade Routes, Seventeenth and Eighteenth Centuries. Map by Bill Nelson.

to encourage trade and diplomatic exchanges between their two realms. This may seem counterintuitive, given the confessional conflict that, from the beginning of the sixteenth century, drove a wedge between these two dynasties and repeatedly served as a rallying cry for war between the Shi'a Safavids and Sunni Uzbeks. Considering the vitriolic exchanges that one finds in the sources, it would be easy to assume that political friction would have stifled all commercial relations. But divergent religious ideologies seem to have had little impact on trade.[23] Both Willem Floor and Audrey Burton reference multiple sources documenting the presence and protection of Bukharan merchants in Safavid territory at the very moment that the two governments were at war.[24] And even as 'Abdallah Khan was developing improved relations with Akbar in India and trying to enlist Akbar in a joint campaign against the "heretical" Safavids, he also exchanged diplomatic

Sengupta and Mirzohid Rakhimov (Kolkata: Maulana Abul Kalam Azad Institute of Asian Studies; Tashkent: Institute of History, Academy of Sciences, 2015), 95–107.

23. Floor, *Economy of Safavid Persia*, 229.
24. Floor, *Economy of Safavid Persia*, 228–32; Burton, *Bukharans*, 438–43.

THE EARLY MODERN SILK ROAD

letters with Shah 'Abbas I (r. 1588–1629), who promised the Bukharans that he would guarantee "assistance and protection to all pilgrims and traders coming from Tūrān."[25] Later Safavid rulers would repeat that message. With the rise of the Toqay-Timurid dynasty following 'Abdallah's death in 1598, Bukharan political relations with the Safavids normalized, and, in addition to improved trade connections, it became even more common for travelers, including especially Bukharan pilgrims undertaking the hajj to Mecca, to pass through Safavid territories.[26]

Considering that both Safavid Iran and Uzbek Central Asia occupied the semiarid zone and could boast populations of only some five to ten million people, the magnitude of their domestic markets was never terribly substantial. This is especially so when compared to the much larger commercial markets of China and India. Local markets were modest, but the central importance of the trade routes passing between the Uzbek and Safavid territories is that they connected those markets to a much larger transit trade that passed through each region, linking Central Asia with the Ottoman Mediterranean and Indian Ocean markets, for example.[27] The transit trade across these regions represents yet another means by which Central Asia was connected to external markets in the early modern era.[28] This remained more or less in place until those routes were temporarily dislocated as Safavid power collapsed in the 1720s.[29]

With only a few notable disturbances, the Mughal administration's favorable trade policies with Central Asia also remained in place until the collapse of Mughal authority in the early eighteenth century, a topic discussed in more detail in the next chapter. Akbar's merchant-friendly fiscal

---

25. Floor, *Economy of Safavid Persia*, 230; Riazul Islam, *A Calendar of Documents on Indo-Persian Relations (1500–1750)*, 2 vols. (Tehran: Iranian Culture Foundation, 1982), 2:227 (tx. 337).
26. Thomas Welsford, "The Re-opening of Iran to Central Asian Pilgrimage Traffic, 1600–1650," in *Central Asian Pilgrims: Hajj Routes and Pious Visits between Central Asia and the Hijaz*, ed. Alexandre Papas, Thomas Welsford, and Thierry Zarcone (Berlin: Klaus Schwarz Verlag, 2012), 149–67. For further discussion of Toqay-Timurid relations with the Safavids, see McChesney, "'Barrier to Heterodoxy'?" For additional insights into the movement of peoples throughout the early modern Persianate world, see Muzaffar Alam and Sanjay Subrahmanyam, *Indo-Persian Travels in the Age of Discoveries, 1400–1800* (Cambridge: Cambridge University Press, 2007).
27. In addition to the work by Rudi Matthee and Willem Floor, cited below and in the bibliography, see the collection of essays on Safavid commerce in part III of Floor and Herzig, eds., *Iran and the World in the Safavid Age*, 207–90.
28. Floor, *Economy of Safavid Persia*, 231.
29. In addition to Floor, *Economy of Safavid Persia*, 230, see Alam, "Trade, State Policy," 216–17 and notes.

policies were expanded upon during Jahangir's reign (r. 1605–1627). There was a temporary disruption in diplomatic relations during the reign of his son, Shah Jahan (r. 1627–1658), who ordered his own son, Aurangzeb (r. 1658–1707), to lead what was ultimately a failed Mughal occupation of Balkh in 1646–1647. Mughal relations with Bukhara suffered as a result. But just one decade later, shortly after word reached Bukhara that Aurangzeb had imprisoned his father and taken the throne for himself, the Bukharan ruler 'Abd al-Aziz Khan (r. 1645–1681) dispatched an embassy to his previous adversary charged with delivering a letter that declared: "Before this period, in the time of the great ones [i.e., Emperor Akbar and 'Abdallah Khan] there was a steady relationship that had become our tradition. We would like the same relations to be protected and continued in this time. The sending of messengers and goods on both sides should be the practice."[30] Aurangzeb agreed, and relations normalized soon thereafter.

Mughal, Uzbek, and Safavid rulers promoted an active caravan trade between their realms. But the intensification of commercial interactions between early modern India and Central Asia is most evident in the fact that, from the middle of the sixteenth century, large numbers of Indian merchants began to establish a network of semipermanent communities across Central Asia. To emphasize, these diaspora communities came into being *at the very historical moment* that the received wisdom vis-à-vis the Silk Road suggests that Central Asia and India would have been growing further apart. And while their numbers in the sixteenth century were modest, in the seventeenth century, the Indian communities in Central Asia expanded significantly in both number and size. One seventeenth-century Bukharan *farmān* (mandate) assures the protection of the khanate's Hindu guests and refers to Indian merchant communities in "Bukhara, Balkh, Badakhshan, Qunduz, Taliqan, Aibek, Ghuri, Baghlan, Shabarghan, Termiz, Samarqand, Nesf [Qarshi], Kish, Shahrisabz, and wherever else they may live . . ."[31]

As the decades passed, the Indians became an even greater presence in the Bukharan Khanate, and their international activities were by no means limited to that one region. Available evidence suggests that, at any given time in the seventeenth century, a circulating population of roughly thirty-five thousand Indian merchants lived for several years at a time in caravanserais and neighborhoods in urban and rural markets across Afghani-

---

30. Mirakshah Munshi, Mullah Zahid Munshi, and Muhammad Tahir Wahid, comps, *Maktubat munsha'at manshurat*, Institut Vostokovedeniia Akademii Nauk, Uzbekistan (henceforth IVANU), Ms. No. 289, fol. 7a.
31. Mirakshah Munshi et al., comps., *Maktubat munsha'at manshurat*, fols. 185b–186a.

stan, Central Asia, and Iran, from where they made their way to Astrakhan, in Russia, and ventured up the Volga River even as far as Moscow and St. Petersburg.[32] These merchants were not simple caravan traders or peddlers. They were trained agents of heavily capitalized Indian family firms with centers of operation in the northwest Indian city of Multan. They were in command of considerable investment capital and employed an array of commercial technologies in their application of that wealth.

A brief summary of the Indians' commercial system illustrates the mechanisms that these firms used to connect Central Asian markets with the Indian Ocean economy. Beginning already in the thirteenth century, the Multani family firms developed highly diversified commercial portfolios with interests in various types of markets across northwest India. The Multanis used those investments to acquire large quantities of merchandise at low prices. In the sixteenth century, they began extending this merchandise to their agents as a capital investment prior to dispatching them to travel to Central Asia, or other locations, where they took up residence. Over a period of years—the average seems to have been about seven—these Indian merchants gradually sold their merchandise for cash, which they then invested in a number of other profit-oriented ventures.[33]

Typically, the Multani firms managed extensive commercial portfolios that included leveraging their network in India to acquire large quantities of merchandise, primarily cotton textiles. The firms would enlist Afghan nomads to transport this merchandise from India to Central Asia as they made their annual migrations; they would participate in partnerships with other merchants, including, of course, Indians as well as Bukharans, Armenians, Tatars, and others; and they would then use their capital to invest in a variety of loans. The loans that the Indians advanced can be divided into two categories: in urban environments, the Indians served as suppliers of a wide variety of short-term loans to artisans and others at high interest, generally made against collateral; in rural environments, they extended longer-term agricultural loans, providing investment capital at planting time in exchange for a percentage of the harvested crops and commonly purchasing the remainder for cash and arranging for its transportation to regional markets.

In this way, the thousands of Indian merchants who occupied cities and villages across early modern Central Asia used their resources as an engine for Central Asian commercial activity and agricultural produc-

---

32. Levi, *Indian Diaspora*, 178.
33. For a more complete summary of the Indians' commercial system, see Levi, *Caravans*.

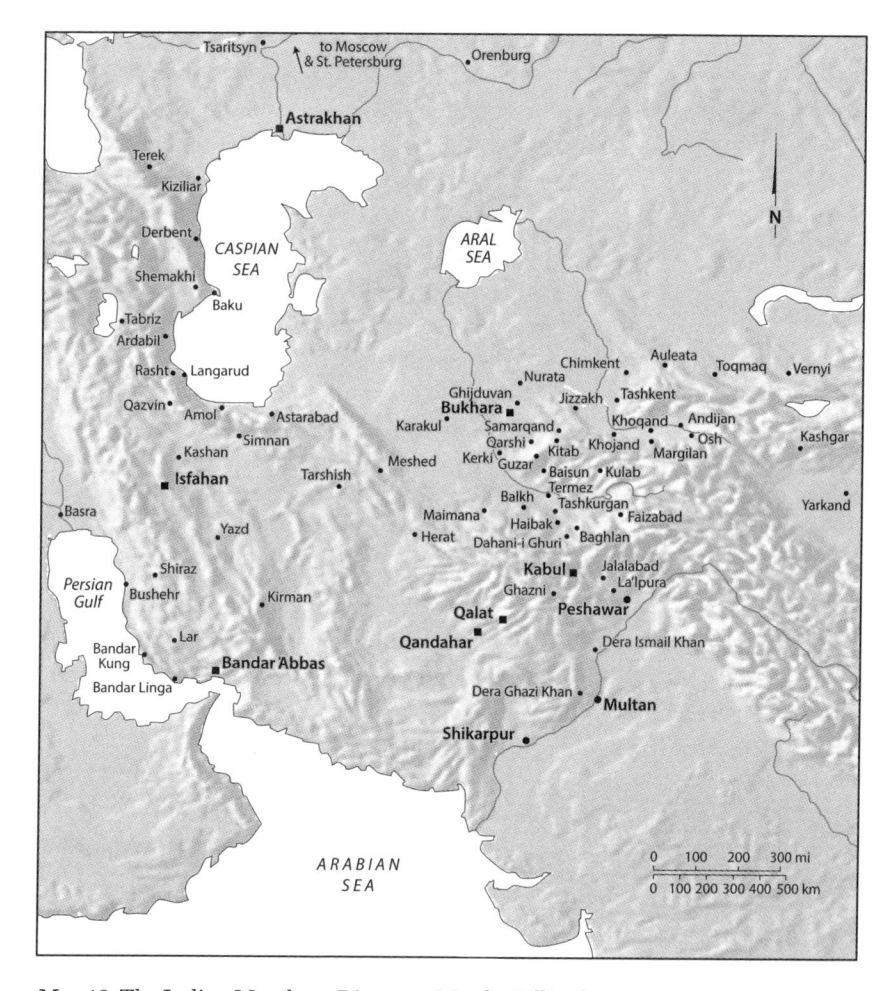

Map 12. The Indian Merchant Diaspora. Map by Bill Nelson.

tion, supplying markets with merchandise and investment capital, and monetizing local economies throughout the region. This had substantial implications for the regional economy, improving agricultural production and diminishing the need for barter, for example, which facilitated the collection of taxes in cash. The Bukharan government placed a great value on the economic services the Indians provided, as evidenced in the Bukharan khans' deliberate efforts to encourage the largely Hindu communities to come to Bukhara. In one seventeenth-century *farmān*, the Bukharan khan declares: "We are thinking about the condition of the greater community of people. Those of other religions [Hindus] obey the *farmāns* that we make and help us very much; for this reason, we will weaken the grip of those who try to oppress them. The goods and property of these people should not become ruined; they are protected. Their protection will come from here and their aspirations should be directed to Bukhara."[34] A few temporary disruptions notwithstanding, Central Asia and India enjoyed a close commercial relationship through the late nineteenth century.

The discussion has thus far focused on Indian agency in this relationship, but it is important to emphasize that the Indian caravan trade with Central Asia was not unidirectional. In addition to serving as bankers and orchestrating the movement of thousands of camel loads of Indian cotton textiles, dyes, rice, spices, and other Indian merchandise, these merchants (alongside others) were also involved in the exportation of Central Asian merchandise to Indian markets. This included large quantities of fresh and dried fruit, precious stones, silks and other textiles, and other locally produced merchandise. It also included goods from elsewhere, including Chinese silks and medicinal herbs, leather goods produced in the steppe, and Siberian furs, all of which were part of an elaborate transit trade that passed through the region. Most important by far, however, were the many tens of thousands of Central Eurasian horses that Indian merchants and other caravan traders exported to Indian markets each year.[35]

For some four thousand years, breeding horses and other livestock represented arguably the Central Eurasian nomads' most important contribution to the Eurasian economy.[36] Each year, nomads traded hundreds of thousands of their horses to their sedentary neighbors in India, China, the Middle East, and Eastern Europe, where they were put to use for transportation, as beasts of burden, and, of course, for military purposes. Indians are known to have imported Central Eurasian horses since antiquity, and the evidence suggests that there was a substantial growth in demand for military steeds for cavalry forces following the establishment of the Turco-Afghan Delhi Sultanate (1206–1526).[37] This trade was therefore nothing new in 1332–1333, when the Tunisian traveler Ibn Battuta (1304–1377)

---

34. Mirakshah Munshi et al., comps., *Maktubat munsha'at manshurat*, fols. 185b–186a.
35. Levi, *Indian Diaspora*, 54–60. See especially the study by Gommans, *Rise of the Indo-Afghan Empire*.
36. Pita Kelekna, *The Horse in Human History* (Cambridge: Cambridge University Press, 2009), 49. See also David W. Anthony, *The Horse, the Wheel, and Language: How Bronze-Age Riders from the Eurasian Steppes Shaped the Modern World* (Princeton: Princeton University Press, 2007).
37. See the discussion in André Wink, *Al-Hind: The Making of the Indo-Islamic World*, vol. 2, *The Slave Kings and the Islamic Conquest, 11th–13th Centuries* (Leiden: E. J. Brill, 1997).

passed through the territory of the Golden Horde and encountered groups of nomads leading multiple herds of some six thousand horses each destined for Indian markets.[38] Significant in the fourteenth century, the horse trade became many times larger in the early modern era. This spike in demand is at least partly a product of the dramatic increase in the size of early modern militaries.

As noted previously, at the turn of the sixteenth century, Babur estimated that between seven and ten thousand horses annually passed through Kabul en route to Indian markets.[39] One might expect that similar numbers passed through the other mountain passes leading into India. Whether or not that is the case, the available evidence indicates that Indian demand rose substantially as the Mughal Empire grew larger and more powerful, and seventeenth-century European observers place the figure much higher. Both Jean Baptiste Tavernier and Jean de Thévenot suggest that some sixty thousand Central Asian horses passed through Kabul on their way to Indian markets each year.[40] Writing at the very beginning of the eighteenth century, near the end of Emperor Aurangzeb's reign, Manucci ventures the highest figure, estimating that the annual horse trade at that time included as many as one hundred thousand horses taken from Central Asia to India, twelve thousand of which were taken directly to Aurangzeb's stables.[41]

In a detailed study on the subject, Jos Gommans calculates that the total number of horses in India at any given point in time in the eighteenth century fluctuated between four hundred thousand and eight hundred thousand, and that he finds that this population needed to be replaced every seven to ten years. This is because of the exceptionally high mortality rates for horses in India, partly because of their application as cavalry steeds but also because of the extremely hot and wet Indian climate, insufficient land reserved as pasture, and poor diet. These factors rapidly rendered mares infertile, limiting the abilities of Indians to breed their own animals.

The magnitude of this trade appears to be substantial, but one must ask: How does this trade compare against other early modern commercial rela-

---

38. Ibn Battuta, *The Travels of Ibn Battuta, A. D. 1325–1354*, 3 vols., trans H. A. R. Gibb (New Delhi: Munshiram Manoharlal, 1993 [1929]), 2:478.
39. Zahir al-Din Muhammad Babur, *Baburnama*, trans. Thackston, 153.
40. Jean Baptiste Tavernier, *Les six voyages de Jean Baptiste Tavernier, Ecuyer Baron d'Aubonne…*, 2 vols. (Utrecht: Guillaume and Jacob Poolsum, 1712), 2:63; Jean de Thévenot, *The Travels of Monsieur de Thevenot, the Third Part, Containing the Relations of Indostan, the New Moguls, and of Other People and Countries of the Indies*, trans. Archibald Lovell (London: H. Faithorne, 1687), 57.
41. Manucci, *Storia do Mogor*, 2:390–91.

tionships? The question of scale is an important one, and it is addressed in more detail below. For now, I observe that several factors contributed to the intensification of Central Asian commercial relations with India over the early modern era. These include the dramatic and sustained increase in the circulation of silver; the impact that this had on intensifying the Indian commercial economy; the willingness and ability of a large number of Indian merchants to relocate to semipermanent communities in Central Asia; the role that the Mughal, Uzbek, and Safavid states played in protecting and encouraging foreign merchant communities in their territories; and the sustained demand within India for horses bred in the Central Eurasian steppe. This remained the case through multiple political transitions, including the collapse of Mughal authority and the rise of the Mughal successor states, and even the collapse of the Bukharan Khanate in Central Asia.[42] Moving beyond notions of Silk Road peddlers and Central Asian isolation, the sustained increase in trade with India represents one important way in which early modern Central Asians became more tightly linked to the global economy.

CHINA

Shifting attention eastward, the Central Eurasian horse trade looms very large in Chinese history as well. Already in the eighth century, Tang armies reportedly maintained as many as seven hundred thousand steeds.[43] Focusing attention on later dynastic periods, Peter Perdue provides valuable insight into the general magnitude of China's horse trade, as well as the fluctuations in the flow of Central Eurasian horses into Chinese stables in the early modern era.[44] In 1415, about eighty years after Ibn Battuta observed Inner Asian nomads leading multiple herds of thousands of horses each destined for markets in India, the third Ming Emperor, Yongle (r. 1402–1424), is said to have had just three hundred thousand horses in the Ming stables. He found that to be insufficient, and within just seven years he had increased that number to some 1.2 million horses.[45] As in India, the Ming had tried, and failed, to breed their own replacements rather than acquire them through trade with their nomadic neighbors (and occasional enemies). Their efforts were doomed to fail, however, as the same ecolog-

---

42. Levi, *Caravans*, 10–27.
43. Edward H. Schafer, *The Golden Peaches of Samarkand: A Study of T'ang Exotics* (Berkeley: University of California Press, 1963), 58.
44. Peter Perdue, *China Marches West: The Qing Conquest of Central Eurasia* (Cambridge, MA: Harvard University Press, 2005), 35.
45. Perdue, *China Marches West*, 70.

ical pressures that millennia earlier had motivated whole communities of people to venture into the vast Inner Asian steppe and develop a pastoral-nomadic lifestyle centered on breeding horses and other livestock ensured that they would continue to monopolize that economic activity into the modern era.

At the core of this explanation is the need for an immense amount of grassland to pasture such a large number of animals. In Rudi Lindner's analysis of pastoral-nomadic economies, he finds that each horse raised in the steppe required approximately twenty-five acres of pasture to maintain it for a year.[46] This was viable in the open steppe, where land was abundant and familial groups could move several thousand horses from one large open pasture to another, grazing along the way. But it was both environmentally and economically unsustainable in China and in India. Early modern agrarian empires such as those ruled by the Ming, the Qing, and the Mughals were in the business of expanding irrigation agriculture to produce food crops to sustain their large populations and cash crops for domestic consumption and for export. They could little afford to set aside enormous tracts of arable land for pasturing animals. At the end of the fifteenth century, it was quite clear to the Ming that the amount of Chinese pasture available was woefully insufficient. Furthermore, those horses that the Chinese did breed were of poor quality and outmatched on the battlefield by those born and raised in the steppe. The Ming had only one option, and that was to acquire the animals through trade.[47]

In exchange for annually supplying China with horses and other livestock, the early modern Chinese empires—both the Ming and the Qing—supplied their nomadic neighbors with large amounts of tea, grain, silk, silver, and more. Because of insufficient silver supplies in the fifteenth century, the Ming at first developed a system whereby the state endeavored to monopolize the horse trade by establishing *chamasi*: dedicated markets where licensed horse dealers could exchange tea, salt, and other merchandise for the animals. Moving into the sixteenth and seventeenth centuries, the sustained increase in China's silver imports, predominantly from Japan and the Americas, propelled the growth of the horse trade. Perdue's explanation regarding the effects this had on the Ming economy merits attention:

> The sixteenth century marked a new high tide in the advance of commercial relations throughout China. The influx of silver, first from Japan and

---

46. Rudi Paul Lindner, "Nomadism, Horses, and Huns," *Past and Present* 92 (1981): 3–19. Cited in Perdue, *China Marches West*, 33–34.
47. Perdue, *China Marches West*, 68–69.

later from the New World, provided the medium for expanding long-distance monetary exchange.... In the late sixteenth century, Beijing sent over 4 million taels of silver per year to the northwest garrisons for purchasing goods from local peasants and frontier merchants. These garrisons formed a vast consumer belt demanding constant replenishment of grain rations and textiles. Their demands fostered the growth of a trading system that linked the northwest to the lower Yangzi, through merchant contracting with the state and through private networks. The military and civilian distribution systems were intertwined through mechanisms of silver payment.[48]

The trend continued: over the course of the early modern era, from 1500 to 1800, conservative estimates suggest that Latin America pumped some 150,000 tons of silver into the global economy.[49] Japan was also a major silver producer during the eighteenth century, as was Russia.[50] As noted previously, this silver flowed into regional economies in India and China, where it stimulated economic growth. It also made it possible, even necessary when one considers the implications of the horse trade for military purposes, for commercial groups to connect regional economies in the Central Asian hinterland with coastal entrepôt more tightly than ever before.

At the same time, emerging political developments in the region made early modern China's westward trade considerably more complex than exchanging silk, tea, grain, and silver for horses. In the middle of the sixteenth century, Russia annexed both the Khanate of Kazan (1552) and the Khanate of Astrakhan (1556), extending Russian imperial authority down the Volga to the northern shores of the Caspian Sea. Over the course of the seventeenth century, the Russian Empire rapidly expanded across Siberia, and this brought Russia into direct commercial contact with China.

Historians have directed some attention to the role that the Treaties of Nerchinsk in 1689 and Kiakhta in 1727 played in increasing Russia's official trade with China.[51] More than twenty-five years ago, Morris Rossabi

---

48. Perdue, *China Marches West*, 73. At roughly 1.3 ounces each, four million taels of silver is the equivalent of approximately 325,000 pounds in weight, or more than 150 tons. See also James A. Millward, "Qing Silk-Horse Trade with the Qazaqs in Yili and Tarbaghatai, 1758–1853," *Central and Inner Asian Studies* 7 (1992): 1–42.
49. Flynn and Giráldez, "Born with a 'Silver Spoon,'" 202.
50. See Ian Blanchard, *Russia's 'Age of Silver': Precious-Metal Production and Economic Growth in the Eighteenth Century* (London: Routledge, 1989).
51. See the analysis of the Russo-Qing negotiations in Peter C. Perdue, "Boundaries and Trade in

argued that because of these treaties there was no early modern decline in the overland transportation of Chinese merchandise to Europe—at least in terms of the northern caravan routes.[52] Rather, he emphasized the role that these treaties played in promoting a peaceful and predictable commercial environment that attracted traders on both sides. As a result, Rossabi found that "Russian merchants streamed into China during the eighteenth century to trade for cotton, silk, tea, tobacco, and rhubarb."[53] More recent work referenced below indicates that it was far more than just Russian merchants who orchestrated this trade, and the trade was much more substantial than Russians supplying the Chinese with fur, leather, woolens, and European manufactured goods. Regardless, Rossabi found the magnitude of Russo-Chinese trade to have been significant and to have increased by a factor of ten over the second half of the eighteenth century, from some 837,066 rubles in 1755 to 8,383,846 rubles in 1800.[54]

This increase was partly a result of the rapidly growing trade in tea, which alongside Siberian furs became more fashionable among European consumers during the eighteenth century. But Chinese rhubarb also made its way across the northern steppe in substantial quantities. While identifying rhubarb as an important commercial commodity may appear so random as to be humorous, rhubarb's importance as an article of trade had nothing to do with pastries; rather, it was quite seriously a response to growing European demand for its reputed medicinal value as a digestive aid.[55] Several factors propelled this trade: European medical authorities at the time were certain that only the root from the variety of rhubarb found in northern China and Mongolia offered the desired pharmacological effects; European botanists were unable to reproduce that variety in their own environments; and, perhaps in response to warnings issued by the merchants who mediated its trade, European physicians and pharmacists were also quite certain that Chinese rhubarb lost its medicinal value if it should be exposed to water or humid environments such as that asso-

the Early Modern World: Negotiations at Nerchinsk and Beijing," *Eighteenth-Century Studies* 43, no. 3 (2010): 341–56.
52. Rossabi, "'Decline' of the Central Asian Caravan Trade," 368.
53. Rossabi, "'Decline' of the Central Asian Caravan Trade," 368.
54. Rossabi, "'Decline' of the Central Asian Caravan Trade," 368.
55. Since antiquity, Chinese rhubarb was considered to be a reliable and effective, yet gentle, purgative. Erika Monahan, "Locating Rhubarb: Early Modernity's Relevant Obscurity," in *Early Modern Things: Objects and Their Histories, 1500–1800*, ed. Paula Findlen (London: Routledge, 2013), 228, 240.

ciated with maritime travel.⁵⁶ Through efforts to market it, one might even say to "brand" it, caravan traders who dealt in the Chinese rhubarb root trade were able to resist the efforts of (especially) Dutch sea traders and European growers to turn it into a commodity that they could monopolize. Chinese rhubarb therefore became a staple of the early modern Eurasian caravan trade. It was produced in abundance in northern China and Mongolia, and, following the Treaties of Nerchinsk and Kiakhta, enormous quantities were transported along trade routes crossing the northern stretches of Central Eurasia, passing through Russia to constipated consumers across Europe.⁵⁷

The establishment of these two treaties had profound implications for Russia and China, both in terms of their relations with each other and also with their Central Eurasian neighbors. In terms of their impact on long-distance overland trade, these treaties encouraged official trans-Eurasian trade between the Russian and Qing Empires. These treaties were also part of a process whereby both imperial powers began to assert an increased imperial presence in the steppe. Perdue succinctly summarizes that "trade continued to increase on the frontier from the seventeenth through the eighteenth centuries, as the Qing rulers carefully used their control of continental trade to extract submission from the nomads. The old Silk Routes shifted to the official border towns, but the same goods and the same merchants moved along them."⁵⁸ While I do not disagree with Perdue's summary, I would add that the impacts of Qing westward expansion during the middle of the eighteenth century were also felt farther to the south, where another Central Asian merchant network had emerged in the Ferghana Valley, at the heart of the Khanate of Khoqand.

Turkic Muslim populations on either side of the Tian Shan range had long maintained regular commercial connections.⁵⁹ In her work on Qing political and economic relations with the Khanate of Khoqand, Laura Newby examines a number of ways that these connections expanded as the rulers of Khoqand leveraged their official relationship with the Qing

---

56. Matthew P. Romaniello, "True Rhubarb? Trading Eurasian Botanical and Medical Knowledge in the Eighteenth Century," *Journal of Global History* 11, no. 1 (2016): 3–23.
57. Caravan traders also transported significant amounts of ginseng, ferum asafetida, and a number of other Chinese medicines to markets in Russia and beyond. Romaniello, "True Rhubarb?" 3–23.
58. Perdue, *China Marches West*, 400.
59. For a survey of Bukharan trade with the Yarkand Khanate in the sixteenth and early seventeenth centuries, see Gulchekhra Sultonova, "Torgoviie otnosheniia mezhdu Bukharskim i Yarkendskim khanstvami v XVI–nachale XVII veka," *Bulletin of IICAS* 11 (2010): 40–48. For

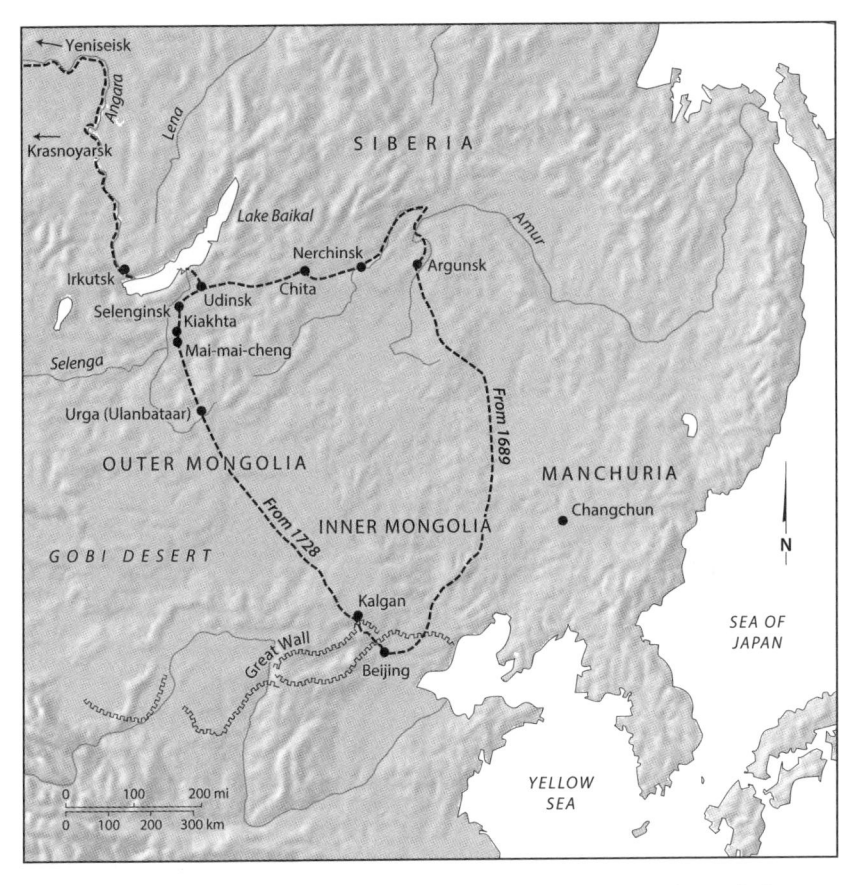

Map 13. Nerchinsk and Kiakhta: Northern Trade Routes in the Eighteenth Century. Map by Bill Nelson.

both to influence Qing foreign policy in the region and to advance their own political and commercial interests.[60] From the Qing conquest of Kashgar in 1759, Khoqand employed a foreign policy that effectively exploited the weak hold that the Qing had over Altishahr, or, as the Qing later came to designate it, Xinjiang, China's "New Frontier."[61] Time and again, Kho-

>an insightful study of the caravan trade in Altishahr during the seventeenth and eighteenth centuries, see Onuma Takahiro, "Political Power and Caravan Merchants at the Oasis Towns in Central Asia: The Case of Altishahr in the 17th and 18th Centuries," in *Xinjiang in the Context of Central Eurasian Transformations,* ed. Onuma Takahiro, David Brophy, and Shinmen Yasushi (Tokyo: Toyo Bunko, 2018), 33–58.

60. Laura J. Newby, *The Empire and the Khanate: A Political History of Qing Relations with Khoqand c. 1760–1860* (Leiden: E. J. Brill, 2005).
61. Also translated as "New Dominion," or "New Province." Although *Altishahr* literally means

Figure 3.2. Kiakhta in the Eighteenth Century. Lithograph produced by Nicolas Louis de Lespinasse and printed in Paris, 1783.

qand managed to force the much larger and more powerful, but distant, Qing government to bend to the will of a comparatively small and much weaker Central Asian khanate. In economic terms, Khoqand's interests included dispatching as many embassies to the capital as the Qing would permit, as the "gifts" that the Qing returned always exceeded the value of the "tribute" Khoqand had remitted, and the Qing permitted the official merchants that accompanied the embassy the right to trade tax-free in Qing markets. But these concerns were minor when compared to other interests, the most important of which was the expansion of a commercial network of "Andijani" traders across Xinjiang that numbered in the thousands.[62] In several important ways, the Andijani network that ema-

"Six Cities," the region is commonly referred to in Khoqandi sources as Yetishahr, or the "Seven Cities" region. Newby notes that the Qing administration actually divided the region into two administrative zones, a western and an eastern, of four cities each. The western cities included Kashgar, Khotan, Yangi Hisar, and Yarkand. The eastern cities included Qarashahr, Qucha, Uch Turfan, and Aqsu. Newby, *Empire and the Khanate*, 64n55.

62. Newby, *Empire and the Khanate*, 45–50, 64–66; Levi, *Rise and Fall of Khoqand*, 62–66. Qing records indicate that some three thousand Andijanis were active in Xinjiang during 1820s. Tôru Saguchi, "The Eastern Trade of the Khoqand Khanate," *Memoirs of the Research Department of the Toyo Bunko (The Oriental Library)* 24 (1965): 85.

nated from the Ferghana Valley into Chinese markets across Xinjiang represented an early modern manifestation of the Sogdians' classical Silk Road merchant diaspora.[63]

While not necessarily from the city of Andijan itself, the Andijanis were likely identified as such because of that city's historical importance in the Ferghana Valley; because they spoke the dialect of Turkic prevalent in the valley as opposed to the dialect spoken in Altishahr; and perhaps also because many would have traveled through that city on their journey across the Tian Shan to Kashgar, Yarkand, and other urban centers in the area.[64] There, they encountered and worked alongside myriad other Turkic Muslim, Indian, and Chinese merchant communities, and developed yet another transregional trade network that connected Central Asia with producers and markets in China, Russia, India, and beyond. Andijanis exported goods produced in the Ferghana Valley, including the ancient staples of fruit and textiles, as well as livestock and larger quantities of other merchandise brought from Bukhara, Khiva, Afghanistan, Persia, and beyond. From China came silks and porcelains, but, as was the case in Kiakhta, these luxury goods were overshadowed by large amounts of bulk goods, such as rhubarb and tea.

The tea trade was substantial in the eighteenth century, and it grew rapidly as the beverage increased in popularity across Europe.[65] It is important to emphasize that, in addition to the well-traveled maritime routes, there were a number of overland avenues by which tea reached markets in Russia and, through Russia, Europe. While the official trade through Kiakhta is the most well documented of these, farther to the south the Andijani merchants took an aggressive role as mediators in a trade that, in the nineteenth century, amounted to millions of kilograms of tea per year. Tea and rhubarb, like many of the other commodities that the Andijanis dealt in, enjoyed great demand in markets farther to the west, and the Andijanis' ability to assert a dominant mediatory role in that transit trade effectively fueled Khoqand's economy.[66]

The commercial activities of the Andijani merchants and the deliberate efforts of the Khoqandi administration to promote that trade are well doc-

---

63. For a comparative view of the Sogdians, see Jonathan Skaff, "The Sogdian Trade Diaspora in East Turkestan during the Seventh and Eighth Centuries," *Journal of the Economic and Social History of the Orient* 46, no. 4 (2003): 475–524.
64. Newby, *Empire and the Khanate*, 66 and note.
65. Newby, *Empire and the Khanate*, 129–35.
66. Newby, *Empire and the Khanate*, 135.

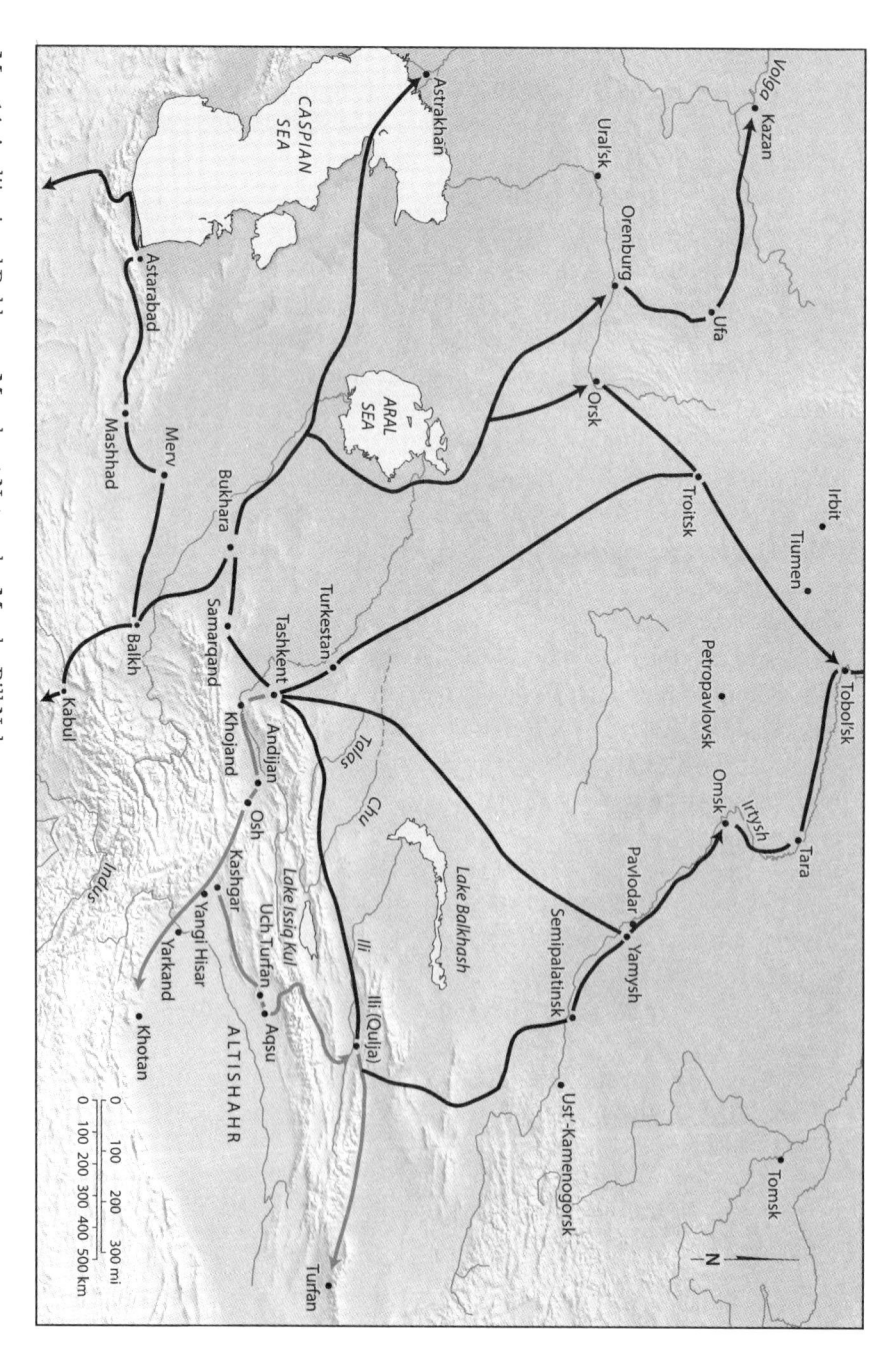

Map 14. Andijani and Bukharan Merchant Networks. Map by Bill Nelson.

umented.[67] But as is often the case, the historical record is heavily biased in favor of sedentary communities. The role that nomadic groups played in transregional trade throughout the region is less well documented. This is because commercial exchanges orchestrated by the Kyrgyz and other nomadic communities in the region often escaped notice in the historical record, or they were written off as smuggling operations because nomads often operated independent of state supervision and, whenever possible, moved merchandise across political boundaries without paying taxes. It is, however, possible to gain some insight into the magnitude of the nomadic mediatory trade between Khoqand and Altishahr in the late eighteenth and nineteenth centuries. In this instance, the nomadic trade appears to have been so substantial that it drew the attention of the Qing border authorities. Qing official reports indicate that nomads moved ("illegally smuggled") an amount of merchandise ("contraband") westward from Qing territory that was approximately equal to the amount of the official ("taxed") trade that the Andijani merchants conducted.

Another important facet of this network is that the expansion of the Andijani network eastward in Qing Xinjiang occurred concomitant to a marked increase in Central Asian caravan traffic northward across the steppe, toward Russia. Over the course of the early modern era, Russian consumers exhibited a growing demand for commodities available in Central Asia, especially tea, rhubarb, and, increasingly, raw cotton, which spurred the expansion of irrigation agriculture and the production of cotton as a cash crop. The results were largely successful, and from 1758 to 1853, the import-export trade of Russia and Khoqand increased by well over ten times, most notably (especially, it seems, in the later decades) in cotton.[68] In exchange, increasing amounts of Russian and Russian-Siberian goods (chiefly silver, treated leather, furs, and manufactured goods) also reached Central Asian markets, including those in the Ferghana Valley. Some of this merchandise was destined for consumption in the khanate, but much was further transported by Andijani merchant communities to Xinjiang, where they were sold for local consumption, or carried onward to markets elsewhere in China or southward across the Karakoram range to India.[69]

During the late eighteenth and nineteenth centuries, the Andijanis were

---

67. In addition to Newby's work, see Saguchi's detailed analysis, "Eastern Trade of the Khoqand Khanate," 47–114.
68. A. A. Askarov, ed., *Istoriya Uzbekistana*, vol. 3, *XVI–pervaia polovina XIX veka* (Tashkent: Fan, 1993), 228.
69. Saguchi, "Eastern Trade of the Khoqand Khanate," 47–114.

not the only merchant group to exploit the improved commercial economy in the Ferghana Valley. It was noted earlier that Indian Multanis were present in Bukhara already from the middle of the sixteenth century, and that seventeenth-century Bukharan sources place them in urban and rural markets across the khanate, though not, it seems, in the Ferghana Valley. Beginning in the 1770s, Khoqand began a century-long effort to expand irrigation agriculture in the valley. At some point, possibly in the late eighteenth century, though certainly by the early nineteenth century, the rulers of Khoqand welcomed Indian merchants into their territory. As had long been their practice elsewhere in Central Asia, the Indians linked local markets in the valley to foreign markets through their long-distance trade networks and also developed a rural credit system to service Khoqand's rapidly expanding agricultural lands.[70]

Early Russian colonial records pertaining to the Ferghana *oblast* (district) portray it as a densely populated agricultural zone, and they document hundreds of Indian merchants inhabiting communities in cities and villages throughout the valley.[71] The Indians owned caravanserais, warehouses, and commercial property, and they were heavily involved in the financing of agricultural production and trade. Beyond the valley, nineteenth-century Russian records also place Indian merchants farther to the north in Kapal, on the border with Xinjiang, and farther to the west in the Khoqandi fortress town of Toqmaq. Nineteenth-century Qing sources similarly locate several hundred Indian merchants in Kashgar, Yarkand, and other locations within the Qing Empire as well.[72]

Qing economic policies on its western frontier highlight another important aspect of Central Asia's foreign commercial interests. Following their conquest of Altishahr in 1758–1759, Qing officials faced a serious problem: their military had been sufficiently strong to conquer the region, but the economic burden associated with garrisoning tens of thousands of troops there rendered their ability to maintain military superiority over the region far less certain. In the long run, the Qing decided that their control over Xinjiang would need to depend more on collaboration than on coercion, and so the Qing administrators devised a mechanism to secure the loyalty

---

70. Levi, *Indian Diaspora*, 29 and note, 109, 132–33, 155–56; Levi, *Rise and Fall of Khoqand*, 112–13.
71. This contrasts sharply with the late fifteenth-century description provided by Babur, the Timurid prince and ruler of the Ferghana Valley in his youth, in which the valley is portrayed as a wilderness paradise. Zahir al-Din Muhammad Babur, *Baburnama*, trans. Thackston, 3–8. This transformation is discussed in detail in Levi, *Rise and Fall of Khoqand*.
72. Levi, *Indian Diaspora*, 155–56.

of the Begs, the local Muslim elite.[73] This involved implementing a series of policies, including land grants and cash incentives, designed to move financial resources into the hands of the Turkic Begs while also providing them incentives to exploit the region's natural resources and expand the agricultural economy.[74] The efforts were highly successful, and between 1772 and the mid-nineteenth century, the amount of arable land in Altishahr roughly doubled and the population increased by a factor of five.[75] According to Qing records, already in 1778, one individual is said to have owned some 8,459 acres of land; a century later, another family had amassed such wealth that they were able to invest more than 6.5 million taels of silver in commercial ventures.[76]

James Millward has examined the most direct mechanism that the Qing employed to achieve their goals in the region. This was the *xiexiang*, the silver stipend that the Qing administration dispatched each year to Altishahr, beginning soon after the conquest and lasting even to 1853. Gathered from regions that achieved a surplus, the xiexiang that the Qing remitted to Altishahr reached into the millions of taels each year.[77] For nearly a century, the Qing efforts were successful, and they enjoyed a sustained peace on their western frontier. The injection of wealth into the region stimulated the regional economy and generally secured the loyalty of wealthy Turkic landowners. It did not, however, always benefit the less fortunate segments of the population. It is important to emphasize that globalizing forces are neither inherently positive nor negative; the same economic forces that provide desirable opportunities for some can also unleash devastating conditions on others.

From the middle of the eighteenth century, the success of Qing authority in Central Asia became inextricably bound to Beijing's ability to divert resources from the eastern seaboard to the population of Xinjiang. To be sure, the Turkic Muslim population of the region was quite capable of cast-

---

73. Kwangmin Kim, *Borderland Capitalism: Turkestan Produce, Qing Silver, and the Birth of an Eastern Market* (Stanford: Stanford University Press, 2016).
74. Kim's research on this particular issue is supported by another recent study, which details how the Shanxi *piaohao*, a Chinese financial institution, flourished primarily by moving silver throughout the Qing Empire to link coastal markets with the hinterland. See Luman Wang, "Money and Trade, Hinterland and Coast, Empire and Nation-State: An Unusual History of Shanxi Piaohao, 1820–1930," PhD diss., University of Southern California, 2014.
75. Kim, *Borderland Capitalism*, 11 and appendices A-1 and A-2.
76. Kim, *Borderland Capitalism*, 7.
77. James Millward, *Beyond the Pass: Economy, Ethnicity, and Empire in Qing Central Asia, 1759–1864* (Stanford: Stanford University Press, 1998), 58–61, 235–37.

ing off the Qing when it was in their best interest to do so.[78] But time and again, the nobility resisted calls for religious uprisings against the Qing, choosing instead to submit to their non-Muslim rulers so long as those linkages were in place and working to their advantage. In general, from the mid-eighteenth century, Qing fiscal and administrative policies in Xinjiang represent yet another avenue through which Central Asia was connected to the globalizing early modern world.

RUSSIA

Pivoting toward the field of Russian history, one also finds a substantial and growing amount of evidence to support the argument that, over the course of the early modern era, Central Asian (and, more broadly, Central Eurasian) markets became more heavily engaged in commercial connections with their neighbors to the north as well. Echoing our discussions of India and China, the most apparent aspect of this trade is again the exportation of Central Eurasian horses and other livestock to Russia, although the extent to which that was the case has been the topic of some debate. In her recent study of Russian commercial expansion in early modern Siberia, Erika Monahan observes that, already in 1474, a large caravan of Tatar merchants brought forty thousand horses along with considerable other merchandise to Moscow.[79] While this suggests a substantial Russian demand for Central Eurasian horses, it should perhaps be emphasized that many of these steeds were destined for markets not in Muscovy but farther to the west in Eastern Europe.

Other evidence provides more modest figures for these early years. Focusing on one set of documents pertaining to Muscovy in the mid-sixteenth century, Michael Khodarkovsky has analyzed Moscow's horse trade with the neighboring Nogai Horde, a successor state to the Golden Horde. In 1548, just two Nogai mirzas together sent Moscow some 18,000 horses, but that was exceptional. Surveying records from 1551 to 1564, Khodarkovsky finds that the Nogai generally provided Moscow with a meager 7,400 horses per year, and that "usually the numbers were far lower."[80] It may very well be that the Russian conquest of the khanates of Kazan in 1552 and Astrakhan in 1556 simply removed the need to purchase horses from the Nogai. But such an explanation is, of course, speculative.

---

78. Levi, *Rise and Fall of Khoqand*, 135–47.
79. Erika Monahan, *The Merchants of Siberia: Trade in Early Modern Eurasia* (Ithaca: Cornell University Press, 2016), 38.
80. Michael Khodarkovsky, *Russia's Steppe Frontier: The Making of a Colonial Empire, 1500–1800* (Bloomington: Indiana University Press, 2002), 26.

What is more certain is that the stark difference in the magnitude of Moscow's demand for horses in comparison with China at this time would largely be a product of demographics: the sixteenth-century population of Muscovy, or indeed all of Eastern Europe, is dwarfed by that of Ming China.

At the same time, other evidence suggests that higher figures may be applicable to the earlier years as well. In an unpublished article on the subject, Cherie Woodworth suggests that, already in the sixteenth century, the Nogai Horde alone supplied Moscow with forty thousand horses each year while also providing Kazan with an additional twenty thousand horses and a comparable number of sheep.[81] For Moscow, similar numbers are also found for the seventeenth century. In the 1660s, one observer placed sales in Moscow at some thirty thousand head per year.[82] According to Brian Davies, in the seventeenth century, Nogai traders alone annually provided Moscow with as many as twenty-seven thousand horses and four thousand sheep.[83] The reasons why Russia would have developed such a substantial demand are easy enough to imagine. En route to Ukraine in the 1630s, the Franco-Polish cartographer Guillaume de Beauplan encountered a single Crimean Tatar campaign against Moscow accompanied by an estimated two hundred thousand horses.[84]

Substantial in the sixteenth century, the importance of Russian livestock markets expanded considerably during the seventeenth and eighteenth centuries. The available figures suggest a relatively steady demand for Nogai steeds in and around Moscow. But this was accompanied by a sharp increase in demand at other locations across the rapidly expanding Russian Empire. In terms of explaining this general trajectory, it is important to note that this pattern is in harmony with the dramatic growth in the size of the Russian army in the seventeenth century, a topic addressed in the next chapter. Throughout this period, one must also recognize that Moscow's trade with the Nogai nomads represented only one facet of Russian

---

81. Cherie Woodworth, "How Many Horses? 14th–16th c. Russia in the Economic System of the Steppe's 'Great Churn,'" unpublished paper presented at the Davis Center for Russian and Eurasian Studies, Harvard University, February 11, 2011, 3. I am grateful to Dr. Woodworth for providing me a working draft of her paper. Dr. Woodworth passed away in 2013, before she was able to revise her essay for publication.

82. Michael Khodarkovsky, *Where Two Worlds Met: The Russian State and the Kalmyk Nomads, 1600–1771* (Ithaca: Cornell University Press, 1992), 28.

83. Brian L. Davies, *Warfare, State and Society on the Black Sea Steppe, 1500–1700* (London: Routledge, 2007), 28.

84. Davies, *Warfare*, 20–21.

horse imports from the steppe; that the trade in horses was accompanied by even larger numbers of other livestock, including camels, cattle, and, especially, sheep; that the livestock trade represents only one aspect of Russians' commercial relationship with their Central Eurasian nomadic neighbors; and that this trade grew substantially as the Russian Empire reached across Siberia to the Pacific throughout the seventeenth and eighteenth centuries. Russian farmers and soldiers were obvious consumers, but in a mirror image of the North American cattle industry, Central Eurasian livestock flowed westward through Russian markets into Europe. In the early nineteenth century, Ian Blanchard finds that an estimated 3.5 million animals (principally horses, camels, sheep, and cattle) were transported each year from the southern steppe to Russian markets.[85] While this was all intra-Russian trade at the time, it emerged from long-standing patterns that had in previous centuries crossed political boundaries.

The primary participants in the livestock trade were not mediatory merchants attached to the smaller agrarian states but the pastoral nomads who bred the animals themselves. The Nogai Horde played an important role in the sixteenth century. Mongolian pastoralists had long been important suppliers to Chinese markets, and during the seventeenth century, Mongolian Qalmaqs (also Oirats) became suppliers of livestock to Russia as well. As Russia pushed its commercial frontier farther into the steppe and a series of factors led to the depletion of the Qalmaq herds, from the 1730s, that role shifted to another pastoral group, the Kazakhs.[86]

As noted in chapter one, in ethnic, linguistic, and political terms, the Kazakhs are descendants of the same group of Qipchaq Turks as the Uzbeks who under the Chinggisid leadership of Muhammad Shibani Khan had departed the steppe at the end of the fifteenth century and displaced Babur.[87] While the Uzbek nomads became the dominant political group in Transoxania, the Kazakhs remained in the steppe under their own Chinggisid leadership. One often encounters references to a single monolithic Kazakh Khanate ruling over the steppe from the mid-fifteenth century into the eighteenth century, and historical evidence can be used to support such a view. But, as was often the case among Central Asian nomadic polities, leadership remained a corporate affair, and the extent to which the Kazakh peoples were truly united under a singular leader during this period remains

---

85. Excepting those years when the trade was obstructed. Blanchard, *Russia's 'Age of Silver'*, 269–70 and note.
86. Khodarkovsky, *Where Two Worlds Met*, 28.
87. Again, see Lee, Qazaqlïq, *or Ambitious Brigandage, and the Formation of the Qazaqs*.

questionable.[88] It is more clear, however, that by the death of Tauke Khan (r. 1680–1718), the Kazakhs had formed three separate, though still loosely organized, political groups: the Senior (Uly), Middle (Orta), and Junior (Kishi) *zhüzes*.[89] To the east, in what is today northeastern Kazakhstan and the northern stretches of Xinjiang, was the Jungar Empire, the last of the great Inner Asian nomadic empires. As noted previously, during the first half of the eighteenth century, these non-Chinggisid Mongols unleashed a series of invasions of Kazakh pastures and represented a persistent thorn in the western flank of the Qing Empire as well. Following the 1757–1758 Qing campaign into Central Eurasia, the Jungars were eliminated and the Kazakhs became the principal suppliers of all varieties of livestock and animal products for the increasing number of Russian, Chinese, and other consumers in the region.[90]

Despite a few obvious differences, one might suggest that the type of analysis that historian William Cronon directed to the nineteenth-century United States some thirty years ago could generate exciting new insights into Central Eurasian history as well. Cronon's classic study, *Nature's Metropolis*, illustrates how Chicago's rise from the mid-nineteenth century was a product of its role in mediating the relationship between the increasing demands of the more densely populated American east with the vast natural resources of the sparsely populated American west.[91] In the process, he explores how rising market demands and eastward commodity flows—including lumber, wheat, and especially livestock—shaped the rise of cities across the Midwest, and the ecological transformation of America.

---

88. Thomas Welsford, "The Disappearing Khanate," unpublished paper, n.d., 1–15. For an original anthropological perspective on the historical misrepresentations and complexities of statecraft among Central Asian nomadic peoples, see David Sneath, *The Headless State: Aristocratic Orders, Kinship Society, and Misrepresentations of Nomadic Inner Asia* (New York: Columbia University Press, 2007).
89. *Zhüz* is often mistranslated as "horde." The word *horde* is etymologically derived from the Turkic word *ordu*, and it carries with it a military connotation that is lacking in the meaning of *zhüz*. For two recent studies of the Kazakhs in this period, see Jin Noda, *The Kazakh Khanates between the Russian and Qing Empires* (Leiden: E. J. Brill, 2016), and Ian W. Campbell, *Knowledge and the Ends of Empire: Kazakh Intermediaries and Russian Rule on the Steppe, 1731–1917* (Ithaca: Cornell University Press, 2017).
90. Millward, "Qing Silk-Horse Trade." For the most thorough treatment of the Qing expansion westward and victory over the Jungar state and Altishahr in the 1750s, see Perdue, *China Marches West*.
91. William Cronon, *Nature's Metropolis: Chicago and the Great West* (New York: W. W. Norton, 1991).

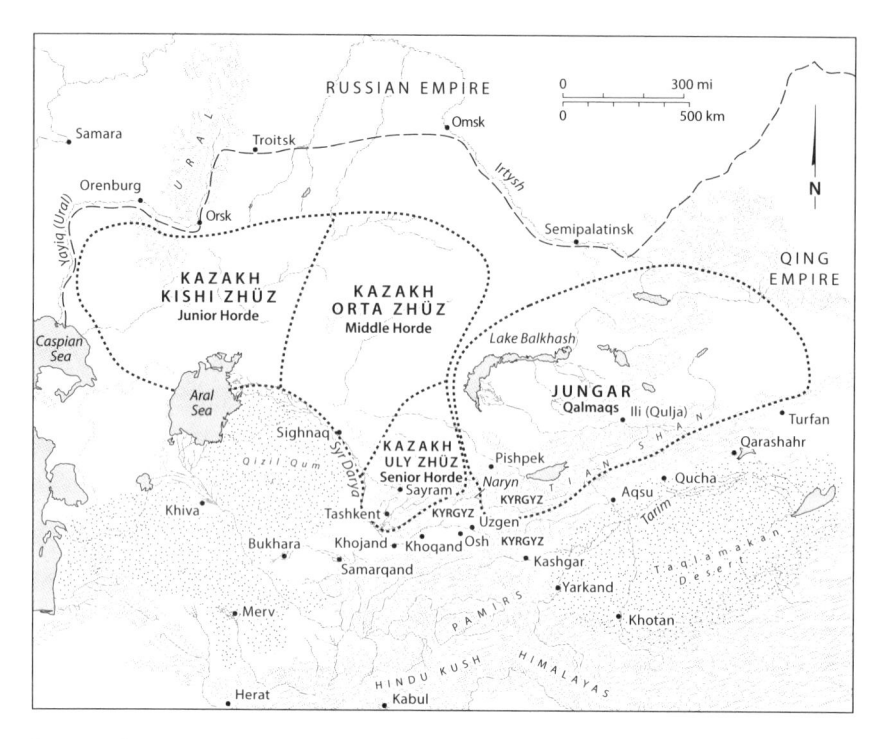

Map 15. Steppe Powers in the Eighteenth Century. Map by Bill Nelson.

More recently, a small number of environmental historians have begun to direct attention to Central Asia, focusing mostly on the late nineteenth and early twentieth centuries. Sarah Cameron advances our understanding of the ways that Russian, and then Soviet, perceptions, aspirations, and agricultural policies transformed the Kazakh steppe and led to the horrific famine of 1930–1933.[92] But there is an earlier story to be told as well, one grounded in the annual movement of livestock from these same pastures westward into Russia and farther into Europe during the eighteenth and early decades of the nineteenth centuries. What sparked the rise in demand in this period? How did Central Asian producers increase their livestock production in response to that demand? How were social and economic

---

92. Sarah Cameron, *The Hungry Steppe: Famine, Violence, and the Making of Soviet Kazakhstan* (Ithaca: Cornell University Press, 2018). See also Ian Campbell, "The Scourge of Stock Raising: Zhŭt, Limiting Environments, and the Economic Transformation of the Kazakh Steppe," in *Eurasian Environments: Nature and Ecology in Russian and Soviet History*, ed. Nicholas Breyfogle (Pittsburgh: University of Pittsburgh Press, 2018), 60–74; Maya Peterson, *Pipe Dreams: Water, Technology, and the Remaking of Central Asia in the Russian Empire and Soviet Union, 1848–1948* (Cambridge: Cambridge University Press, 2019).

structures devised to manage this flow of commodities, even before the age of the railroad? What were the political implications of this trade in the steppe? Did the intertwined and evolving relationships among urban and rural consumers in the Eurasian west and the livestock producers in the Inner Asian steppe leave lasting environmental legacies of the type that Cronon identifies in North America? If so, do these legacies remain visible and relevant in the twenty-first-century world? It does not seem too bold to suggest that engaging seriously with such questions stands to generate valuable insights into the ways that early modern Central Asians responded to changes in external economic and political forces, and also into the historical foundations of some of the most pressing environmental issues that confront the region in the present day.

Returning to the subject at hand, other scholars have observed that Russia's southward trade was not limited to the acquisition of livestock from nomadic neighbors: throughout the early modern era, merchant groups from the sedentary zone in Central Asia proper were also involved in trade with Russia. The expansion of Bukharan trade with markets in Russia and Siberia, as well as China, India, and elsewhere, is illustrated in considerable detail in Audrey Burton's comprehensive study of Bukharan politics and trade over a century and a half, from 1550 to 1702.[93] Burton's densely packed study marshals evidence from an array of Persian- and Russian-language manuscripts and primary sources to construct an elaborate portrait of the Bukharans' international commercial interests in this period. She examines Bukharan political efforts to enhance commercial traffic within the region, their efforts to use diplomacy to create opportunities for their merchants in foreign markets, the primary trade routes that Bukharan caravans traversed, and the impressive expanse of the Bukharan commercial network. Burton also documents the merchandise that the Bukharans dealt in, which included some items produced in and around Bukhara, but mostly items that they retrieved from elsewhere: Chinese silks, rhubarb, and other medicinal herbs; manufactured goods from Russia as well as Siberian furs, horses and other livestock from the steppe; all varieties of Indian textiles and dyes imported from India and Persia; Qarakul lambskins, wool, and other merchandise from Safavid and Ottoman domains, as well as slaves, jewelry, weapons, agricultural goods, and much, much more.[94]

Astrakhan, which from 1556 served as Russia's commercial center at the mouth of the Volga, represented one of several central hubs where much of this trade took place. From at least as early as the 1640s and throughout

---

93. Burton, *Bukharans*.

the eighteenth century, Russian sources document a community of several hundred Bukharan merchants in Astrakhan.[95] In some ways, the Bukharan trade network, like that of the Indians referenced earlier, represents a continental version of what the Julfa Armenians established in the maritime world.[96] These networks overlapped, and archival records show that they also collaborated. In addition to moving merchandise to and from Central Asia, the Bukharan merchant communities participated in a wide variety of commercial partnerships with official Russian merchants, local Tatars, Qalmaqs, Indians, Armenians, and Persians, as well as with each other.

As was the case with the Multani Indians and Armenians, during the seventeenth and eighteenth centuries, the Russian government provided Bukharan merchants a *dvor* (residence) in Astrakhan, and from there their commercial interests extended outward and up the Volga to Moscow. At the same time, Astrakhan was but one outpost. Into the eighteenth century, Bukharan trading communities were present in both Safavid and Mughal markets as well. But perhaps the most interesting dimension of their trade was the extension of their network northward into Siberia, where they mediated the movement of goods, people, animals, wealth, and information between Siberian settlements and the sedentary stretches to the south, and elsewhere. During the early decades of the eighteenth century, even as (and perhaps partly because) the Bukharan political crisis grew critical, Central Asian commercial groups expanded their reach into Russian markets.[97] These Siberian markets were something much greater than isolated campsites frequented by a handful of caravan traders.

Erika Monahan has conducted an impressively detailed study of the role that the expanding Muscovite commercial economy in early modern Siberia played in the development of the Russian state, and her work demonstrates another way that Russian interests in the region promoted

---

94. Burton, *Bukharans*, 363–90.
95. For intercommunal partnerships in the seventeenth century, see K. A. Antonova, N. M. Gol'dberg, and T. D. Lavrentsova, eds., *Russko-indiiskie otnosheniia v XVII v., sbornik dokumentov* (Moscow: Nauka, 1958), docs 18, 169, 170, 203, 206, 207. For the eighteenth century, see K. A. Antonova and N. M. Gol'dberg, eds., *Russko-indiiskie otnosheniia v XVIII v., sbornik dokumentov* (Moscow: Nauka, 1965), docs 82, 87. Both volumes include abundant references to Bukharan traders.
96. Sebouh David Aslanian, *From the Indian Ocean to the Mediterranean: The Global Trade Networks of Armenian Merchants from New Julfa* (Berkeley: University of California Press, 2011).
97. In addition to sources cited below, cf. D. A. Makeev, *Rossiisko-vostochnie torgovie sviazi na rubeje Srednevekov'ia i Novogo vremeni (XVI–pervaia chetvert' XVIII veka)* (Vladimir: VIT-print, 2013), 116–43, and A. I. Yukht, *Torgovlia c vostochnimi stranami i vnutrenniy rinok Rossii (20–60-e godi XVIII veka)* (Moskva: Nauk, 1994), 149–75.

Central Asian commercial engagement with globalizing forces. For example, Monahan focuses some attention on Lake Yamysh, a remote salt lake midway along the Irtysh River in what is today northeastern Kazakhstan, situated on trade routes that at that time led eastward to Kiakhta. Yamysh was long known to have been a source of exceptionally high-quality salt: an ingredient critical for the preservation of the food that made it possible to survive the long Siberian winters and also to process the leather and furs that drove the region's economy. Etymologically, Monahan notes that the Russians adopted the name Yamysh from the Turkic *yam*, which suggests that it was likely to have been used as a postal weigh station during the Mongol era.[98] But it was the salt that made the location desirable, drawing traders from throughout the region. At Yamysh, Monahan finds an exceptional case study: "a glimpse of the too-little documented dynamics of trade between Russians, Bukharans, Qalmaqs, Kazaks, Dzhungars—a juncture at which the (too) classically defined 'settler-nomad' societies met." Her detailed microhistorical analysis of this remote salt lake examines its development over the course of the seventeenth and eighteenth centuries, as it transformed from a remote commercial trading post into an important regional market. Monahan finds that "not only does Lake Yamysh testify to the growth in the trade between Russia and China. It presents a counterstory to the problematic commonplace that early modern overland trade declined against the competition of European maritime trade."[99]

Geographically remote, Yamysh flourished primarily because of its location along routes that connected Bukhara with Kiakhta. In the seventeenth century, long before the 1727 Treaty of Kiakhta, the annual Yamysh fair occurred in late summer. Monahan describes the following:

> Livestock, fabrics, and slaves were the main products Russians bought or exchanged for leather, furs, and 'Russian goods' at Lake Yamysh. Kalmyks drove livestock—horses, camels, sheep, goats—to the lake and traded for Russian items as well as for tobacco. Fabrics made up the bulk in nearly every caravan arriving from the east, but even herein the variety was enormous, from thick, coarse cottons to the finest Chinese silks, in all manner of colors. Livestock, dried fruits (raisins, dates), roots such as rhubarb and ginseng, slaves, Indian spices, Chinese tea, sometimes precious gems, paper, and ivory were some of the goods that weighed Russian flat-bottomed river boats down as they sat low in the water on the return journey down-

---

98. Monahan, *Merchants of Siberia*, 183.
99. Monahan, *Merchants of Siberia*, 176.

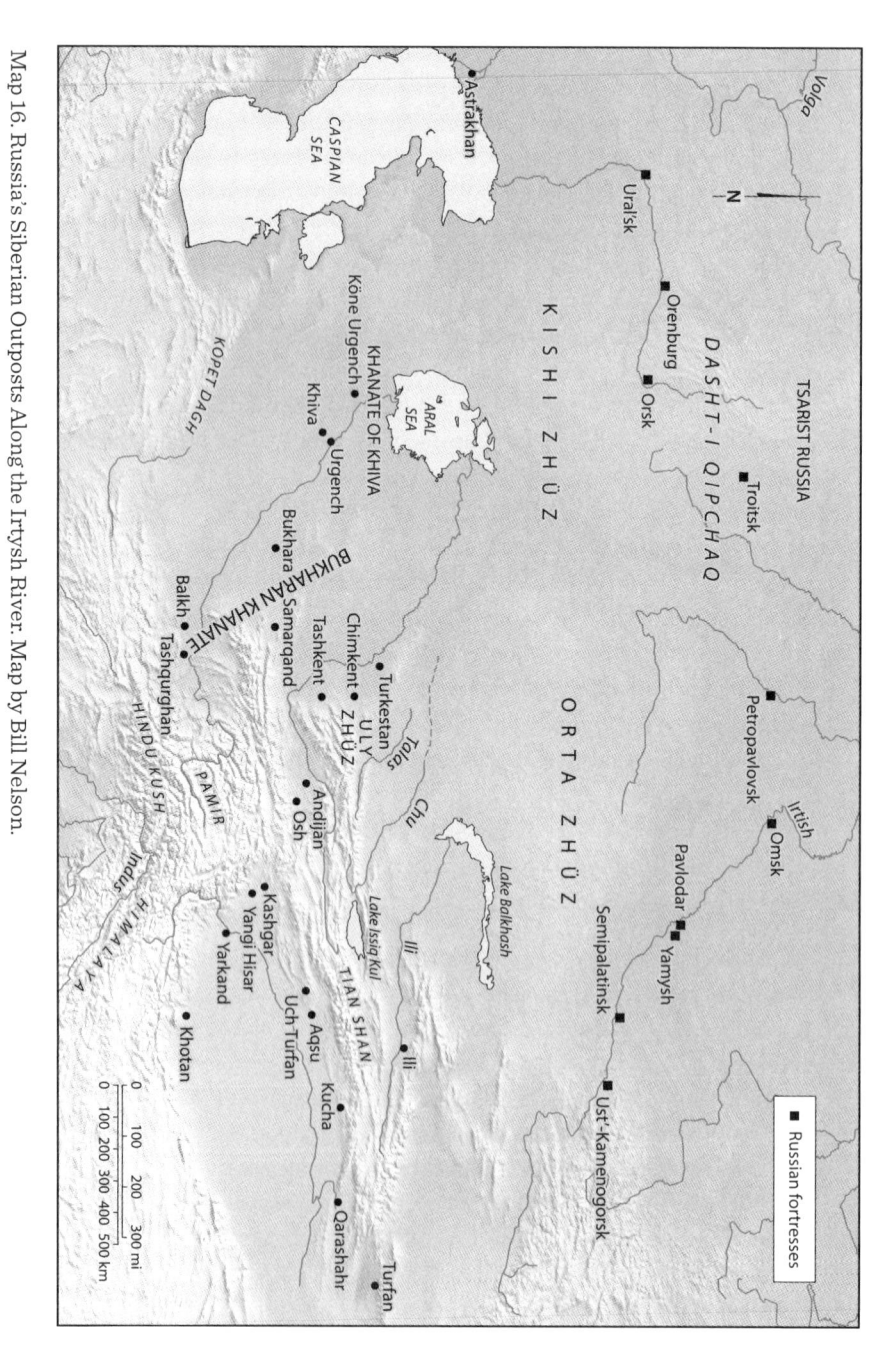

Map 16. Russia's Siberian Outposts Along the Irtysh River. Map by Bill Nelson.

stream. Merchants from the east, meanwhile, departed with furs, leather hides, English wool, fry pans, axes, utensils, mirrors, nails, needles, thread, knit socks, boots, and occasionally clocks or mirrors fixed to the backs of camels and horses for the overland portion of the journey.[100]

Among the participants in this trade, Monahan locates a variety of classes of Russian merchants, including agents of the privileged *gosti*, as well as commoners. Perhaps most striking, and certainly most relevant to our present interest, is her conclusion that "the merchants who turned out at Lake Yamysh in the greatest numbers were likely Bukharans, from Siberia and Central Asia."[101] As was the case with the Andijanis mentioned previously, the label identifies individuals as part of a commercial community, but it does not necessarily identify the city or even the region of origin. To clarify, Siberian (or to the Russian administrators, "yurt") Bukharans were those merchants who had migrated from the Bukharan Khanate (or the surrounding areas) to Siberia and permanently relocated to the region. Central Asian (or "transit") Bukharans were those who had traveled to Siberia by caravan to conduct their trade, after which they would continue onward to other Russian outposts or China, or return southward to make their way back home. In a sense, these were not so much two separate communities of Bukharans as they were a number of distinct merchant families whose commercial activities overlapped. For example, the transit Bukharans are also known to have spent extended periods of time—even months—living among the yurt Bukharans before moving onward.[102]

These Bukharan merchants served an important mediatory role in overland Eurasian trade. Bukharans in Siberia were well-known traders and suppliers of cotton textiles, the majority of which would have been produced in India and transported to Central Asia by Indian merchants working with Afghan nomads. From there, Bukharan merchants assembled their own caravans and transported them onward to Siberia, or elsewhere. They are also known to have traveled great distances themselves in order to gain direct access to their merchandise.[103] Near the end of the seventeenth century, the Dutch statesman Nicolaes Witsen took a great interest in Siberia and reported that Bukharans traveled across much of Asia, they regularly took their camels and horses to China and India, and they pro-

---

100. Monahan, *Merchants of Siberia*, 192–93.
101. Monahan, *Merchants of Siberia*, 194.
102. Monahan, *Merchants of Siberia*, 264.
103. Burton, *Bukharans*, 363–90.

vided critical services for the Siberian markets that they passed through along their way. He noted that the Bukharans returned with silken textiles and spices, but most interesting to him was their use of "Chinese Tobacco," which was available in various colors, including brown, yellow, and green. Describing the method of smoking, Witsen cautioned that the brown variety produced a pleasant aroma, but that smoking it tended to make one "fall unconscious."[104]

Drawing on archival research in Tiumen Oblast, and particularly in the west Siberian city of Tobolsk, Monahan also provides a case study of the Shababin family, one of the most important multigenerational Bukharan merchant families in early modern Siberia.[105] The Shababin were descendants of Shaba Seitov (perhaps Saba Sayyid), a Bukharan merchant to whom, in 1657, Tsar Alexei I (r. 1645–1676) granted more than nineteen hundred acres of land across the Tura River from the city of Tiumen (see Map 14, above). This area later became known as the "Bukharan Neighborhood" (*Bukharskaia sloboda*).[106] In terms of their business interests, from their arrival in Siberia the Shababin family was primarily engaged in transregional trade, which they augmented with animal husbandry and leather production. Their property holdings expanded over time, and by the mid-eighteenth century, the Shababin were the most successful of the many Bukharan merchant families in the region. To no small extent, their commercial success was built on Russo-Bukharan collaboration.

Monahan's study also sheds light on the Russian state's motivations in encouraging Muslim merchants from Bukhara to relocate to this recently acquired and sparsely populated Siberian territory. For their part, the Shababin served the Russian state through their commercial activities, by investing in the development of the regional commercial infrastructure, and in more official capacities by serving as officers in the customs administration, for example. Her study focuses on the Shababin, but she takes care to examine that family in the context of the many other Bukharan merchant families in Siberia during the seventeenth and eighteenth centuries. By the end of the seventeenth century, some three thousand Bukharan merchants had settled just in the Siberian region around Tiumen and Tobolsk.[107] These numbers multiplied in subsequent decades—again, perhaps propelled by

---

104. N. Witsen, *Noord en Oost Tartarye* . . . , 2nd edition (Amsterdam: François Halma, 1705), 377.
105. Monahan, *Merchants of Siberia*, 254–301.
106. Monahan, *Merchants of Siberia*, 254–59.
107. Monahan, *Merchants of Siberia*, 260.

the growing Bukharan political crisis of the early eighteenth century—and contemporary sources estimate that by 1775 more than twenty thousand Bukharan men had taken up residence in the Russian Empire.[108] Quite apart from enforcing policies designed to suppress Islam, the Russian administrators encouraged the Siberian Bukharan merchants as they partnered with Christian Russians and other Muslims, including, of course, large numbers of transit Bukharans.

This Bukharan network linked Central Asian markets to the growing Russian trade with China across the northern steppe, as well as the growing Russian commercial economy in general during Russia's eighteenth-century "Age of Silver." Considering the imperial economy as a whole, Russian exports during the eighteenth century increased from 3.6 million rubles in 1710 to 100 million rubles in 1799.[109] And despite its reputation as a remote wilderness, Monahan emphasizes both that Siberian trade represented a substantial component of Russian commercial expansion in this period and that Bukharan merchants were heavily involved in Siberian trade. If this appears revelatory, it is because scholarly attention has long been focused on Russian commercial markets farther to the west. But in the early eighteenth century, Yamysh customs receipts actually compared favorably to the trade fairs in western Siberia.[110] Furthermore, the Bukharans served as important intermediaries in Russo-Chinese trade, both before and after the Treaty of Kiakhta.[111]

The magnitude of this trade was substantial in the first half of the eighteenth century, and, along with the Russian economy, it increased over time. The Uzbek economic historian Hamid Ziyaev references mid-eighteenth-century sources indicating that groups of hundreds of Bukharan merchants regularly made their way to Yamysh, or passed through it en route to Tobolsk and other Siberian markets.[112] In 1744, as the Toqay-Timurid regime in Bukhara teetered and neared utter collapse, customs records

---

108. Monahan, *Merchants of Siberia*, 260–61. Monahan references the account of a German scholar who observed this while traveling through Siberia at that time, Johann Gottlieb Georgi, *Russia: Or, a Compleat Historical Account of All the Nations Which Compose That Empire*, 4 vols. (London: J. Nichols, 1780), 2:127, 129.
109. Monahan, *Merchants of Siberia*, 201. Figures from A. I. Aksenov et al., *Ekonomicheskaia istoriia Rossii*, vol. 1 (Moscow: Rosspen, 2009), 403.
110. Monahan, *Merchants of Siberia*, 195.
111. Monahan, *Merchants of Siberia*, 200. Monahan's revelation contradicts earlier assumptions that it was only Russians, and not Bukharans, who conducted trade in these new border towns.
112. Hamid Ziyaev, *Ekonomicheskie sviiazi Srednei Azii s Sibiriu v XVI–XIX vv.* (Tashkent: Fan, 1983), 77, 84.

indicate that some 565 Bukharan merchants traveled through Yamysh in a period of just two months, and the following year a caravan of some 150 merchants passed through in a single day.[113] It is true that Central Asian merchants found the relative importance of the Yamysh trade to diminish in later years, but this was not because Bukharan trade there declined. In fact, the case was quite the opposite. Monahan observes that "in the sense that a rising tide raises all ships," it was because Bukharans' commercial activities at other Siberian commercial outposts had increased more rapidly and outpaced the Yamysh trade.[114]

Multiple factors contributed to the steady advancement of this process, as well as to the growing importance of Central Asia's mediatory role in overland Eurasian trade. In addition to Russia's obvious commercial interests in the region, the Russian steppe fortresses served both as military outposts and important trading entrepôt. As such, they attracted Russian and Tatar merchants, Kazakhs and other nomadic peoples of the steppe, and large numbers of caravan traders from Bukhara and other points in Central Asia.[115] In the seventeenth century, Russia's Siberian outposts were important commercial centers for nomads. During the early eighteenth century, the fortresses established along the Irtysh became even more important as the Caspian trade diminished in the wake of the 1722 Ghilzai uprisings and the resulting political disruptions in Safavid Iran.

Thus, in the year 1735, as the Bukharan khan's authority barely extended beyond the capital and just two years before Nadir Shah's Persian forces launched their first invasion of Central Asia, the newly established Orenburg Dispatch Department issued a summons for an Indian merchant to be brought from Astrakhan to Orenburg for an interview.[116] The stated objective was to increase Russian trade with Bukhara, and the Indian who was selected is identified in Russian archival records as "Marwari Baraev" (the "Great Marwari," or head of that particular Indian merchant community). According to Baraev, the ongoing disturbances in Nadir Shah's Persia had dislocated foreign trade networks leading to Astrakhan. But he suggested to the Russian authorities that these very problems could work to the Russian advantage in their trade with Central Asia, and, should the route from Bukhara to Orenburg be adequately protected, the Russians could expect to attract large numbers of Bukharan merchants and "at least 600 Indian mer-

---

113. Monahan, *Merchants of Siberia*, 206.
114. Monahan, *Merchants of Siberia*, 202.
115. Audrey Burton, "Bukharan Trade, 1558–1718," Papers on Inner Asia, no. 23 (Bloomington: Indiana University Research Institute for Inner Asian Studies, 1993), 66–77.
116. Antonova and Gol'dberg, eds., *Russko-indiiskie otnosheniia*, doc. 69, 1735, 128–33.

chants every year."[117] The Russians' invitation to trade in Orenburg was all the encouragement needed. Shortly thereafter, both Bukharan and Indian merchants began shifting their trade away from Astrakhan and toward Orenburg.[118]

Materials from the Orenburg State Archive shed additional light on Russia's early successes in this venture. In a letter dated 1745, just five years after Nadir Shah's second invasion of Bukhara, a Bukharan merchant identified as Irnazar Massudov informed Orenburg officials that, as instructed, he had done everything possible to motivate "not only Bukharan traders, but also Indian traders, to participate in the Orenburg Fair." Massudov reported that "as a result, Indians (alone) went to Bukhara with ... goods worth about 300,000 rubles."[119] In 1750, a new trade fair was opened in Troitsk, situated between Orenburg and Omsk, with prices listed in both rubles and rupees.[120] In 1751, the Russian Senate Collegium of Foreign Affairs endorsed the governor of Orenburg's proposal to establish a new Orenburg Company to further advance Russia's trade with Central Asia and, through Central Asia, with India.[121] By the mid-eighteenth century, Orenburg had an established position as an important center for Russian trade with the Central Asian khanates, and it retained that position as Russia's southward trade expanded over the following century.[122]

A QUESTION OF SCALE

The evidence presented in this chapter highlights the dynamic nature of Central Asia's early modern commercial economy. At the same time, another body of evidence highlights the destabilizing processes that also confronted the region during this same period. Related events include multiple Jungar invasions, including the especially devastating occupation of Kazakh pastures in 1723; the resulting Kazakh mass migration southward and the devastation it caused; a growing fiscal crisis and eco-

---

117. Antonova and Gol'dberg, eds., *Russko-indiiskie otnosheniia*, doc. 69, 1735, 129.
118. In 1747, the year Nadir Shah was assassinated, a Russian census shows Astrakhan's Indian community to have numbered only fifty-one people. Antonova and Gol'dberg, eds., *Russko-indiiskie otnosheniia*, doc. 132, 1735, 265–69.
119. Orenburg District State Archive, fond 3, opis' 1, delo 8, list 10. Also discussed in Levi, *Indian Diaspora*, 238–39.
120. E. Ia. Liusternik, *Russko-indiiskie ekonomicheskie sviazi v XIX v.* (Moscow: Nauka, 1958), 12.
121. Antonova and Gol'dberg, eds., *Russko-indiiskie otnosheniia*, doc. 139, 1751, 283–84.
122. G. A. Mikhaleva, *Torgovie i posol'skie sviazi Rossii so Sredneaziatskimi khanstvami cherez Orenburg (vtoraia polovina XVIII–pervaia polovina XIX v.)* (Tashkent: Fan, 1982).

nomic hardship; and a rise in conflict among the Kazakh zhüzes during the second quarter of the eighteenth century, which encouraged parasitic attitudes toward travelers and efforts to disrupt caravan traffic in rivals' territories.[123] I address these themes in greater detail in the next chapter. For now, it is necessary to ask what one can make of two contradictory bodies of evidence. How is it that Bukharan trade in Siberia appears to have expanded at precisely the same time that the Bukharan political climate descended into crisis and travel throughout the region became more precarious?

Complexity is not a vice. As historians, we evaluate arguments, critically investigate sources, scrutinize our evidence, and weigh that evidence for bias and reliability as we endeavor to improve our understanding of the past. In doing so, we must also endeavor to appreciate the nuances of historical circumstance and the importance of contingency. In this case, a meaningful analysis must take both bodies of evidence into account. That is to say, even as the Bukharan political climate deteriorated to the point of collapse in the first half of the eighteenth century, Bukharan merchants were still willing to trust their established networks and relationships, and, assessing the risk and deeming it worthwhile, venture into Siberia in pursuit of their fortunes. One might even argue that increasingly uncertain circumstances at home made foreign markets appear that much more desirable. In this way, rather than regional decline and isolation, the destabilization of the Bukharan state may actually be seen as having propelled outward commercial expansion and long-term integration. In the end, some of these many thousands of Bukharans met with success, finding newly emerging and unexploited opportunities. Others met with failure, ending up impoverished, enslaved, or worse. It is also worth noting that these processes may have had other lasting effects in the region, such as contributing to the considerable Bukharan influence in intellectual currents among Muslim communities in the Russian empire at the same time.[124]

An accurate portrait of early modern Central Asia is neither one of abject crisis nor of unbridled vitality. Rather, as some trends were unweaving the fabric of the regional economy, other trends were busily stitching new patterns. Such is the nature of transition. Focusing more precisely on the early decades of the eighteenth century, the establishment of a network of Rus-

---

123. Holzwarth, "Relations between Uzbek Central Asia," 199–201.
124. See Allen J. Frank, *Bukhara and the Muslims of Russia: Sufism, Education, and the Paradox of Islamic Prestige* (Leiden: E. J. Brill, 2012).

sian fortresses in southern Siberia enhanced Central Asian trade with Russia, and with China through Russia. This happened even as the Bukharan Khanate descended into a decades-long political crisis that brought Chinggisid rule to an end.[125]

It may also be instructive to pull the lens back further still and ask how commercial patterns in early modern Central Asia compared to those that were unfolding in the Indian Ocean at the same time. Such a comparison is, of course, impossible to advance with any degree of accuracy. This is partly because of the extraordinary geographical breadth of both commercial arenas, partly because our interests cover a period of several centuries, and partly because of the uneven availability of commercial records.

Scholars working in the field of Indian Ocean history have for some time recognized that the generations of research in the companies' comparatively well-kept and accessible records have produced a biased perspective of European activities along the Indian Ocean littoral. With few exceptions (e.g., the Dutch control over the spice trade), the notion of European commercial dominance in the Indian Ocean (at least prior to the nineteenth century) is a lasting legacy of this imbalance.[126] This notion is based on impression, not evidence, and so long as it persisted it threw shade on the vastly more complex commercial arena dominated by many less well-documented non-European commercial groups. I will refrain from digressing into a survey of the many achievements to emanate from the field of Indian Ocean history in recent years. But I will note that the dichotomy between overland and maritime trade is to no small extent a false one, and that many Asian and African merchant networks thrived by linking together the bustle of the maritime entrepôt with the vast resources of the hinterland.[127]

Nevertheless, there is merit in pursuing an answer to these pressing historiographical concerns by establishing some sense of scale between the companies' activities in the Indian Ocean and the magnitude of Central Asian trade at roughly the same time. Extensive research into the official records of the Dutch V.O.C. and the English (later British) East India Company provides valuable insights into the European trade, and its subtleties. For example, the English East India Company and the V.O.C. both engaged

---

125. Monahan, *Merchants of Siberia*, 205–6; John LeDonne, "Building an Infrastructure of Empire in Russia's Eastern Theater, 1650s–1840s," *Cahiers du monde russe* 47, no. 3 (2006): 581–608; Ziyaev, *Ekonomicheskie sviiazi*, 83–100; Levi, *Indian Diaspora*, 233–50.
126. This is examined in more detail in Levi, "India, Russia," 522–26.
127. For a recent example of how this operated along the Swahili coast, see Thomas F. McDow, *Buying Time: Debt and Mobility in the Western Indian Ocean* (Athens: Ohio University Press, 2018).

in a vibrant Euro-Asia trade. The Dutch, however, were particularly successful at exploiting their monopoly over the Southeast Asian spice trade and their singular access to Japanese markets to leverage profits in the intra-Asian trade. Working with Dutch records, the economic historian Om Prakash finds that over the forty-eight-year period stretching from 1640 to 1688, the V.O.C. paid out some 67 million florins (also guilder, minted with 10.61 grams of silver in 1680) in dividends.[128] The Euro-Asia trade was significant, but, Prakash suggests, the revenue behind these payments, which averaged 1.4 million florins per year, was derived primarily from the intra-Asian trade. This revenue was so important to the success of the V.O.C. that the board of directors considered it to be the very "soul of the Company." The value of intra-Asian trade far exceeded the amount of revenue achieved through sale of Asian merchandise in Europe by either the Dutch or the English.[129]

For several reasons, the case of Bengal in northeast India provides a useful point for comparison and for contrast: unlike Central Asia, Bengal was densely populated and agriculturally rich, enjoyed direct maritime links to both the South and Southeast Asian commercial arenas, and was a major center of Portuguese activity in the sixteenth century, and of both English and Dutch activity in the seventeenth century. Moving into the eighteenth century, the English would emerge dominant in Bengal. The English outpost at Calcutta (Kolkata) was established in 1690 and rapidly transformed from a small outpost of some ten thousand people in 1704 into a major urban center of four hundred thousand people in 1756, eclipsing Hooghly and other thriving seventeenth-century commercial centers.[130] The following year, Robert Clive infamously defeated the Nawab of Bengal at the Battle of Plassey (Palashi) and took over the Bengal Subah in the name of the company.

European commercial interests in Bengal were substantial. In the early years of the eighteenth century, from about 1709 to 1718, Om Prakash calculates that the V.O.C. annually procured an average of 2.27 million rupees' worth of merchandise in Bengal, and the English procured another 1.88 million rupees.[131] The Bengal trade focused on textiles, which Bengali labor-

---

128. Om Prakash, *Bullion for Goods: European and Indian Merchants in the Indian Ocean Trade, 1500–1800* (Delhi: Manohar, 2004), 68–86.
129. Prakash, *Bullion for Goods*, 17.
130. Tirthankar Roy, *The East India Company: The World's Most Powerful Corporation* (New Delhi: Penguin, 2012), 165.
131. Prakash, *Bullion for Goods*, 265. Rupees struck in this period are of variable weights, but they generally contained a higher silver content than the florin, with one rupee approximately equal

ers produced in abundance principally for export. Prakash calculates that, each year during this period, the Dutch purchased on average more than 4.1 million square yards of cloth and the English purchased another 5.5 million yards.[132] Both the Dutch and the English offset these acquisitions primarily with precious metals: bullion and coins were used to cover some 92 percent of the Dutch costs and 76 percent of English costs. Rather than cause inflation, the sustained injection of precious metals into Bengal's economy appears to have driven an increase in production and, in general, contributed to a vibrant commercial economy.[133] On the one hand, European demand in the early eighteenth century was substantial enough to drive Bengali farmers to shift their production from rice and other foods to cash crops for export. On the other hand, it is important to recognize that the Dutch and English achieved this position after sixty years of trading in Bengal, and their collective business interests still represented only between only 8.69 and 11.11 percent of the total Bengali market.[134]

How does Central Asia's commercial environment compare? The discussion above has aimed to demonstrate that overland trade through Central Asia was multivectored, multifaceted, and orchestrated by many different groups with both complementary and competing interests. Bukharan merchants ventured northward to engage the commercial routes from China that passed westward through Kiakhta and Irkutsk, and across Siberia. Estimates suggest that the annual value of that trade rose by a factor of ten over the course of the eighteenth century.[135] Shifting southward, China's westward trade with the Turkic Muslim peoples of Central Asia was a feature of the region's economic life in the seventeenth century, and it became a foundational element of it following the Qing conquest of Xinjiang in the 1750s. We have also seen that Russia's southward commercial interests grew substantially during the seventeenth century and became another foundational element of Central Asia's regional economy from the early decades of the eighteenth century.

We have established that the vast majority of the overland trade that passed into and through Central Asia, and Central Eurasia more broadly, included bulk goods rather than luxury items. Turning to specifics, one might recall the reference above to the V.O.C. agents who, in the seventeenth

to one and a half florin. Om Prakash, *The Dutch East India Company and the Economy of Bengal, 1630–1720* (Princeton: Princeton University Press, 1985), 70.

132. Prakash, *Bullion for Goods*, 272.
133. Prakash, *Bullion for Goods*, 267.
134. Prakash, *Bullion for Goods*, 280. See also Prakash, *Dutch East India Company*, 242.
135. Rossabi, "'Decline' of the Central Asian Caravan Trade," 368.

century, reported that each year caravans moved some twenty-five thousand to thirty thousand camel loads of cotton textiles from India to Persia.[136] Those estimates may be reasonably precise, or they may greatly exaggerate the magnitude of the overland trade in an effort to advance some undeclared agenda. Proceeding cautiously, even if we were to take the V.O.C. estimates and divide them in half, the remaining thirty-five million yards of cloth that camel caravans transported from India to Persia would be more than three and a half times greater than the total amount of cloth that the English and Dutch purchased each year from Bengal in the early eighteenth century. In terms of the implications for Central Asia in particular, I recognize, of course, that only a fraction of that cloth would make its way northward into Central Asia's transit trade. Nevertheless, this example provides an important insight into the magnitude of the early modern caravan trade. No less important is that contemporary sources report that caravan traders annually transported many thousands of camel loads of bulk goods, including textiles, directly from India to Central Asia in the same period.

In terms of the commodities that originated in Central Asia, one would find considerable value in all of the fruits, furs, silks, and other items annually exported to foreign markets. But it is highly doubtful that anything would approach the value of the horses that were bred in the steppe and sold in markets in India, China, Russia, and elsewhere. Focusing on India, we have seen multiple references to the movement of many tens of thousands of horses each year across Afghanistan to markets in India. Estimates run as high as one hundred thousand horses per year for the seventeenth century and roughly half of that for later in the eighteenth century. Gommans is careful to stress the tenuous nature of his calculations in assessing the value of this trade, but given the available evidence, he suggests that the annual value of this trade amounted to some twenty million rupees.[137] Mughal records indicate that the *turki* horses, those sturdy and reliable steeds bred in the Central Eurasian steppe, were especially in demand because of their strength and stamina, and they sold in India for at least four hundred rupees each.[138] Even if this trade constituted only thirty thousand animals per year, its value would still amount to some twelve million rupees, or three times

---

136. Steensgaard, *Asian Trade Revolution of the Seventeenth Century*, 410–11.
137. Gommans suggests that this amount is equal to "more than three times the total of Bengal exports to Europe by the English and Dutch East India Companies together." Gommans, *Rise of the Indo-Afghan Empire*, 89.
138. Gommans, *Rise of the Indo-Afghan Empire*, 88 and note. Especially fine horses could sell for several thousand rupees, and, Gommans notes, weaker horses such as the indigenous *tātū* breed fetched a much lower price, between fifteen and one hundred rupees.

the combined average annual value of Dutch and British exports from Bengal during the period from 1711 to 1720.[139]

The success of this trade had serious implications for Central Asian nomadic communities, South Asian militaries, and multiple mediatory groups. Gommans observes, for example, that profits from mediating the Indo-Central Asian horse trade represented a critical economic foundation underpinning the mid-eighteenth-century rise of the Durrani Afghan state. Although the magnitude of the trade diminished as cavalry forces were eclipsed by infantry in later years, Indian markets remained dependent upon Afghan mediatory traders and Central Asian suppliers for their horses even to the turn of the twentieth century. In popular culture, this is illustrated in the novel *Kim*, which Rudyard Kipling published in 1901. In the novel, set in the years following the Second Anglo-Afghan War (1878–1880), the British agent Mahbub Ali was a Pashtun horse trader, a figure so ubiquitous that the spy could hide in plain sight as he passed northward from India, making his way across the Hindu Kush, "far and far into the Back of Beyond."[140]

These figures give the reader much to consider, but they must also be approached with caution. On the one hand, it is important to remember that Bengal represents only one—albeit significant—component of Dutch and English trade in the Indian Ocean commercial arena. It is also important to stress that the two points of reference used for this comparison are, in fact, two different economic categories. The problem is not just that we are comparing apples (Bengali textiles) to oranges (Central Asian horses); we are also comparing the value of apples purchased at the orchard with the value of oranges purchased at the market. That is to say, the English and Dutch textile acquisitions in Bengal are wholesale transactions, whereas the Central Asian horses sold in Indian markets are retail transactions. For every Central Asian horse sold in India, the estimated purchase price of four hundred rupees included the collective profits and expenses recovered by the horse dealers in India, the merchant-financiers (Multanis, Bukharans, and others), the Pashtun horse traders, and also the nomadic breeders. On the other hand, while there are no documentary records from which to conduct a thorough analysis of Central Asia's annual horse trade with India, it is also important to emphasize that the figure of thirty thousand horses per year through the end of the eighteenth century is a conservative estimate. Our sources suggest that, for the seventeenth century, a figure twice

---

139. Based on the figures presented in Prakash, *Dutch East India Company*, 82.
140. The first edition was released as Rudyard Kipling, *Kim* (London: Macmillan, 1901).

that high would be reasonable, and even that figure is dwarfed by the flow of Central Asian livestock to markets in both China and, especially from the eighteenth century, Russia.

Considered alongside the movement of cotton textiles, tea (from the eighteenth century), slaves, furs, rhubarb and other medicinal herbs, narcotics, chemicals, weapons, rice and other grains, sugar, fruits, precious metals, and countless other items, the available evidence clearly demonstrates that early modern Central Asia was far from marginal to the global economy. Compared to Bengal, Central Asia was a sparsely populated semiarid zone with limited agricultural potential. Nevertheless, it maintained an active commercial economy bolstered both by a substantial (if slow-moving) transit trade as well as the large-scale export of livestock and other commodities produced within the region. Even deep in the hinterland of Central Asia, as in Bengal, commodity prices fluctuated in harmony with global patterns, and farmers also shifted from food crops to cash crops when it was in their best interest to do so.[141]

EARLY MODERN CONNECTIONS

From the early decades of the sixteenth century, European maritime traders began to inject enormous amounts of American silver into the Chinese and Indian Ocean economies. Rather than causing a decline in the overland "Silk Road" trade through Central Asia, the evidence presented here supports the conclusion that Central Asia became more tightly linked to the emerging early modern global economy. While assembling a comprehensive commercial history of the early modern Silk Road trade is beyond the parameters of the present study, this chapter has documented a number of the more important components of that trade. These include: the sixteenth-century expansion of the Indian merchant diaspora into the region, which involved Indian traders using their resources to support the Central Asian agricultural economy and effectively link the region to the rapidly growing Indian Ocean economy; the eighteenth-century expansion of Chinese commercial interests westward and the deliberate use of silver and other commercial incentives to facilitate Qing governance in Xinjiang; the development of new commercial arteries across the northern steppe; the advancement of Russian interests down the Volga, deep into Siberia, and along the Irtysh River; the flow of merchandise and wealth into the region from India, China, and Russia in exchange for horses, other livestock, leather, furs, fruits, and other commodities; and, most interestingly, the

---

141. McChesney, *Central Asia*, 41–43.

concomitant outward expansion of two Central Asian merchant networks, the Andijanis and the Bukharans. While neither of these designations referred specifically to merchants from either particular city, they did apply to Central Asian merchants that ventured outward into a particular market. The Bukharans were Central Asian merchants from in and around the vicinity of Bukhara who traveled northward into Siberia and the Russian Empire, and the Andijanis were Central Asian merchants from in and around the Ferghana Valley who traveled eastward into Altishahr and the Qing Empire.

This discussion presents an image of the region that contrasts sharply with the standard narrative of the Silk Road. During the early modern era, the region was neither isolated nor marginal, and its inhabitants were anything but passive in their relations with their more populous and increasingly powerful neighbors on the Eurasian periphery. Moving beyond unsupported assumptions about caravan traders moving thousands of camels loaded with luxury goods between China and Europe, we find that two critical forces drove the early modern Central Asian commercial economy. First, commercial groups from both within and beyond the region orchestrated a multivectored transit trade that involved the movement of a great variety of merchandise, mostly textiles and other bulk goods, great distances from producers to consumers across much of Eurasia. Second, many of these same commercial groups, and others, worked with multiple nomadic communities to move extraordinarily large numbers of Central Asian horses alongside other livestock, furs, leather, and agricultural commodities produced within the region to the bustling commercial markets of the vast Eurasian periphery.

I have argued that an improved understanding of the commercial dynamics that underpinned the "Silk Road exchange" is critical to advancing research on Central Asian social and political history. At this same time, this does not change the fact that the Bukharan Khanate underwent a major political crisis in the first half of the eighteenth century, accompanied by widespread economic hardship. Setting aside the collapse of the Silk Road trade and Central Asian isolation as a causal factor, we are now in a better position to understand what precipitated this crisis and why it unfolded when it did and the way it did.

FOUR

THE CRISIS REVISITED

The previous chapter examined scholarship emanating from a number of fields in an effort to offer a more holistic representation of Central Asia's involvement in early modern Eurasian trade. The discussion argued that there were a number of significant commercial developments in the region during the early modern era, and that none of these constituted anything resembling a collapse of the region's commercial infrastructure. In place of rugged but simple traders leading long camel caravans along dusty trails back and forth across the Eurasian landmass, researchers have begun to construct a more comprehensive understanding of Central Asian commercial history. This includes directing attention to the activities of multiple overlapping trade networks, each of which involved thousands of trained merchants. Central Asian merchants exploited their location at the heart of a dynamic web of exchange by extending their interests outward, and merchants from the large sedentary civilizations on the Eurasian periphery similarly sought to reap the benefits to be had at the heart of the web. Aside from the effects of a general increase in commercial activity and the commodification of cotton, tea, and certain other goods, early modern Central Asian commercial patterns exhibited a striking similarity to early periods.

At the same time, one cannot deny the fact that the Bukharan Khanate and other early modern Central Asian states persisted at a significantly less elevated stature than had been the case under the Timurids and earlier regional powers. For centuries, Central Asian rulers had been able to draw upon the abundant nomadic manpower in the region and use it to their military advantage. They launched successful invasions into their agrarian neighbors, subjugated foreign powers, and returned home heavy with treasure and tribute. Such extractive activities had long benefited powers in the region. But, already in the early sixteenth century, the Shibanid rulers in Bukhara found their military strength matched by Safavid Persia. This was largely due to the proliferation of gunpowder weaponry, which the Safavids had incorporated to an extent that was limited by comparison to their Ottoman neighbors to the west but considerably greater than the Uzbeks to the northeast.

Throughout the seventeenth century, the Bukharan Khanate was generally able to maintain the status quo. But in the first half of the eighteenth century, Bukhara suffered debilitating invasions from both Persia and the steppe, exacerbating a growing political crisis that culminated with the collapse of the state and the end of Chinggisid rule in the region. In addressing this crisis, there has been little success at moving beyond the theory that early modern Central Asia became economically isolated as Eurasian commerce shifted from overland routes to the maritime shipping lanes. But the available evidence does not support such a conclusion. Returning attention to the crisis as introduced in chapter one, our discussion now aims to identify a number of causal factors that available evidence does support.

In what follows, I suggest that there was no single cause for the Bukharan crisis. Rather, I identify multiple causal factors, some independent and some related, some of which unfolded gradually over the course of the seventeenth century whereas others shocked the region more abruptly. These historical strands converged in the first half of the eighteenth century, sending the political economy of the Bukharan Khanate into a severe crisis from which it would not emerge. Growing recognition that the khanate's Chinggisid rulers were no longer able to govern effectively, protect their subjects, and manage the needs and demands of their subordinate Uzbek tribal amirs terminally undermined their claim to legitimacy. In 1747, this culminated with the termination of Toqay-Timurid Chinggisid rule in Bukhara and the rise of a new model of governance across the region that placed executive authority in the hands of the Uzbek tribal leadership.

BUKHARA IN CRISIS, ANOTHER LOOK

In an essay on the three main Uzbek tribal dynasties that emerged in the eighteenth century and governed until the Russian colonial period—the Manghit in Bukhara, the Qongrat in Khiva, and the Ming in Khoqand—Yuri Bregel summarizes the regional context as follows: "In the first half of the eighteenth century the sedentary regions of Central Asia experienced, to various degrees, a political and economic crisis, which manifested itself in the decline of the ruling dynasties in the two Uzbek khanates, Bukhara and Khiva, the weakening or even the total collapse of the central governments, the resurgence of tribal forces, increasing interference by steppe nomads in the affairs of the sedentary states, and the disruption of economic life."[1] Bregel's discussion continues with a description of the rebellious actions of Uzbek amirs across the region, the collapse of Chinggisid authority in the middle of the century, and the rise of the Uzbek Manghit, Qongrat, and Ming tribal dynasties. As a whole, there is little with which one could object in Bregel's characterization of the crisis that confronted the final two Toqay-Timurid rulers, 'Ubaydullah Khan (r. 1702–1711) and his brother Abu'l Fayz Khan (r. 1711–1747). One might suggest that Bregel advances a decidedly state-centered perspective of eighteenth-century Central Asia, but such a critique would unfairly miss the mark as "the state" is the deliberate focus of his essay.

From its inception, the political structures of the Bukharan Khanate were built upon nomadic traditions of shared power that the Uzbeks had inherited from the Mongols, and the Mongols had inherited from other nomadic states before them. These nomadic traditions were enshrined in the Chinggisid yasa, or legal code, although by the time of the sixteenth-century Shibanids these had been infused with certain Islamic practices.[2] Following their victory over the Timurids, the Shibanids reintroduced the traditional Mongolian appanage system, replacing Timurid heirs and their dependents with an inherently decentralized political system that divided power and resources among the ruling family. This set it apart from the more centralized (though certainly not absolutist) governmental structures of the Ottomans and Mughals, for example. McChesney explains,

---

1. Bregel, "New Uzbek States," 392.
2. Robert D. McChesney, "Zamzam Water on a White Felt Carpet: Adapting Mongol Ways in Muslim Central Asia," in *Religion, Customary Law, and Nomadic Technology*, ed. Michael Gervers and Wayne Schlepp (Toronto: Joint Centre for Asia Pacific Studies, 2000), 63–83.

The Abu'l-Khayrid Shibanids reintroduced the appanage system of territorial administration and the institution of the quriltai or royal clan conclave. The appanage system was the practical application of the policy that every male member of the ruling Chinggisid clan had a right to a portion of the territory under Chinggisid suzerainty and the quriltai was the instrument for distributing that territory. The khan himself presided at quriltais but was little more than a first among equals. Although Islamicate historians felt bound by a traditional outlook to focus on the khan as 'king,' in fact every member of the royal clan was king in his own appanage.[3]

We have seen above that several Bukharan rulers tried to overcome the appanage system and impose a more centralized governmental structure, and that those efforts met with failure. Thus, the Bukharan khans governed through the management of a perpetually negotiated relationship with other members of the royal family, and also with the leadership of the Uzbek tribes. It will be seen below that this relationship grew increasingly fraught from the mid-seventeenth century, weakening the already limited authority of the Bukharan khan. During this period, the Toqay-Timurid leadership suffered a diminished capacity to manage and control the Uzbek tribal aristocracy, whose support was the cornerstone of their dynastic power and whose loyalty remained the basis of their legitimacy and right to rule.

In the early eighteenth century, Jungar forces launched multiple damaging invasions into the region. In an effort to assert greater authority, 'Ubaydullah Khan and Abu'l Fayz Khan shifted their patronage to Kazakh and Karakalpak nomads, Persian slaves, and others, at the expense of the Uzbek tribes that had engineered their rise and retained a claim to share in the power of the state. Bukharan efforts to garner the tax income needed to modernize the military and subjugate the Uzbek amirs met with failure, and they had the doubly negative effect of further alienating the Uzbeks and provoking widespread rebellions. From the vantage point of those leading the government in Bukhara, the situation in the early eighteenth century was grim, and growing even more so with each passing year.

Surveying travel literature and other sources produced within the region, one can find abundant references to support images of hardship and decline throughout this period.[4] The account left by 'Abd al-Karim Kash-

---

3. McChesney, "Chinggisid Restoration," 279.
4. As noted above, Sela's summary of these sources can be found in his chapter "Central Asia in Turmoil, 1700–1750," in Sela, *Legendary Biographies*, 117–40.

miri is a particularly good example. A well-educated man, 'Abd al-Karim had traveled from his native Kashmir to Delhi to request permission to go on the hajj at the unfortunate moment of Nadir Shah's invasion and sack of the Mughal capital. Nadir Shah was impressed by the man and reportedly offered him a position in his administration. It was for this reason that 'Abd al-Karim happened to accompany Nadir Shah in 1740, as he led his army's second invasion of the Bukharan Khanate.

Several years later, 'Abd al-Karim recorded his experiences in Nadir Shah's service, and his account includes a harsh depiction of local conditions in Bukhara at the time.

> The inhabitants of Turan, when compared with those of Turkey, Persia, and Hindustan, may be said to be poor in point of money and the luxuries of life, but in lieu thereof the Almighty has given them abundance of most exquisite fruits; with robust forms, and healthy constitutions, the greatest of earthly blessings. In reflecting upon the poverty of Turan and Arabia, I was at first at a loss to assign a reason why those countries had never been able to retain wealth, whilst, on the contrary, it is daily increasing in Hindustan. Timur carried into Turan the riches of Turkey, Persia, and Hindustan, but they are all dissipated; and during the reigns of the four first Caliphs, Turkey, Persia, part of Arabia, Ethiopia, Egypt, and Spain, were their tributaries; but still they were not rich. It is evident that this dissipation of the riches of a state must have happened either from some extraordinary drains, or from some defect in the government. Hindustan has been frequently plundered by foreign invaders, and not one of its Kings ever gained for it any acquisition of wealth; neither has the country many mines of gold and silver, and yet Hindustan abounds in money and every other kind of wealth. The abundance of species is undoubtedly owing to the large importation of gold and silver in the ships of Europe and other nations, many of whom bring ready money in exchange for the manufactures and natural productions of the country. If this is not the cause of the prosperous state of Hindustan, it must be owing to the peculiar blessing of God.[5]

The interpretation 'Abd al-Karim presents is a familiar one: except for its wonderful fruit, eighteenth-century Central Asia has become an impoverished backwater no longer able even to defend itself from external threats. Its wealth paled in comparison to that of his native India, and the reason

---

5. Scott C. Levi and Ron Sela, eds., *Islamic Central Asia: An Anthology of Historical Sources* (Bloomington: Indiana University Press, 2010), 260–64.

for this was that European merchants and others busily pumped gold and silver into the Indian economy in exchange for its agricultural production and textiles, while Central Asia remained external to global trade patterns. The legendary achievements of Timur were lost.

'Abd al-Karim's account is genuine, insofar as the author was present in Central Asia in 1740 and one can assume that his description accurately reflects his experiences.[6] His assessment of the Indian economy echoes those of earlier observers referenced above. But there are good reasons to question how far one can take the author's conclusions regarding Central Asia, as well as the usefulness of his account as a reliable reference point beyond Bukhara and its environs in the year 1740. Recall, for example, that Kashmiri's observations were based on little more than perception alone and were filtered through the eyes of his Bukharan hosts: the very nobles who represented the teetering central government near the end of a crisis that had grown in severity over more than half a century. He references Timur's legendary wealth, acquired through conquest, but he provides no analysis of the Central Asian economy in the interim and has no basis from which to determine how standards of living had changed over the centuries. Further, it seems ill advised to attempt to draw meaningful conclusions from observations made at the precise historical moment that the region itself was suffering a second hostile occupation in four years. His account is a testament to his experiences in that context, not proof of a centuries-long civilizational decline.

To be clear, drawing attention to the weaknesses of 'Abd al-Karim's account is not meant to imply that the wealth and power of the Bukharan Khanate did not decline during the decades leading up to his visit. As noted in chapter one, it most certainly did, and the crisis was both widespread and traumatic. But I wish to make equally clear that I find efforts to characterize the region as a whole as "in decline" to be imprecise, to be lacking in analytical value, and to obscure more than they illuminate. In essence, the notion elevates one (albeit important) aspect of the region's historical experience above all others and imposes it as a stereotype for all of Central Asia. It is one thing to argue that the Bukharan Khanate suffered a decline in its wealth, power, and authority in this period, and something quite different to write off the entire region and its people as being "in decline." Not only is this contradicted by historical evidence presented above and below, but, as James Pickett rightly observes in regard to his work on the Keneges

---

6. Alam and Subrahmanyam approach Kashmiri's account less critically. See Alam and Subrahmanyam, *Indo-Persian Travels*, 243–95.

in Shahrisabz, while some suffered in this period others "found opportunity in upheaval."[7]

Even as the crisis in the Bukharan Khanate became critical, some segments of Central Asian society managed to adjust and even thrive. Monahan's work on the expansion of the Bukharan commercial network into Siberia and the Bukharans' role mediating Russian trade with China following the establishment of the Treaties of Nerchinsk in 1689 and Kiakhta in 1727, surveyed in the previous chapter, is one such example. Wolfgang Holzwarth has argued that the development of this new Russian-Chinese trade through the "Siberian corridor" negatively affected the commercial positions of Central Asian traders in the area. In his words, "the new route enabled Russian tradesmen to reach China without touching Kazak or Jungar territories, and thus undermined the intermediary role of Central Asian merchants and steppe peoples in Inner Asian trade. Subsequently, the so-called Siberian Bukharians, representing the northern outposts of the joint Kazak-Bukharan trade network, lost their quasi monopoly of Asian trade in Russian Siberian towns."[8] Monahan's evidence contradicts this statement and demonstrates that the Siberian situation was more complicated: first, because the Bukharan merchant network never really enjoyed any sort of quasi monopoly in Russian commercial outposts, and second, because throughout the first half of the eighteenth century, the Bukharan traders themselves remained heavily involved in the mediation of Russo-Chinese trade along this very route. The subsequent expansion of Bukharan trade with Russia through the new Siberian outposts at Orenburg, Omsk, and elsewhere from the 1730s forward represents another example of Central Asian integration during the heart of the Bukharan crisis.

In this same period, the Ferghana Valley began to receive immigrant communities from several regions, including the Pamirs ("Kohistanis"), Kashgar, and nearby Samarqand—at that time, a severely suffering Bukharan city.[9] In this matter, Bukhara's loss was Ferghana's gain, as those refugees

---

7. James Robert Pickett, "The Persianate Sphere during the Age of Empires: Islamic Scholars and Networks of Exchange in Central Asia, 1747–1917," PhD diss., Princeton University, 2015, 13. See also James Robert Pickett, *Polymaths of Islam: Power and Networks of Knowledge in Central Asia* (Ithaca: Cornell University Press, forthcoming). For a more focused study on the Keneges ruling dynasty of Shahrisabz, see James Robert Pickett, "Written into Submission: Reassessing Sovereignty through a Forgotten Eurasian Dynasty," *American Historical Review* 123, no. 3 (2018): 817–45.
8. Holzwarth, "Relations between Uzbek Central Asia," 191 and notes.
9. This theme is discussed in chapter one of Levi, *Rise and Fall of Khoqand*, 14–49. Beisembiev adds to this Jankatis, though he is uncertain as to their region of origin. Beisembiev, "Migration in the Qöqand Khanate," 36.

who fled Samarqand settled in the valley and gradually formed prosperous agricultural communities. Then, even as Nadir Shah's armies invaded Bukharan territory for a second time, the leader of the Uzbek Ming, 'Abd al-Karim Biy, abandoned his father's capital in favor of a new one near the valley's only entrance not naturally protected by mountains. The city was named Khoqand (modern Qo'qand), it was founded in 1740, and over time it grew to become the most populous city in the valley.[10] The Uzbek Ming ruling dynasty of Khoqand rose to power from 1709, and the state they gave rise to fostered the expansion of irrigation agriculture and increased urbanization within the valley; transregional contacts with China, India, Russia, and the Ottoman Empire; and a vibrant, if brief, Islamic cultural renaissance.[11] By 1840, Khoqand's territory would expand to cover some 250,000 square miles (thirty times larger than the Ferghana Valley) with some three million sedentary subjects and another two million pastoralists.[12] Khoqand's most significant achievements in this regard did not begin to take shape until near the end of the eighteenth century. But the Bukharan crisis of the first half of the eighteenth century set those processes in motion.

The depopulation of Samarqand in the 1720s, discussed in chapter one, is another topic that may benefit from deeper investigation. We have seen that the Timurids' ancestral capital emptied in the wake of the Aqtaban Shubryndy, the Kazakhs' "Barefooted Flight," of 1723. For several years, the Kazakhs occupied and overwhelmed the region, and they permitted their herds to graze on crops in the fields, which led to famine and then flight. We have also seen that many of the Samarqandis sought refuge among the Uzbek Ming in the Ferghana Valley, while an estimated twelve thousand are said to have left Central Asia entirely and made their way to India.[13]

This event has been presented as an indication that the regional crisis was so severe that, giving up all hope for their homeland, these Samarqan-

---

10. Levi, *Rise and Fall of Khoqand*, 31–32. The Khoqand chronicles represent the principal sources for the history of the khanate, and I discuss a number of these in some detail in the preface to Levi, *Rise and Fall of Khoqand*, xxii–xxviii. For a comprehensive treatment of the Khoqand chronicles, see the monumental study by Timur. K. Beisembiev, *Kokandskaiia istoriografiia: Issledovaniie po istochnikovedeniiu Srednei Azii XVIII–XIX vekov* (Almaty: TOO Print-S, 2009).
11. See the discussion in Levi, *Rise and Fall of Khoqand*.
12. See Levi, *Rise and Fall of Khoqand*, 134, 157; Timur K. Beisembiev and Scott C. Levi in "Kokand Khanate," *Encyclopaedia Iranica*, s.v., forthcoming.
13. Again, for a description of the Kazakh occupation, see Holzwarth, "Relations between Uzbek Central Asia," 193–98. For the Samarqandis' migration to India, see Beisembiev, "Migration in the Qöqand Khanate," 35.

dis fled to go live among the Hindus in the sweltering heat of the subcontinent. That may be so, but one might also wonder if there is more to the story. What happened to these Samarqandis? Did they reach the Indian frontier as destitute refugees whose only recourse to escape death was to work as laborers or sell themselves, or their children, into slavery? Or did a different fate await them on the southern slopes of the Hindu Kush? Unfortunately, at present very little is known about what happened to these Samarqandis once they reached India. But the one narrative about which I am aware suggests that the situation may have been more complicated than "they were running for their lives under brutal and dreadful circumstances."[14]

On December 27, 1797, a baby boy was born to a Muslim family in the north Indian city of Agra. The boy was named Muhammad Asadullah Beg Khan, and later in life he became famous under the pen name of Ghalib. As an intensely introspective poet and public figure, Ghalib remains arguably the most celebrated of all the Urdu poets. As an adult, he earned his fame as an erudite witness to the dissolution of the last vestiges of the Mughal Empire and the rise of the British Raj in the wake of the 1857 Sepoy Mutiny. Less well known is that, throughout his life, Mirza Ghalib (as he was commonly called) emphasized the nobility of his ancestry and their proud heritage as military commanders, which he traced through his father to his grandfather, a Turkic nobleman named Mirza Qoqan Beg Khan, who, according to tradition, had lived in Samarqand until he left for India and joined the services of Nawab Muin al-Mulk in Lahore. Later, Mirza Qoqan moved onward to Delhi, where he eventually earned a high post in the Mughal army of Shah 'Alam II (r. 1759–1806) and a *pargana* (land grant) "for his personal expenses and the maintenance of the cavalry of which he was the Commandant."[15]

The specific circumstances surrounding Mirza Qoqan's departure from Samarqand remain unknown, and no available source references the year that he departed for India or how old he would have been when Ghalib's father was born. Indeed, several versions of Ghalib's family history exist,

---

14. Sela, *Legendary Biographies*, 121.
15. Arifshah C. Sayyid Gilani, *Ghalib: His Life and Persian Poetry* (Karachi: Azam Books, 1962), 14–15. See also Ralph Russell and Khurshidul Islam, *Ghalib, Life and Letters* (London: George Allen and Unwin, 2010 [1969]), 27. I am grateful to Justice Aftab Alam of the Indian Supreme Court for informing me of Ghalib's ancestral heritage in Central Asia and the circumstances surrounding his family's migration to India. Ghalib's claim about his connection to Samarqand seems convincing as other family members supported it. Less convincing is his claim that his ancestry could be traced through his grandfather to the Seljuk Turks and, through them, to the ancient Persian kings Afrasiyab, Faridun, and Jamshid.

and some of the timelines they present are in conflict. But considering that Samarqand is said to have become completely depopulated by the end of the 1720s and that it remained vacant for several decades after, it seems most likely that his departure for India took place in the wake of the Kazakh's Barefooted Flight.[16] Additionally, if Mirza Qoqan was, in fact, an amir, as Ghalib's family tradition maintains, then it also seems likely that he would have left the region accompanied by many of his Central Asian followers and their families. If a few other Turkic amirs elected to join him, then one could reasonably explain how twelve thousand Samarqandis would have decided to relocate to India. Again, advancing such an observation is not meant to deny the terrible circumstances that led the Samarqandis to flee their homes. But, alongside these circumstances, one must also consider the possibility that these refugees made a strategic decision to depart Central Asia in pursuit of desirable opportunities in Mughal India. That is to say that they fled, but with purpose.

Central Asia's history in this period is complicated, and it requires careful analysis and answers to important questions, not the least of which is: What caused the eighteenth-century crisis? There is clear evidence that the Bukharan treasury and those dependent upon it suffered in this period, and there is also evidence of Bukharan efforts to gain revenue by increasing taxation to an extent that provoked rebellion in several provinces. One can be quite certain that the cause of this crisis had nothing to do with a general pattern of European traders usurping the Silk Road trade. But if it is in some way linked to the Indian Ocean economy—that is to say, if Central Asia was so integrated with the Indian Ocean economy that a temporary dislocation of southward-reaching commercial arteries in the first half of the eighteenth century was sufficient to send the region spiraling into economic and political crisis—then one still must explain why it grew critical precisely at that historical moment. Why did it not impact the region so severely in the seventeenth century? And what changed to ensure that the crisis did not extend into the second half of the eighteenth century? One thing is quite certain: for such a dislocation to have occurred, but to have been restricted only to the first half of the eighteenth century, the argument in favor of Central Asia's early modern isolation would not only have to be wrong—it would have to be very wrong indeed.

---

16. Citing Bartold, Sela notes that there were only some one thousand families inhabiting the city's fort in the year 1740, and the city was not fully rebuilt until the end of the eighteenth century. Sela, *Legendary Biographies*, 126.

ECONOMIC FACTORS

Setting aside the binary "overland trade versus maritime trade" dichotomy, there is evidence to support an argument that certain economic factors external to the region exerted a negative impact on the Central Asian economy during the early eighteenth century. The evidence, however, is quite different from that which has previously been cited, and it includes much more than just European activities in the Indian Ocean arena. In fact, in terms of economic factors, the most important considerations appear to stem from developments to the east and not to the south.

In Qing China during the first half of the eighteenth century, Dennis O. Flynn and Arturo Giráldez identify a combination of factors including rapid population growth and imperial expansion that caused the value of silver within Qing territory to swell by some 50 percent.[17] Economic historian Richard von Glahn similarly describes the Chinese demand for silver during this same period as "voracious" and a key factor that must be considered in any analysis of the early modern global economy.[18] In explaining this dynamic, von Glahn observes that the population of China nearly doubled during the first half of the eighteenth century, from 140 million to 260 million, largely through the expansion of agriculture and the settlement of previously marginal lands in the interior. One result of this spike in population growth was a dramatic intensification in demand for "media of exchange." As silver circulated between commercial firms as large ingots and imports were insufficient to meet demand and keep local markets sufficiently monetized, the Qing turned to bronze as a supplementary medium of exchange.[19] Peter Perdue cautiously notes that one should be careful not to exaggerate the silver economy during the Ming era (1368–1644), but he also finds that "the Qing would embrace the commercial economy much more wholeheartedly and push the impact of money out to its farthest frontiers."[20]

In their collaborative work on this subject, von Glahn, Flynn, and Giráldez are primarily concerned with the relationship between the rising value of silver in Qing markets and specie flows from the Americas during a period in which Qing economic policies placed considerable emphasis on interna-

---

17. Flynn and Giráldez, "Cycles of Silver," 407.
18. Richard von Glahn, "Money Use in China and Changing Patterns of Global Trade in Monetary Metals, 1500–1800," in *Global Connections and Monetary History, 1470–1800*, ed. Dennis O. Flynn, Arturo Giráldez, and Richard von Glahn (Aldershot: Ashgate, 2003), 187.
19. Von Glahn, "Money Use," 192–201.
20. Perdue, *China Marches West*, 382–83.

tional maritime trade.[21] But it also stands to reason that, as the value of silver in China increased along with demand, the affects would have been felt to the west, in Central Asian markets, too. That is to say, the Qing economy's voracious thirst for silver drew silver circulating in Central Asia eastward into China—principally as highly coveted currency in exchange for goods.

Numismatic evidence indicates that Central Asian silver reserves became severely depleted in this same period. In one of her earlier publications, the economic historian Elena Davidovich carefully charts the steady debasement of Bukharan silver coins over much of the seventeenth century and notes that this problem became even more acute in the early decades of the eighteenth century. Specifically, her research indicates that silver coinage during the reign of the early Toqay-Timurid ruler Wali Muhammad (r. 1605–1611) was quite strong at 90 percent pure. During the reign of Imam Quli Khan (r. 1611–1641), this dropped to 80 percent (in c. 1615), then to 70 percent (in c. 1618), and then again to 65 percent (in c. 1623). During the short reign of Nadir Muhammad Khan (r. 1641–1645), silver coinage remained relatively stable at 60 percent pure (in c. 1642).

Problems became considerably worse during the reign of 'Abd al-'Aziz Khan (r. 1645–1681), and the silver content of his coinage dropped to 35 percent pure (in c. 1656). Purity levels during Subhan Quli Khan's reign (r. 1681–1702) appear to have fluctuated, but at a generally lower level, with a high reaching to 30 percent (in c. 1699).[22] Davidovich elaborates on the coinage of Subhan Quli Khan's reign, noting that he issued three types of silver coins, all of which were exceedingly low in silver and one of which had a content of only some 12.18 percent.[23] Matters worsened even further under 'Ubaydullah Khan (r. 1702–1711), whose horrendous monetary reform in 1708 brought the silver content of his coinage down to just 9 percent purity.[24] We have observed that this severe debasement led to a popular rebellion in 1708–1709.[25] At this point, Bukharan coinage included so little silver that it was rendered essentially worthless for international trade.

---

21. For Qing maritime commercial policies and their effects, see Gang Zhao, *The Qing Opening to the Ocean: Chinese Maritime Policies, 1684–1757* (Honolulu: University of Hawai'i Press, 2013).
22. Statistics are drawn from chart 37 in Davidovich, *Istoriia monetnogo dela Srednei Azii XVII–XVIII vv.*, 101.
23. Davidovich, *Istoriia monetnogo dela Srednei Azii XVII–XVIII vv.*, 117, chart 46.
24. Davidovich, *Istoriia monetnogo dela Srednei Azii XVII–XVIII vv.*, 139–40. For an analysis of the reform, see 145–56.
25. Holzwarth, "Relations between Uzbek Central Asia," 191 and note.

Purity of Bukharan Silver Coinage, 1600–1750

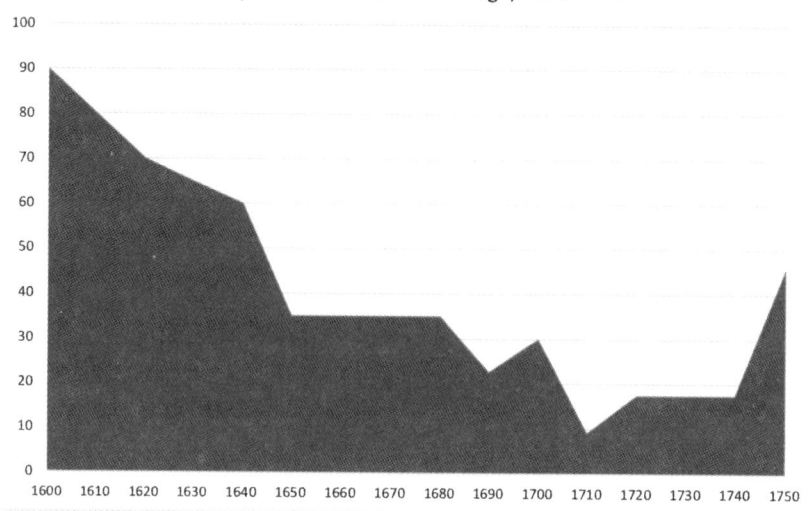

Chart 4.1. Silver Purity of Bukharan Coinage, 1600–1750. Based on numismatic evidence made available in E. A. Davidovich, *Istoriia monetnogo dela Srednei Azii XVII–XVIII vv.* (Dushanbe: Nauk, 1969).

Davidovich's conclusions in this area are supported by numismatist Boris Kočnev, who also finds that the coins the Toqay-Timurids minted early in the seventeenth century "were of comparatively high quality," but that by the reign of Subhan Quli Khan they were only 30 percent silver and debased even further during the reign of his son, 'Ubaydullah Khan.[26]

During his longer, but ultimately failed, reign, Abu'l Fayz Khan (r. 1711–1747) sought to bring some relief to the Bukharan currency crisis by increasing efforts to mine gold from local sources, principally along the Syr Darya and in Badakhshan. The proceeds from these efforts were used to mint gold coins, called the *ashrafī*, or the *ṭilā*.[27] These coins were able to satisfy commercial needs within the region and also used to offset trade imbalances with Russian markets. Their introduction even appears to have had a mildly salutary effect on Bukharan silver currency as well, which increased from 9 to 17.45 percent pure.[28] This was a slight improvement, but it was still

---

26. Boris D. Kočnev, "The Last Period of Muslim Coin Minting in Central Asia (18th–Early 20th Century)," in *Muslim Culture in Russia and Central Asia from the 18th to the Early 20th Centuries*, ed. Michael Kemper, Anke von Kügelgen, and Dmitriy Yermakov, vol. 1 (Berlin: Klaus Schwarz Verlag, 1996), 433.
27. Davidovich, *Istoriia monetnogo dela Srednei Azii XVII–XVIII vv.*, 178, 192–93.
28. Davidovich, *Istoriia monetnogo dela Srednei Azii XVII–XVIII vv.*, 160.

abysmally low, and, predictably, the chronic shortage of silver throughout much of Abu'l Fayz Khan's reign remained a cause of serious hardship. But toward the end of his reign, the story becomes more interesting. Looking more closely, Davidovich finds that there were actually two different types of silver coins minted during Abu'l Fayz Khan's reign, and the second variety was a staggering (in its context) 45.62 percent pure.[29] Analyzing the available evidence, Davidovich concludes that this second, much richer silver coin was introduced after 1741.[30]

Additional research confirms that Central Asia's silver crisis did indeed come to an end in the mid-eighteenth century, and it appears to have been a result of historical developments that unfolded both to the south and to the east. The first of these was Nadir Shah's infamous sack of Delhi in 1739 and his dethesaurization of hundreds of millions of rupees worth of silver, gold, precious stones, and other wealth from the Mughal treasury. We will return to this event below. For now, it is sufficient to note that the sudden surge in silver circulation had an immediate impact on both the Indian and Persian economies, with ramifications that rapidly extended far beyond those markets. For example, we have observed that, already in the 1730s, Russian officials were working to encourage Central Asian and Indian merchants to trade in Orenburg, and that their efforts met with some early successes. We have also seen that, at that time, the Bukharan economy had been starved of silver for several decades. But in the wake of Nadir Shah's sack of Delhi, Central Asian markets appear to have become so flush with precious metals that Bukharan merchants began dealing in gold and silver bars as an export commodity that was in high demand in Russian markets. Referencing Russian records, Davidovich finds that between 1748 and 1755, Bukharan merchants *exported* to Orenburg some 50 *pud* (more than 1,800 pounds) of gold and nearly 4,600 pud (more than 166,000 pounds, or 83 tons) of silver.[31] Looking beyond the singular event of Nadir Shah's sack of Delhi, one should also keep in mind the rapid rise of the Durrani state in Afghanistan following Nadir Shah's death in 1747 and its efforts to secure revenue by promoting India's commercial traffic with Persia and regions to the north of the Amu Darya.[32]

These developments to the south helped to lift Bukhara out of its crisis and drive the fiscal recovery from midcentury. But in terms of sustaining

---

29. Davidovich, *Istoriia monetnogo dela Srednei Azii XVII–XVIII vv.*, 160.
30. Davidovich, *Istoriia monetnogo dela Srednei Azii XVII–XVIII vv.*, 163.
31. Davidovich, *Istoriia monetnogo dela Srednei Azii XVII–XVIII vv.*, 195.
32. Gommans, *Rise of the Indo-Afghan Empire*.

this economic trend, events unfolding to the east were more important. Most immediately, as the value of silver in Chinese markets decreased from midcentury onward, it became easier for the Central Asian markets to retain silver.[33] Beyond that, from the mid-eighteenth century to the mid-nineteenth century, the Qing Empire became more directly engaged with Central Asia's commercial economy. Instead of absorbing Central Asian silver, as had been the case in the early decades of the eighteenth century, China's economic relationship with Central Asia essentially inverted. In the wake of the Qing annexation of the territory that would become known as Xinjiang in 1758, the Qianlong Emperor (r. 1735–1796) implemented a new policy that favored injecting silver into the region in support of his efforts to pacify his western frontier.[34] We have seen in chapter three that this had a number of positive implications for Central Asian commercial interests, including most notably the Andijani merchants of Khoqand. Later in the eighteenth century, Davidovich references multiple reports indicating that Chinese silver ingots flowed westward into Bukharan markets through the hands of Central Asian traders based in Kashgar.[35] With only a few brief disruptions, Qianlong's policy was retained until 1853.[36]

The numismatic evidence presented here helps to illustrate the worsening Bukharan fiscal crisis and also several factors that, from midcentury, enabled the Manghit leadership to chart a course into recovery. But we must now return attention to the causal factors that drove the crisis. In this regard, the political disruptions that occurred to the south of Bukhara represent yet another factor that merits consideration. Mughal and Safavid government officials had long fostered transregional trade between their realms and also with the Bukharan Khanate. That support disappeared as both empires began to decentralize and collapse: in India, over the decades following Emperor Aurangzeb's death in 1707; and more abruptly in Iran, after the Ghilzai Afghan invasion in 1722. One might be tempted to suggest that this would have completely dislocated Bukhara's connections to the Indian Ocean economy. But on closer analysis, the extent to which that was the case remains questionable.

---

33. For Chinese silver values, see Flynn and Giráldez, "Cycles of Silver," 411–12.
34. Cf. Millward, *Beyond the Pass*; Newby, *Empire and the Khanate*; Kim, *Borderland Capitalism*; and Levi, *Rise and Fall of Khoqand*.
35. Davidovich, *Istoriia monetnogo dela Srednei Azii XVII–XVIII vv.*, 196. Her sources include the account of the Russian Major Blankennagel, who visited the region in 1793–1794. Blankennagel emphasizes the role of Bukharan traders in Kashgar, but they most certainly would have been Andijani merchants.
36. Millward, *Beyond the Pass*, 235–36.

In India at the time of Aurangzeb's death, the Mughal treasury held gold and silver worth an estimated 240 million rupees.[37] That began to diminish as Bahadur Shah (r. 1707–1712) fought his brothers for the right to ascend the throne and provincial rulers elected to retain their tax income rather than dispatch it to a ruler unable to force them to do so. Emperor Aurangzeb (d. 1707) had worked feverishly throughout his long reign to force recalcitrant subjects into submission. With his death, Sikhs, Rajputs, Marathas, Afghans, and others tore at the fabric of the empire, and widespread rebellions made quick work of the Mughal imperial system. Following years of intense fighting, multiple Mughal successor states had solidified their own particular regional power structures at the expense of the Mughal center, which by the 1730s had diminished considerably.[38]

According to Muzaffar Alam, whereas the Punjab, in northwestern India, had "registered unprecedented growth in the seventeenth century," imperial collapse and military conflict caused serious setbacks in the early decades of the eighteenth century. This rendered travel along the trade routes connecting India with Persia and Central Asia more difficult and more dangerous.[39] It also had a negative, though temporary, impact on the Indian family firms centered in Multan, the principal Indian commercial agents orchestrating long-distance trade beyond the northwest frontier.[40] There is abundant evidence illustrating the nearly complete collapse of Indian commercial activity in Safavid territory during the second quarter of the eighteenth century.[41] Those disruptions were the result of specific policies targeting the predominantly Hindu merchant communities that the Afghan invaders enforced and that Nadir Shah perpetuated. There is no available evidence to suggest that foreign merchant communities suffered anything resembling that same type of abuse in Bukhara. However, it does

---

37. John F. Richards, *The Mughal Empire* (Cambridge: Cambridge University Press, 1993), 253.
38. It is well established in Indian historiography that the collapse of the Mughal Empire caused economic disruption and deurbanization in the imperial center, but that it led to increased prosperity in the provinces. For a number of classic studies, cf. André Wink, *Land and Sovereignty in India: Agrarian Society and Politics under the Eighteenth-Century Maratha Swarajya* (Cambridge: Cambridge University Press, 1986); Muzaffar Alam, *The Crisis of Empire in Mughal North India, 1707–1748* (Oxford: Oxford University Press, 1986); C. A. Bayly, *Rulers, Townsmen and Bazaars: North Indian Society in the Age of British Expansion, 1770–1870* (Cambridge: Cambridge University Press, 1983); Richard Barnett, *North India between Empires* (Berkeley: University of California Press, 1980); and J. S. Grewell, *The Sikhs in the Punjab* (Cambridge: Cambridge University Press, 1990).
39. Alam, "Trade, State Policy and Regional Change," 224.
40. See Levi, *Caravans*, 78–86.
41. Levi, *Indian Diaspora*, 168–69.

stand to reason that, as the commercial environment in Multan suffered, Indian commercial connections with Central Asia suffered as well.

In the field of Iranian history, Rudi Matthee has charted the gradual process of Safavid decline. Matthee argues that Safavid power and authority began to follow a downward trajectory after the reign of Shah Abbas I (d. 1629), and he finds that, especially from the late seventeenth century, Safavid rulers grew comfortable and further removed from affairs of the state, "preferring the cushions of the palace to the rigors of the saddle."[42] Matthee identifies a number of other factors that, together, undermined the structural strength of the Safavid dynasty. These include a limited amount of arable land, poor management of the arable land they had, limited economic productivity, poor monetary policies, a widely dispersed population, the presence of nomads, the oppression of religious minorities, and a notoriously poor infrastructure.

Matthee's list is quite comprehensive, but there are other factors that should also be taken into account. In his recent study of the history of modern Iran, Abbas Amanat suggests that scholars should also consider the effects of the seventeenth-century global climate crisis on the Safavid agricultural economy and the nomadic populations occupying the Safavid periphery.[43] We will turn attention to this subject directly as it relates to a similar process of decentralization in the Bukharan Khanate. Also echoing the situation in Central Asia, Safavid numismatic studies illustrate a serious pattern of debasement already during the last quarter of the seventeenth century, indicating a weakening state economy.[44] By the early eighteenth century, there was so little holding the state together that as Mughal and Safavid control over their Afghan border territories diminished, a relatively small band of Afghan raiders were able to take Isfahan and topple the Safavid Empire.

Matters only became worse as Nadir Shah pushed the Afghan forces from Iran and waged a number of successful campaigns, including his 1739 sack of Delhi. The wealth that the Mughals had amassed over the previous two centuries was immense, and the weakened Mughals were unable to protect it from the Persian invaders. Nadir Shah's spoils included, for exam-

---

42. Rudi Matthee, *Persia in Crisis: Safavid Decline and the Fall of Isfahan* (London: I. B. Tauris, 2012), 243–55. A similar argument can be found in Roger Savory, *Iran under the Safavids* (Cambridge: Cambridge University Press, 1980), 226.
43. See the discussion "Climate, Insolvency, and Invasion," in Amanat, *Iran*, 136–42.
44. Rudi Matthee, "Mint Consolidation and the Worsening of the Late Safavid Coinage: The Mint of Huwayza," *Journal of the Economic and Social History of the Orient* 44, no. 4 (2001): 505–39. This is also addressed in Amanat, *Iran*, 139–40.

ple, Shah Jahan's fabled Peacock Throne, a solid gold marvel that weighed some 2,500 pounds and was adorned with thousands of pearls, emeralds, rubies, and other precious jewels—including the 186-carat Koh-i Nur (Mountain of Light) diamond.[45] Nadir Shah took the throne, emptied what remained in the Mughal treasury, and returned to Iran. Estimates place the total amount of wealth that Nadir Shah and his troops looted from India at more than 700 million rupees.[46] But rather than using those resources to build a viable commercial infrastructure in Iran, he quickly squandered it by distributing it to his supporters in exchange for their temporary loyalty and purchasing favor through populist tax moratoriums. In essence, Nadir Shah's shortsighted, predatory, and exploitative policies suddenly put an enormous amount of silver into circulation, but they did nothing to bolster Iran's commercial infrastructure.

The Iranian political and economic crisis would have had a disruptive, if temporary, impact on Central Asia's engagement with the Indian Ocean economy. But the pattern of decentralization in Central Asia had begun long before Aurangzeb's death in 1707, let alone the Ghilzai invasion of Iran in 1722. Furthermore, as Matthee correctly notes, Safavid trade with Central Asia had always been "limited" in its magnitude.[47] It therefore seems reasonable to suggest that the Safavid collapse would have had only a muted effect on Central Asia's commercial economy.

To an extent, the same is true for the Indian economy, though for different reasons. To be sure, Central Asian markets were more tightly bound to Mughal India than they were to Safavid Iran, and the Mughals had long enforced policies designed to promote overland trade with Central Asia. A breakdown in those relations therefore stood to have a greater impact on

---

45. The value of the Peacock Throne is difficult to assess. Tavernier, a jeweler, estimates it at 107,000 lakh rupees, which at more than ten billion rupees is certainly an error. The editor, Valentine Ball, suggests that Tavernier most likely meant to place its value at the more believable figure of 107 million rupees. Jean-Baptiste Tavernier, *Travels in India*, 2nd ed., 2 vols., ed. William Crooke and trans. V. Ball (New Delhi: Munshiram Manoharlal, 1995 [1676]), 2:384–85 and note. Bernier suggests that it was worth 4 crore (40 million) rupees. Bernier, *Travels in the Mogul Empire*, 268–69. The Koh-i Nur diamond is counted among the crown jewels of the United Kingdom, and it is on display at the Tower of London.
46. If accurate, the current value would far exceed USD $100 billion. Michael Axworthy, *The Sword of Persia: Nader Shah, from Tribal Warrior to Conquering Tyrant* (London: I. B. Tauris, 2006), 10. The extraordinary increase in the circulation of rupees following Nadir Shah's sack of Delhi may explain why, in 1750, the aforementioned Russian trade fair in Troitsk would have listed prices in both rubles and rupees. Liusternik, *Russko-indiiskie ekonomicheskie*, 12.
47. Matthee, "The Safavid Economy," in Floor and Herzig, eds., *Iran and the World in the Safavid Age*, 34–36.

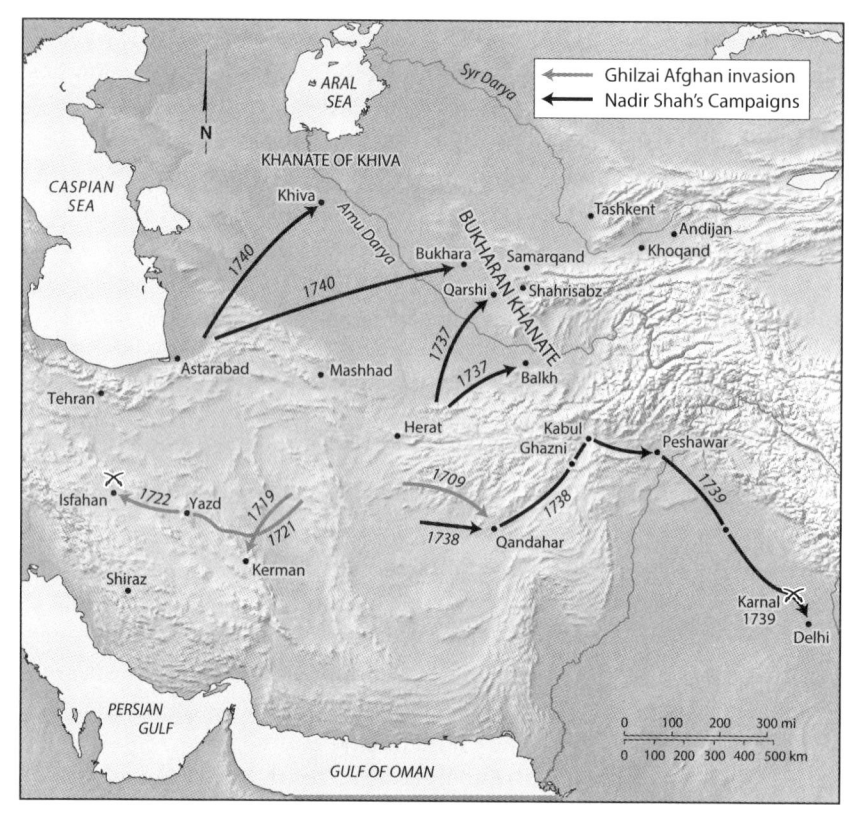

Map 17. Nadir Shah's Campaigns. Map by Bill Nelson.

the Central Asian economy than the Safavid imperial collapse. But there are other reasons to question the magnitude of the impact that the Mughal collapse had on Central Asia. In a survey of recent work on Mughal economic history, Sumit Guha finds that commercial disruptions stemming from the collapse of the empire were actually minimal, that the Mughal economy was much more diversified than has previously been appreciated, and, ultimately, that "the breakdown of the empire did not mean an end to profitable commerce."[48] Rather, local power brokers redirected their efforts into developing provincial economies and investing in regional trade centers because, "as the apocryphal bank robber said, that was where the money was."[49] Thus, the long-standing Mughal mint town of Multan diminished in

---

48. Sumit Guha, "Rethinking the Economy of Mughal India: Lateral Perspectives," *Journal of the Economic and Social History of the Orient* 58, no. 4 (2015): 569.
49. Guha, "Rethinking the Economy of Mughal India," 569.

importance, but nearby Shikarpur rapidly rose to take its place, and, pursuing Durrani patronage, many of the Multani commercial families that had prospered under the Mughals soon became known as Shikarpuris.[50]

Another factor to consider is that the Mughal and Safavid imperial collapse would have had little impact on pastoral nomadic mediatory traders, such as the Afghan Powindas, who required no state-supported commercial infrastructure and generally moved across the intermediary territories with impunity. Additionally, as discussed in chapter three, even as political collapse created obstacles to Central Asian connections to the Indian Ocean economy, the region remained thoroughly integrated in other Eurasian commercial infrastructures. During the first half of the eighteenth century, Bukharans and other Central Asian traders expanded existing trade networks northward into Russia and, through Siberia, to China. One must therefore conclude that the collapse of the Mughal and Safavid states should be considered a minor contributing factor, not a key causal factor, for the Bukharan crisis. The drain of silver into Chinese markets during the early decades of the eighteenth century was clearly more significant. But even that represents only part of the story.

A GLOBAL ENVIRONMENTAL CRISIS

Our discussion thus far has not strayed far from transregional trade, specie flows, and other commercial considerations. At first glance this may seem logical, as scholars have long identified a weakened economy as one of the principal features of the eighteenth-century Bukharan crisis. But one must look beyond the economy to identify the causal factors behind the crisis. Throughout history, one can point to incidents of widespread, wholesale civilizational decline caused by invasion, disease, and famine. In Central Asia itself, the Mongol onslaught resulted in the massacre of millions of people and the destruction of urban infrastructure and irrigation networks.[51] No less damaging was the plague pandemic in the fourteenth century, which devastated urban areas across much of Eurasia.[52]

While early modern Central Asians were certainly not immune to the ravages of disease, there is no indication that anything of the sort was present in sufficient magnitude to explain the steady erosion of Bukharan political legitimacy from the mid-seventeenth century to the mid-eighteenth century. As in the Safavid case, contemporary Central Asian sources and

---

50. Levi, *Indian Diaspora*, 112–19.
51. David Morgan, *The Mongols*, 2nd ed. (Oxford: Blackwell, 2007), 64–73.
52. For Central Asia, see Philip Slavin, "Death by the Lake: Mortality Crisis in Early Fourteenth-Century Central Asia," *Journal of Interdisciplinary History* 50 (2019): 59–90.

scholarly analyses often point to the familiar trope of lazy, incompetent, decadent, and despotic rulers who were uninterested in ruling, ineffective at marshaling the support of the Uzbek tribes to defend their people from adversaries, and incapable of shepherding their state into recovery. Recalling Douglas Howard's work on Ottoman decline narratives, the historian must ask how much trust we should place in our sources when, even though the authors experienced the crisis firsthand, the assessments they present bear a striking resemblance to a harsh polemic on a newspaper's op-ed page.[53] While such contemporary critiques may be more or less accurate, they may also be very human reactions made by frustrated firsthand observers critical of their rulers' inability to govern effectively in the face of causal factors beyond their ability even to understand in the moment, much less manage. Such a factor can be found in climate change.

It has long been recognized that the Earth's climatic patterns fluctuate and that these fluctuations impact human societies.[54] Until relatively recently, most have assumed that, at least until the beginning of the industrial age, such environmental shifts unfolded gradually, over long periods of time, and that this left human settlements adequate opportunity to adapt as once arable borderlands became less so, then passed into tundra or desert. In recent decades, scholars have come to appreciate that climate change can also be rapid, and historians have found that sudden climatic disturbances have had widespread impacts throughout history, unleashing catastrophes quite literally on a global scale. Such was the case in the seventeenth century, during the harshest period of the "Little Ice Age."[55]

It is now more widely understood that global cooling patterns disrupt human societies not by lowering the average temperature in a region by a degree or two but by causing global weather patterns to shift. Even a slight drop in temperature wields a powerful impact as air temperature is directly

---

53. Howard, "Ottoman Historiography and the Literature of 'Decline.'"
54. See the literature on the Little Ice Age, including especially Brian Fagan, *The Little Ice Age: How Climate Made History, 1300–1850* (New York: Basic Books, 2000).
55. Geoffrey Parker, *Global Crisis: War, Climate Change and Catastrophe in the Seventeenth Century* (New Haven: Yale University Press, 2013). Parker's study builds on the pioneering study by Jack Goldstone, *Revolution and Rebellion in the Early Modern World* (Berkeley: University of California Press, 1991). The early stages of the debate surrounding this theme as it played out on the global scale are outlined in Geoffrey Parker and Lesley M. Smith, eds., *The General Crisis of the Seventeenth Century*, 2nd ed. (London: Routledge, 1997). In their more recent works, Geoffrey Parker and Sam White (cited below and in the bibliography) provide detailed historiographical surveys of the copious literature on the subject. See also John L. Brooke, *Climate Change and the Course of Global History: A Rough Journey* (Cambridge: Cambridge University Press, 2014), 380–84, 444–51.

related to air pressure, which is a driving force behind seasonal weather patterns. The sustained cooling experienced in the seventeenth century, therefore, unleashed a profound disruption of "normal" weather patterns. In some areas, this included a reversal of wind direction that subjected temperate agricultural zones to severe drought or flooding.

In analyzing the ways that seventeenth-century climate change affected societies across the globe, one can identify two causal factors that propelled the catastrophic events of the period, both of which are beyond the realm of human agency. First is a sustained historic low in sunspot activity, which is indicative of a decrease in the amount of solar radiation emitted from the sun. This contributed to a period of sustained cooling of the Earth that has become known as the Little Ice Age, which had its earliest precursors in the late thirteenth century and continued into the early eighteenth century. This extended period of diminished solar radiation reached its greatest severity in the latter half of the seventeenth century, a period that climate scientists refer to as the "Maunder Minimum." A second factor is a significant rise in volcanic activity that began in the late sixteenth century and grew especially pronounced during the 1630s and 1640s.[56] The result was exceptionally destructive: decreased solar activity resulted in global cooling, erratic weather patterns, and wind reversals, and volcanic eruptions spewed millions of tons of ash into the atmosphere, where it further blocked solar radiation.[57] Together, solar minima and volcanic eruptions shaped a particularly cold epoch—the classic Little Ice Age—running from the 1560s into the 1710s. Notably lower temperatures and drought are documented across the globe throughout much of the century, and they were most severe in the 1640s.

Historians are now in a position to combine information available in textual sources with new research into a vast reserve of evidence that scientists have found in such "natural archives" as tree rings, glacial ice, and sediment samples acquired from locations across the globe. This evidence helps to explain the reasons why, throughout the long seventeenth

---

56. For two recent studies of how volcanic activity impacts climate and society, see William K. Klingaman and Nicholas P. Klingaman, *The Year without Summer: 1816 and the Volcano That Darkened the World and Changed History* (New York: St. Martin's Press, 2013); Gillen D'Arcy Wood, *Tambora: The Eruption That Changed the World* (Princeton: Princeton University Press, 2014).
57. Parker suggests that the two phenomena were linked. He notes that the reversal of winds during the El Niño years also impacts tidal flows, which causes a rise in ocean levels in tectonic zones not accustomed to carrying such weights, which leads to an increase in volcanic activities. Parker, *Global Crisis*, 16.

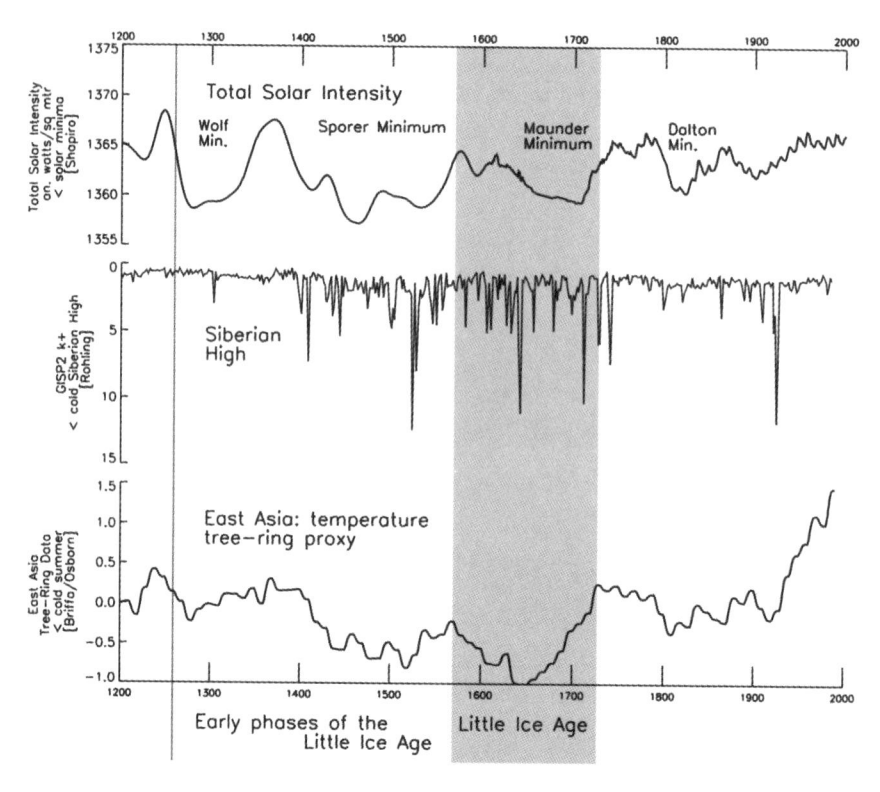

Chart 4.2. Solar Strength, the Siberian High, and East Asian Summer Temperatures. Chart compiled by John Brooke from data developed by A. I. Shapiro et al., "A New Approach to Long-Term Reconstruction of the Solar Irradiance Leads to Large Historical Forcing," *Astronomy and Astrophysics* 529 (2011): A67; E. J. Rohling et al., "Holocene Atmosphere-Ocean Interactions: Records from Greenland and the Aegean Sea," *Climate Dynamics* 18 (2002): 587–93; regional temperature proxies [c. 800–present] developed by Timothy Osborn and Keith Briffa for Box 6.4, Figure 1, E. Jansen, "Palaeoclimate," in *Climate Change 2007: The Physical Science Basis. Contribution of Working Group I to the Fourth Assessment Report of the Intergovernmental Panel on Climate Change*, ed. Susan Solomon et al. (Cambridge: Cambridge University Press, 2007), available at http://www.cru.uea.ac.uk/~timo/datapages/ipccar4.htm.

century, societies across much of the planet were confronted by substantially shorter growing seasons and recurrent failed harvests interspersed with too few successful harvests to provide meaningful relief. Parker's extensive work on the subject focuses on the Northern Hemisphere, but he does chart the impact that the widespread famines had on societies across much of the globe, from Japan to sub-Saharan Africa and England, and from Jamestown and Huron to Mexico City, Potosí, and beyond.[58]

The more densely populated agricultural societies suffered the most. In China, as elsewhere, weather patterns went wild. Southern China experienced its worst drought since before the Mongol conquests. In the four years preceding the Qing revolution that brought an end to Ming dynastic rule in 1644, northern China suffered the two coldest years it had experienced in a millennium. In his investigation of the factors leading to the Ming collapse, Timothy Brook analyzes the widespread, sustained devastation that "a confusing patchwork of severe drought in some places and severe flood in others" unleashed across Chinese territories.[59] Whether it was not enough water or too much, the end was the same: failed harvests, famine, starvation, and death.[60] A Chinese couplet penned in 1616 in Shandong, in the northeast, became a "tagline" characterizing the horrors of the time:

> Mothers eat their children's corpses,
> Wives strip off their dead husbands' flesh.[61]

Matters only worsened as the Ming moved further into the seventeenth century. Brook notes that considerably more serious famines began to appear in 1632, and that "no emperor of the Yuan or Ming faced climatic conditions as abnormal and severe as Chongzhen (r. 1627–1644) had the misfortune of doing."[62] Dry conditions worsened severely in 1637, and for the next seven years Ming China "suffered droughts on an unprecedented scale." The historical record is replete with accounts of soaring prices for

---

58. See the charts in Parker, *Global Crisis*, 15. Reviewing Parker's work, Gregory Cushman finds that "the very latest reconstructions of global climate over the past millennium emphatically confirm both the existence and exceptionality of the Little Ice Age." Cushman emphasizes that "this conjuncture of events is no figment of historians' revolution-obsessed imaginations, and it demands that historians of all stripes begin to reckon with the Little Ice Age (LIA) when considering the foundations of the modern world." Gregory Cushman, review of *Global Crisis: War, Climate Change and Catastrophe in the Seventeenth Century*, by Geoffrey Parker, *American Historical Review* 120, 4 (2015): 1429–31.
59. Timothy Brook, *The Troubled Empire: China in the Yuan and Ming Dynasties* (Cambridge, MA: Belknap Press, 2010), 243.
60. As they apply to the period from 1600 to 1840, these conclusions, and the devastating role that climate change played in undermining the agrarian economy of late imperial China, are supported by the evidence recently presented in Qing Pei et al., "Temperature and Precipitation Effects on Agrarian Economy in Late Imperial China," *Environmental Research Letters* 11, no. 6 (2016): 1–9.
61. Brook, *Troubled Empire*, 243.
62. Brook, *Troubled Empire*, 249.

grain and villagers stripping bark off of trees for food, then eating flesh off of corpses, and finally turning to cannibalism.[63] This was followed by plague, then rebellion.

Local observers and historians have advanced a multitude of theories to explain the Ming collapse and Manchu invasion. These include Ming decadence, inept leadership, and even the argument that the Ming "shift away from classical literary style" undermined the dynasty's cultural foundations and sent it into a lengthy period of decline.[64] Here, Brook rightly observes that "it is useful to distinguish the outcome from the conditions that produced it."[65] Considering the climate crisis and the severity of its effects on China in particular, he finds that "the greatest puzzle might well be to figure out how the Ming remained standing for as long as it did."[66]

This conclusion is supported by von Glahn, who dismisses theories that the causal factor behind the Ming collapse was a scarcity of silver resulting from a deterioration of international trade. Instead, he finds that failed harvests caused a surge in grain prices in the 1630s but only a nominal decrease in silver imports during the 1640s. In harmony with Timothy Brook and William Atwell, von Glahn finds that "the evidence of trade flows, prices, and exchange ratios all point instead toward an acute subsistence crisis precipitated by catastrophic harvests and popular rebellions." Weighing the evidence, he concludes that "Atwell is much more persuasive in attributing the harvest failures of 1638–42 to the climatic disturbances and cold weather experienced across the whole of the northern hemisphere during the seventeenth century."[67]

Russia experienced similarly unpredictable weather patterns throughout the seventeenth century, including extreme cold and drought followed by uncontrollable floods. In his analysis of Russia's "first civil war" in the early seventeenth century, Chester Dunning illustrates how the climate

---

63. Brook, *Troubled Empire*, 250.
64. Brook, *Troubled Empire*, 241.
65. Brook, *Troubled Empire*, 242.
66. Brook, *Troubled Empire*, 242.
67. Richard von Glahn, *The Economic History of China: From Antiquity to the Nineteenth Century* (Cambridge: Cambridge University Press, 2016), 311 and notes. Von Glahn cites William S. Atwell, "Some Observations on the 'Seventeenth-Century Crisis' in China and Japan," *Journal of Asian Studies* 45, no. 2 (1986): 223–44; William S. Atwell, "A Seventeenth-Century 'General Crisis' in East Asian History?" *Modern Asian Studies* 24, no. 4 (1990): 661–82. See also William S. Atwell, "Another Look at Silver Imports into China, c. 1635–1644," *Journal of World History* 16, no. 4 (2006): 467–89.

crisis functioned as one of several causal factors—a list that includes population growth during the sixteenth century, gradually rising prices that spiked at the turn of the seventeenth century, and a number of social tensions among the Russian elite—that converged to destabilize the Russian government and contribute to the outbreak of civil war. Dunning summarizes, "The second half of the sixteenth century was a time of rising population, prices, taxes, state budgets, and bad weather as well as increasing crop failures, poverty, famines, plagues, mortality levels, war, banditry, mass migrations, and popular uprisings throughout much of Europe. All of these problems were strongly present in the catastrophic 1590s, which saw the conjunction of the most severe weather, the worst food crises, and the largest number of rebellions of the entire early modern period. Glacial advances and dense volcanic dust veils also peaked at the very end of that decade."[68] Severely cold weather in 1601–1603, partly attributable to the massive volcanic eruption of Mount Huaynaputina in Peru in 1600, caused a devastating famine that thrust Russia deeper into its legendary Time of Troubles (1598–1613). In those two years alone, more than one hundred thousand people died of starvation in Moscow, and some two million died across the empire. The rise of the Romanov dynasty brought political changes, but the crisis continued. The 1640s registered as the coldest decade that Russia had experienced in half a millennium.

Across the globe, the results of the climate crisis were revolutionary: insufficient resources to mitigate famine led to weakened state structures, a rise in banditry and warfare, a dramatic increase in the overthrow of governments, and, according to Parker, the loss of as much as one-third of the world's population.[69] Recent work on the environmental history of the early modern Ottoman Empire illustrates the role that climate crisis had in undermining state institutions and nearly bringing an end to the empire during the Celali Rebellion in the 1590s.[70] Climate played a destabilizing

---

68. Chester S. L. Dunning, *Russia's First Civil War: The Time of Troubles and the Founding of the Romanov Dynasty* (University Park: Penn State University Press, 2001), 21–22 and notes. See also Dunning's analysis of how famine was precipitated by "abnormally cool and rainy weather" in the summer of 1601, culminating in August frosts that killed crops before they could ripen for harvest (97).
69. Parker, *Global Crisis*, 2. There may be some reason to question as to whether the loss of human lives was quite so severe. See the critical (and rather acrimonious) review essay by Paul Warde, "Global Crisis or Global Coincidence," *Past and Present* 228 (2015): 287–301.
70. Sam White, *The Climate of Rebellion in the Early Modern Ottoman Empire* (Cambridge: Cambridge University Press, 2013).

role in Iran as well. Abbas Amanat finds that "from the middle of the seventeenth century not only the periphery but also the Safavid heartlands suffered hardship due to intemperate weather," and, according to contemporary observers, "from the 1650s to [the] 1670s, agricultural production fell drastically, perhaps by as much as half. Repeated crop failures and recurring droughts coincided with the shrinking of the agricultural hinterlands, decline of trade in Persian Gulf and Mediterranean ports, and the depopulation of the cities."[71] One might also suggest that this sustained crisis and the nearly constant warfare it provoked forms the backdrop for the seventeenth-century advancements in gunpowder weapons technologies, discussed below.[72]

Central Asia did not go unaffected.[73] It was during the heart of the crisis, in 1646, that the Mughal emperor Shah Jahan placed his son Aurangzeb in charge of a highly ambitious and ill-fated effort to reconquer his Timurid homeland. Climate may have played some role in shaping Shah Jahan's motivations to launch this campaign. Paleoclimatic research suggests that seventeenth-century temperature fluctuations contributed to recurrent failed Indian monsoons.[74] While India does not appear to have suffered to the same extent as China, Europe, and other regions in the northern hemisphere, the resulting droughts were especially pronounced in Gujarat and the Deccan in the 1620s and 1630s.[75] It is impossible to state with any certainty whether such droughts informed Shah Jahan's calculations regarding if and when he should launch his campaign. Even if it did, one must also appreciate that Shah Jahan had inherited ample motivation to justify his

---

71. Amanat, *Iran*, 137.
72. Wayne E. Lee, *Waging War: Conflict, Culture, and Innovation in World History* (Oxford: Oxford University Press, 2016), 243–44.
73. In a recent study, Jürgen Paul engages the paleoclimatic literature to support his argument that Richard Bulliet overstates the role that climate played in causing the Seljuk migrations of the eleventh century. Paul observes that while the evidence for sustained cooling across the Central Asia region is unclear for the eleventh century, "cooling is mostly reported for later periods, in particular the 17th century." Jürgen Paul, "Nomads and Bukhara: A Study in Nomad Migrations, Pasture, and Climate Change (11th century CE)," *Der Islam* 93, no. 2 (2016): 527.
74. Cf. Gayatri Kathayat et al., "The Indian Monsoon Variability and Civilization Changes in the Indian Subcontinent," *Science Advances* 3, 12 (2017): e1701296; Ashish Sinha et al., "A Global Context for Megadroughts in Monsoon Asia during the Past Millennium," *Quaternary Science Reviews* 30 (2011): 47–62.
75. Nicola Di Cosmo has observed that climate change often leads to famine and war, but militaries require fodder and so they must wait for the famine to subside in order to campaign. Nicola Di Cosmo, "State Formation and Periodization in Inner Asian History," *Journal of World History* 10 (1999): 1–40. See also Brooke, *Climate Change*, 278–79, 285–87.

efforts: at one time or another, every Mughal emperor from Babur through Aurangzeb devised a plan to recover Central Asia from the Uzbeks.[76] For Shah Jahan, his receipt of a message from the Toqay-Timurid ruler Nadir Muhammad Khan requesting aid in his conflict with his son, ʿAbd al-ʿAziz, provided the perfect pretext for an invasion.

In 1646, as the Mughal forces made their way northward across the Hindu Kush, they passed from one climatic zone into another and unwittingly marched headlong into the blistering cold of the Little Ice Age. The circumstances surrounding the Mughal campaign are addressed in multiple historical sources, produced by both Mughal and Uzbek chroniclers.[77] These sources make it clear that the Mughal army benefited from large numbers and their possession of superior artillery and war elephants. But the Uzbeks were able to use hit-and-run tactics to their advantage, and the severe cold wore down the Mughal troops as they wintered in Balkh.

One Central Asian chronicler, Muhammad Yusuf Munshi, reports that the Mughals arrived in the region during a famine so severe that a single donkey-load of grain was valued at one thousand rupees. The addition of a large force of occupying troops naturally exacerbated the shortage of food, and it was made even worse as the weather was so excruciatingly cold that people could not even venture beyond the city walls to forage for food.[78] Ultimately, the Mughals were forced to abandon Balkh and flee southward across the Hindu Kush.[79] Those who remained behind were killed, and those who fled burned everything they had to stay warm as they made their way across the mountain passes. Even this would not be enough. Muhammad Yusuf reports that fierce winds blew out their fires and the Uzbek "wolves" captured the fleeing Indian "slave-sheep," marched them back northward, and sold them in the markets of Samarqand, Turkestan, and Tashkent.[80]

---

76. Foltz, "Mughal Occupation," 49.
77. These are surveyed in Foltz, "Mughal Occupation"; Burton, *Bukharans*, 234–54; Levi, "Hindus beyond the Hindu Kush," 280. Burton draws on Mughal, Bukharan, and even Russian sources to provide by far the most detailed description of the Mughal campaign against Balkh. She does not single out climate as a factor that contributed to the Mughal defeat, but she does point to the unusually "intense cold" (253) and food shortages alongside the military tactics of the Uzbek soldiers. These included efforts to cause disease among the Mughal troops by polluting their water supply with the carcasses of dead animals. Burton, *Bukharans*, 246.
78. Muhammad Yusuf Munshi bin Khwaja Baqa, *Tadhkira-i Muqīm Khānī*, IVANU, Ms. No. 609/II, f. 323a–b.
79. Muhammad Yusuf Munshi, *Tadhkira-i Muqīm Khānī*, f. 324a. Referencing a French translation of this same source, Foltz adds that "men burned themselves in fires they lit for warmth, and no one left their house for fear of being frozen." Foltz, "Mughal Occupation," 57.
80. Muhammad Yusuf Munshi, *Tadhkira-i Muqīm Khānī*, fols. 323b–24a.

This resulted in such an enormous influx of Indian slaves that their market value dropped by nearly two-thirds. Whereas judicial records dating to 1589 indicate that a healthy Indian male slave sold in Samarqand for 225 tanga, the price for an Indian slave after the Mughal retreat dropped to a mere 84 tanga.[81]

The evidence that climate played a role in undermining the seventeenth-century Bukharan agricultural economy is compelling. But one might liken climatic conditions to the natural canvas on which human history takes shape: they enforce particular constraints on societies, but they do not dictate the ways that people respond to those constraints. That is to say, it is one thing to argue that the scientific evidence demonstrates that the Little Ice Age is a historical phenomenon that merits careful consideration in understanding the historical vicissitudes of early modern Central Asia.[82] It is something different to identify the specific ways that climatic conditions affected local economies and those dependent upon them. This has been achieved for specific societies in certain places, but climate patterns were by no means uniform across the globe and such a study is yet to be written for early modern Central Asia.[83] However, a number of climate research teams have directed their attention to Central Asia, and the evidence that they have produced indicates that Central Asian weather patterns were indeed abnormally cold throughout the seventeenth century.[84]

---

81. See the discussion in Levi, "Hindus beyond the Hindu Kush," 280. This discrepancy in value is magnified when one considers that a tanga minted in 1589 contained substantially more silver than one minted in the 1640s.
82. The literature is effectively surveyed and presented in an accessible format in John L. Brooke and Henry Misa, "Earth, Water, Air, and Fire: Toward an Ecological History of Premodern Inner Eurasia," *Oxford Research Encyclopedia of Asian History* (forthcoming).
83. The present discussion aims to encourage new work in that field as environmental history stands to bring an entirely different body of sources to bear in furthering our understanding of early modern Central Asian history. Scholars have for some time appreciated that environment played a role in the medieval rise of the Mongol Empire and the spread of the plague pandemic a century later. For a thorough introduction to the latter, see the inaugural double issue of the journal *The Medieval Globe* 1, nos. 1–2 (2014), edited by Monica Green. See also the recent essay by Nicola di Cosmo, "Why Qara Qorum? Climate and Geography in the Early Mongol Empire," *Archivum Eurasiae Medii Aevi* 21 (2014–2015): 67–78.
84. Cf. I. Boomer et al., "Advances in Understanding the Late Holocene History of the Aral Sea Region," *Quaternary International* 194 (2009): 79–90; Jan Esper, Fritz H. Schweingruber, and Matthias Winiger, "1300 Years of Climatic History for Western Central Asia Inferred from Tree-Rings," *Holocene* 12, no. 3 (2002): 267–77; Jens Fohlmeister et al., "Winter Precipitation Changes during the Medieval Climate Anomaly and the Little Ice Age in Arid Central Asia," *Quaternary Science Reviews* 178 (2017): 24–36; Xiangtong Huang et al., "Dust Deposition in the Aral Sea: Implications for Changes in Atmospheric

In trying to explain this phenomenon, John Brooke's deep history of the imperceptible (in the moment) and uncontrollable impact that fluctuations in climate conditions had on the full duration of human history is instructive. Pulling back the historian's lens to an even greater extent for a moment, it is well established that the Siberian High weather pattern dominates Eurasian winters, sending outbursts of frigid, wet Arctic air southward into Central Asia. In the early fourteenth century, with the onset of the Little Ice Age after centuries of relative quiet, the Siberian High intensified dramatically (as indicated in Chart 4.2, above). Evidence from near the Aral Sea and the Pamir-Alay Mountains south of the Ferghana Valley suggests that, with this shift, semiarid and steppe Central Asia suffered particularly long, uncharacteristically cold and wet winters—exactly the conditions that our documentary sources describe the Mughal troops as having suffered in Balkh during the winter of 1646–1647.[85]

Such a weather pattern had devastating implications for both nomadic and sedentary populations. For the nomads, sustained bouts of cold, wet weather could make it exceedingly difficult, or even impossible, to provide pasture for their livestock. In the worst cases, the nomads may suffer a *zhŭt*, a Kazakh term that describes a sudden freeze leaving a thick layer of ice on the ground. This ice renders pasture inaccessible to livestock and can lead to the complete devastation of a herd.[86] Sedentary farming populations were also vulnerable, and research into the documentary sources provides

---

Circulation in Central Asia during the Past 2000 Years," *Quaternary Science Reviews* 30 (2011): 3661–74; Hedi Oberhansli et al., "Climate Variability during the Past 2,000 Years and Past Economic and Irrigation Activities in the Aral Sea Basin," *Irrigation and Drainage Systems* 21 (2007): 167–83; E. J. Rohling et al., "Holocene Atmosphere-Ocean Interactions: Records from Greenland and the Aegean Sea," *Climate Dynamics* 18 (2002): 587–93; Philippe Sorrel, "The Aral Sea: A Paleoclimate Archive" (PhD diss., Universität Potsdam, 2006); Philippe Sorrel et al., "Control of Wind Strength in the Aral Sea Basin during the Holocene," *Quaternary Research* 67 (2007): 371–82; Philippe Sorrel et al., "Climate Variability in the Aral Sea Basin (Central Asia) during the Late Holocene Based on Vegetation Changes," *Quaternary Research* 67 (2007): 357–70; Christian Wolff et al., "Precipitation Evolution of Central Asia during the Last 5000 Years," *Holocene* 27, no. 1 (2017): 142–54; Bao Yang et al., "Late Holocene Climate and Environmental Changes in Arid Central Asia," *Quaternary International* 194 (2009): 68–78. See also Fa-Hu Chen et al., "Moisture Changes over the Last Millennium in Arid Central Asia: A Review, Synthesis and Comparison with Monsoon Region," *Quaternary Science Reviews* 29 (2010): 1055–68, though Chen's conclusions are more relevant for Xinjiang than they are for areas west of the Tian Shan.

85. Brooke, *Climate Change*, 380–81.
86. Campbell, "Scourge of Stock Raising," 60–61. Campbell observes that a particularly deleterious *zhŭt*, such as what the Kazakhs experienced in 1855–1856, might result in the death of as much as 70 percent of the livestock in an affected area.

further insight into this matter. Focusing on the Bukharan Khanate in the early seventeenth century, Thomas Welsford describes how local peoples experienced a pattern familiar across the globe: the occasional few years of good harvests were insufficient to bring relief to areas that had suffered a series of failed harvests. Welsford then illustrates in fine detail how various groups confronted with recurrent famine weighed the inertia of political loyalties against rising uncertainty costs associated with a weakening economy, agrarian crisis, and famine.[87]

Moving past the seventeenth century, an inquisitive reader may wonder if climate change had something to do with the extension of the Bukharan crisis into the first half of the eighteenth century, which ultimately did end in revolution. To answer this question on the global scale, the answer is that it did not, or at least not exactly. Climate research indicates that, while the Maunder Minimum faded after the first two decades of the eighteenth century, the intensified Siberian High pattern continued sporadically until roughly 1740.[88] Climatic factors may, therefore, have contributed to some of the traumatic historical events of that period, including the 1723 Jungar-Kazakh wars that precipitated the highly disruptive Kazakh invasion of Bukharan territory.

But in terms of global climate patterns, the eighteenth century marks a significant break with, and improvement over, the dramatic climatic lows of the seventeenth century. Climate scientists chart a steady recovery and a sustained warm stretch beginning in the early eighteenth century, which Brooke identifies as an "optimum" period.[89] At the end of that century, the climate shifted again and entered the "Dalton Minimum" phase, characterized by lower temperatures into the 1840s. But by comparison with the seventeenth century, this cooling trend was only a minor concern. Brooke concludes, "The Dalton was mild relative to the Maunder Minimum of more than a century before. Even if it played a role in world events, climate did not fundamentally constrain the human condition in the northern latitudes during the eighteenth and nineteenth centuries."[90]

Taking that all into consideration as we return to the question of the role that climate played in the Bukharan crisis, the available evidence suggests that the change in climate patterns would have had a signficant and sustained negative affect on the seventeenth-century Toqay-Timurid state. As

---

87. Welsford, *Four Types of Loyalty*, 152–55 and notes.
88. Brooke, *Climate Change*, 468.
89. Brooke, *Climate Change*, 468–71.
90. Brooke, *Climate Change*, 471.

in China, Russia, Iran, Anatolia, and elsewhere, cooler summers punctuated with unseasonable freezes in late spring and early fall contributed to a decrease in agricultural production, an increase in failed harvest, a decrease in tax revenues, and rising political stresses as the state failed to alleviate the effects of recurrent famine.[91] In economic terms, this is reflected in the steady debasement of Bukharan coinage over the course of the seventeenth century, as discussed above. The Bukharan Khanate's fiscal crisis and weakened tax base provides insight into the inability of the Toqay-Timurid khans to maintain the loyalty of the Uzbek amirs—those same regional power holders who, it has long been recognized, pressed for increased autonomy in this very period.[92]

While the available evidence supports the argument that climate change shaped this process, I emphasize that it was one factor among several, and that additional research will be required to determine Central Asia's actual agrarian patterns over the course of the early modern period.[93] But the available evidence does suggest that the stresses brought about by climate change exacerbated the Bukharan Khanate's decentralizing tendencies, and this became increasingly pronounced during the latter half of the seventeenth century. Without a dramatic course correction, this pattern would have carried over into the eighteenth century.

In terms of their direct impact in the moment, other than the possible correlation of the final decades of sporadically severe cold at the end of the Little Ice Age with the 1723 Kazakh-Jungar wars, climatic factors appear to have had little to do with the reasons why the Bukharan crisis grew critical in the first half of the eighteenth century. Rather, the evidence suggests that the dramatic spike in Chinese demand for silver, the concomitant decentralization of the Mughal Empire, and the collapse of Safavid authority all had wide-ranging effects that also adversely affected the Central Asian

---

91. Although he does not address Central Asia, these factors mimic the larger pattern laid out in detail in Jack A. Goldstone, *Revolution and Rebellion in the Early Modern World: Population Change and State Breakdown in England, France, Turkey, and China, 1600–1850*, 2nd ed. (New York: Routledge, 2016). Goldstone takes care to note that the crisis was a powerful catalyst. While societies experienced the crisis in similar ways, its impact across the early modern world was very different as those same societies emerged from crisis and entered a new age.
92. McChesney, "Amīrs of Muslim Central Asia in the XVIIth Century," 33–70.
93. The classic studies by Pavel P. Ivanov and Olga D. Chekhovich would be a good place to begin such a study. See especially P. P. Ivanov, *Iz arkhiva sheikhov dzhuibari: Materialy po zemel'nym i torgovym otnosheniiam Srednei Azii XVI veka* (Moscow: Nauka, 1938–1954); P. P. Ivanov, *Khoziaistvo dzhuibarskikh sheikhov: K istorii feodal'nogo zemlevladeniia v. Srednei Azii v XVI–XVII vv.* (Moscow: Nauka, 1954); and O. D. Chekhovich and A. K. Arends, *Dokumenty k istorii agrarnykh otnoshenii v bukharskom khansve XVII–XIX vv.* (Tashkent: Fan, 1954).

economy. These exacerbated the problems that had plagued the Bukharan Khanate throughout the latter half of the seventeenth century, and they represented formidable obstacles to any recovery efforts. In essence, they ensured that Central Asia's seventeenth-century pattern of decentralization continued into the eighteenth century.

These are not the only factors to consider. Indeed, there remains at least one final factor that underpinned the political crisis in Bukhara. This is the impact that technological advancements in gunpowder weaponry had on the Central Asian state during the later period of the early modern Military Revolution. The shift from traditional mounted archery to gunpowder weaponry in Central Asia was a long, slow process that had begun in the sixteenth century and, encountering fierce local resistance, reached its tipping point only two centuries later, during the first half of the eighteenth century. In the end, as innovations in gunpowder weaponry made their way into Central Asian warfare at a time of increasingly severe political and economic crisis, they effectively undermined core elements of Chinggisid legitimacy and paved the way for the eighteenth-century rise of the Uzbek tribal dynasties.

FIREARMS AND THE NOMADIC MILITARY TRADITION

The introduction of gunpowder weaponry in early modern Central Asia and its impact on Central Asian peoples and society is a topic that has drawn only a small amount of attention.[94] The vast majority of work on Central Asian military history pertains to earlier periods, and in the few studies that continue into the early modern era, the final centuries are presented as a sort of denouement on the eve of colonization: a sad whimper at the end of an epic age.[95] This is because the early modern improvement and proliferation of gunpowder weaponry gradually eroded the nomadic military advantage that had long benefited Central Asian powers and shifted that advantage to the much larger, wealthier, and more populous agrarian empires on the Eurasian periphery. In his recent survey of Central Asian history, Peter Golden summarizes: "In the mid-1600s, there may still have been parity between the nomad's composite bow and the matchlock musket. A century later, the flintlock rifle was becoming the superior

---

94. Wolfgang Holzwarth's pathbreaking work in this area, referenced below and in the bibliography, represents the most significant contribution.
95. In addition to Di Cosmo, ed., *Warfare in Inner Asian History (500–1800)* (Leiden: E. J. Brill, 2001), see Erik Hildinger, *Warriors of the Steppe: A Military History of Central Asia, 500 B.C. to 1700 A.D.* (Cambridge, MA: Da Capo, 1997).

weapon. Some nomads rejected the new technology as not suited to their traditional modes of warfare. Others were willing to use it, but largely lacked the industrial capacity to produce the new weapons or the money to buy them. Overall, they fell behind in the arms race. The heyday of the nomad-warrior had passed."[96] Golden succinctly characterizes the shift in military advantage away from Central Asian nomadic archers and toward the artillery forces of the larger agrarian states. But his study, like nearly all others, says little about how the introduction of gunpowder weapons to the region changed Central Asian states and society. The objective here is to identify a number of ways that technological advancements in gunpowder weaponry introduced political tensions that shaped events at the local level.

Firearms and other gunpowder weapons technologies made their way into Central Asia at various times and through multiple avenues, though in general at a slower rate than elsewhere in Eurasia.[97] During the sixteenth century, when firearms were ubiquitous in Ottoman warfare and were an established part of the hybrid military forces that the Safavids and Mughals employed, they remained little used in Central Asia, and some evidence suggests that they had yet even to reach certain parts of the region. En route from Urgench (modern Köne Urgench, in Turkmenistan) to Bukhara in December 1558, for example, the Muscovy Company agent Anthony Jenkinson (1530–1609) encountered a group of highwaymen who sought to rob him and his companions. In his report to the company investors, Jenkinson explains:

> When the thieves were nigh upon us, we perceived them to be in number 37 men well armed, and appointed with bows, arrows and swords, and the captain a prince banished from his country. They willed us to yield ourselves, or else to be slain, but we defied them, wherewith they shot (arrows) at us all at once, and we at them very hotly, and so continued our fight from morning until two hours within night, some men, horses and camels being wounded and slain on both parts: and had it not been for 4

---

96. Golden, *Central Asia in World History*, 105. I am in general agreement with Golden's assessment. I note, however, that rifling was introduced even prior to the sixteenth century and that, throughout the early modern era, the vast majority of muskets, including flintlock muskets, were smooth bore and were not, in fact, rifles. Golden cites Kenneth Chase, *Firearms: A Global History to 1700* (Cambridge: Cambridge University Press, 2003), 124, 203.
97. For a survey of this subject, see Scott C. Levi, "Asia in the Gunpowder Revolution," *Oxford Research Encyclopedia of Asian History*, April 2018, http://asianhistory.oxfordre.com /view/10.1093/acrefore/9780190277727.001.0001/acrefore-9780190277727-e-186.

handguns (arquebuses) which I and my company had and used, we (would have) been overcome and destroyed: for the thieves were better armed, and were also better archers than we; but after we had slain some of their men and horses with our guns, they dared not approach so close, which caused them to come to a truce with us until the next morning, which we accepted.[98]

While Jenkinson does not venture a guess as to whether these men had ever previously encountered gunpowder weapons, it is clear that they had none in their possession, and that despite his opponents' superior archery skills his own four guns tilted the balance in favor of his company. Firearms had reached Bukhara well before this time, but the quantities were limited and the models dated. This is illustrated by Jenkinson's report that, in Bukhara, 'Abdallah Khan himself found such great marvel in the technology that he "caused us to shoot in handguns before him, and did himself practice the use thereof."[99]

In Iran, the Safavids began to incorporate gunpowder weaponry into their military in a meaningful way after Shah Ismail's decisive defeat at Chaldiran in 1514. In Central Asia, where the prestige of cavalry warfare ran high and cultural biases against such technologies were at least as strong as in Safavid Iran, it is not surprising to find that firearms were adopted even more slowly. Firearms do not appear to have been involved whatsoever at the Battle of Merv in 1510, where Shah Ismail's Qizilbash troops routed the Shibanid Uzbeks and killed Muhammad Shibani Khan. And while the Safavids began adopting them for limited use, references to the Uzbek armies utilizing firearms in battle remain scarce until the end of the century, when 'Abdallah Khan began importing artillery primarily to aid in siege warfare. Some of these weapons are said to have been brought from as far away as Europe.[100] The Uzbeks reportedly used mortars during their siege of Herat in 1587, and they are said to have begun producing their

---

98. Charles Henry Coote and Edward Delmar Morgan, *Early Voyages and Travels to Russia and Persia by Anthony Jenkinson and Other Englishmen, with Some Account of the First Intercourse of the English with Russia and Central Asia by Way of the Caspian Sea*, 2 vols., 1st ser., nos. 72–73 (London: Hakluyt Society, 1886), 1:78. Here and below, I have taken the liberty of slightly altering Jenkinson's sixteenth-century language to reflect modern spelling and word usage.
99. Coote and Morgan, *Early Voyages*, 1:86.
100. J. Kh. Ismailova and L. G. Levteieva, *U'zbekiston Harbii San'ati Tarikhi* (Toshkent: U'zbekiston, 2012), 150–51; D. Kh. Ziyaeva, *U'zbekistonda harbii ish tarikhidan (Qadimgi davrdan hozirgacha)* (Tashkent: Sharq, 2012), 121.

own cannons soon thereafter.[101] Reports indicate that the Toqay-Timurids in Bukhara were able to employ both muskets and cannons at Balkh in 1602 and 1603 because the Bukharan troops had benefited from an "agreement for military aid" with Istanbul. This involved the significantly more technologically advanced Ottomans sending to Bukhara some twenty guns and two hundred arquebuses to aid in their fight with their mutual enemy, the Safavids.[102] Ottoman munificence toward their Turkic brethren in Central Asia continued well beyond the Safavid period.

Even as gunpowder weapons gradually penetrated the Eurasian interior, their use in the steppe remained limited. Toward the end of the seventeenth century, Qalmaq nomads are said to have shunned firearms in favor of fast-moving cavalry archers.[103] The nomads' preference for relying on traditional weapons and equestrian skills may have contributed to a cultural aversion to gunpowder weaponry. However, more pragmatic factors must also be considered. These include their access to a large number of horses, the tactical advantages that cavalry forces enjoyed in terms of speed and maneuverability, the difficulty of using firearms—especially heavy and clumsy early models—on horseback, the relative superiority of their handmade traditional weaponry in terms of precision and reliability, the lack of walled cities on the steppe that would require siege weaponry, and the lack of a local gunpowder-making industry. Faced with the option to shift over to gunpowder weaponry, the nomads' decision to retain traditional strategies and weapons technologies was clearly a logical and pragmatic one.[104]

Another deterrent was the considerable expense associated with acquiring such weapons. Even when nomads did begin to acquire firearms, available sources suggest that they were either outdated or lacked essential technological components. In 1720, a report to the Russian Ministry of Foreign Affairs refers to Russian Cossacks who claimed that two Kazakh khans had amassed fierce cavalry forces numbering some sixty thousand men armed

---

101. Ziyaeva, *U'zbekistonda harbii ish tarikhidan*, 119; Chase, *Firearms*, 124; Matthee, "Unwalled Cities and Restless Nomads," 406. See the detailed discussion in Robert D. McChesney, "The Conquest of Herat 995–6/1587–8: Sources for the Study of S.afavid/Qizilbāsh-Shībanid/Ūzbak Relations," in *Études Safavides*, ed. Jean Calmard (Paris: Institut Français de Recherche en Iran, 1993), 69–107.
102. Steensgaard, *Asian Trade Revolution*, 223. Cited in Rudi Matthee, "Unwalled Cities and Restless Nomads," in *Safavid Persia: The History and Politics of an Islamic Society*, ed. Charles Melville (London: I. B. Tauris, 1996), 406.
103. Matthee, "Unwalled Cities and Restless Nomads," 406 and notes.
104. This point is further developed in Levi, "Asia in the Gunpowder Revolution."

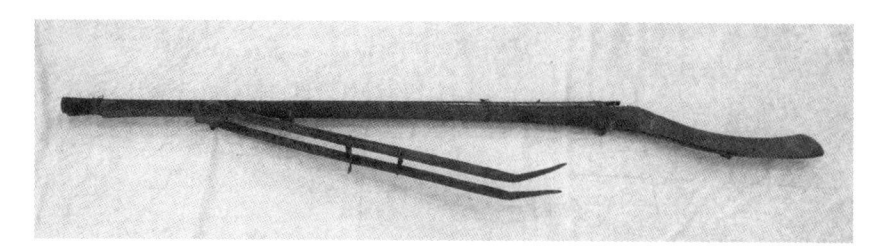

Figure 4.1. Central Asian Lockless Musket with Rest, date unknown. Photo courtesy of Dr. Dono Ziyaeva.

with *dzhagrami bez zamkov*, or lockless muskets, as well as bows, spears, and swords.[105] These lockless muskets would have been relatively inexpensive to acquire, but they were also exceptionally slow and required two people to operate with any precision, one to hold the weapon and aim and the other to light the gunpowder charge.

Two decades later, following a conflict between Russian and Kazakh forces in 1740 in which both sides employed firearms, Russian troops reported that they were able to issue ten rounds against their Kazakh opponents before the Kazakhs could return even one volley.[106] In 1736, the adventurer and member of Russia's Orenburg Expedition John Castle made his way into the steppe armed with a German flintlock pistol that, he reports, attracted great interest among his Kazakh hosts as they had never before seen a flintlock.[107] Castle elsewhere observed a small group of nomads in the steppe firing muskets with impressive accuracy, but overall his account supports the impression that, throughout the first half of the eighteenth century, the Kazakhs strongly favored traditional weaponry.[108]

The invention of the flintlock in the early seventeenth century represents a major advance in the efficiency of gunpowder weapons. Whereas

---

105. A *dzhagra* is a type of *pal'nik*, or a long stick with a wick that was lit and inserted into the touchhole to ignite the powder in rudimentary "Tatar muskets," which were commonly not equipped with a lock. I. N. Tasmagambetov, ed., *Istoriia Kazakhstana v Russkikh istochnikakh XVI–XX vv.*, vol. 2 (Almaty: Dayk-Press, 2005), doc. 16, 295–99. I am grateful to Michael Hancock-Parmer for bringing this reference to my attention.
106. Wolfgang Holzwarth, "Bukharan Armies and Uzbek Military Power, 1670–1870: Coping with the Legacy of a Nomadic Conquest," in *Nomad Military Power in Iran and Adjacent Areas in the Islamic Period*, ed. Kurt Franz and Wolfgang Holzwarth (Wiesbaden: Dr. Ludwig Reichert Verlag, 2015), 292.
107. Beatrice Teissier, ed., *Into the Kazakh Steppe: John Castle's Mission to Khan Abulkhayir (1736)* (Oxford: Signal Books, 2011), 29, 63.
108. Teissier, ed., *Into the Kazakh Steppe*, 97. Castle explicitly states that the Kazakhs were not using flintlocks.

matchlock muskets depend upon an open flame to ignite the gunpowder, flintlocks rely on a piece of flint clamped in a hammer that, when released, comes into contact with a concave piece of metal called the frizzen. The resulting friction sends sparks into the flash pan and ignites the gunpowder charge, eliminating the need to maintain a lit match and significantly decreasing the time soldiers needed to reload their weapons. Informed estimates suggest that using a flintlock increased the ability of a trained infantry soldier to issue volleys by a factor of two to three times over the matchlock.[109] Additionally, it further increased the utility of firearms through improved reliability in damp and windy conditions, and it could also be fired from horseback. In technological terms, the flintlock remained unchallenged well into the nineteenth century, when it was replaced by the still faster and more reliable trigger-released hammer and percussion cap mechanism. This technology gradually made its way into Central Asia, and the early decades of the eighteenth century represent the tipping point in the process by which flintlock muskets permanently eclipsed the effectiveness of traditional nomadic warfare.[110]

Not all nomads were slow to embrace gunpowder weapons. The Jungars, most famously, eagerly sought out weapons-production technologies and cartographic knowledge from European sources in the seventeenth century.[111] By the 1680s, the Jungar ruler Galdan Khan (1644–1697) had overseen the development of a local mining infrastructure to obtain ore, which he had cast into cannons, matchlock muskets, and mortars. The Jungars even refined saltpeter and acquired sulfur to produce their own gunpowder, and for more than a century, they employed a highly effective hybrid military force. Endeavoring to succeed in their role as the primary agents protecting the Dalai Lama, in the 1720s the Jungars sought new means to expand their military capacity, and they experimented with military reforms that included establishing a European-style standing army.[112] Three decades later, the Qing military would launch a massive campaign that would overwhelm the Jungar forces and bring that state to an end. But until then, the Jungars were a powerful military force in the region, and, as

---

109. Wayne E. Lee, personal communication. According to Lee, reload speed varied by training and how often the weapon had been fired recently, fouling the barrel with unburned powder. The creation of a single paper cartridge, roughly contemporaneous with the introduction of the flintlock, also greatly increased reload speed for military forces equipped with them.
110. Again, I develop this point further in Levi, "Asia in the Gunpowder Revolution."
111. James A. Millward, *Eurasian Crossroads: A History of Xinjiang* (New York: Columbia University Press, 2007), 90.
112. Perdue, *China Marches West*, 304–6; Holzwarth, "Relations between Uzbek Central Asia," 210.

Figure 4.2. Flintlock Musket, 1816. Author photo.

we have noted, a highly disruptive one for their Kazakh neighbors and the Central Asian states farther to the south as well. Other developments to the north provide additional insight into how the introduction of gunpowder weapons contributed to the Bukharan crisis.

Donald Ostrowski's work on the introduction of gunpowder weaponry in the Muscovite military provides some insight into the impact this technology had on steppe warfare.[113] Ostrowski observes that in the early seventeenth century, the traditional composite reflex bow was considerably more effective and reliable than contemporary firearms, and it was undeniably the superior weapon. While it was possible to fire a carbine—a short, lightweight musket commonly used at the time—from horseback, the weapon had a limited range and reloading was a slow and complicated affair that required the soldier to dismount. By contrast, mounted archers were able to issue between six and fifteen accurate shots per minute, and, depending upon the skill and strength of the archer, their projectiles had a range of between three hundred and five hundred yards.[114] For these reasons, in

---

113. Donald Ostrowski, "The Replacement of the Composite Reflex Bow by Firearms in the Muscovite Cavalry," *Kritika: Explorations in Russian and Eurasian History* 11, no. 3 (2010): 513–34.

114. Cf. Ostrowski, "Replacement of the Composite Reflex Bow," 513–14; Tim May, *The Mongol Art of War* (Yardley, PA: Westholme, 2007), 50.

Figure 4.3. Flintlock. Author photo.

the heat of battle even those cavalry troops that were armed with carbines would fire the weapon a single time and then put it away in favor of their bow. Another factor to consider is that, unlike most European powers, the Muscovite military suffered no shortage of available horses to support its cavalry. Taking this all into consideration, at first glance it seems puzzling that the Muscovite army would willingly shift from highly mobile cavalry archers to a comparatively sluggish, expensive, and less reliable artillery-based military, which provided no advantage over Muscovy's fierce and fast-moving nomadic neighbors. Nevertheless, they did just that.

On further analysis, Ostrowski concludes that the Muscovite military changed strategies for reasons that had very little to do with the superiority of firearms.[115] Rather, the central problem that drove Muscovy's move toward gunpowder technology was a chronic shortage of skilled Russian archers. While nomads were adept at crafting their own superlative weapons and famously honed their skills and trained their muscles through regular practice, competition, and elaborate hunting exercises, Russians were peasants, not nomads. Thus, even though firearms were inferior, they became the preferred weapon among Russian troops as they required substantially less skill and training to operate in an effective manner.[116]

---

115. Ostrowski, "Replacement of the Composite Reflex Bow," 514.
116. Ostrowski, "Replacement of the Composite Reflex Bow," 516–19.

This became more important over the course of the exceptionally tumultuous seventeenth century, as Russia endured one internal crisis after another and came into conflict with Sweden, the Ottoman Empire, and other powers that had effectively integrated gunpowder weaponry into their militaries.[117]

Brian Davies sheds additional light on the gradual and uneven way that this process unfolded in his analysis of Russia's emergence as a major early modern power. Davies observes that Tsar Mikhail (r. 1613–1645) implemented a number of early military reforms designed to elevate artillery in the Russian military, but that these failed when the Russians lost the Smolensk War in 1634.[118] Sweeping military reforms were introduced again under Tsar Aleksei I (r. 1645–1676), who had considerable success in restructuring the military organization across the empire. Like armies elsewhere in Europe, during the seventeenth century the Russian military had expanded in size, with significantly larger numbers of infantry soldiers equipped with and able to operate firearms. By the end of the 1680s, Ostrowski concludes, "the bow virtually disappears from our sources about military use by the Muscovite cavalry."[119] While individual nomadic soldiers may have been more effective, the story from the mid-seventeenth century forward is one of Russia's progressively larger armies of slow-moving, artillery-based infantry confronting nomadic powers and advancing into their territory. Arguably more important than the technology, however, was the concomitant development of a military administration capable of overseeing logistics and maintaining reliable supply lines.[120]

Developments farther to the south, in sedentary Central Asia, followed a different trajectory. In his study of the Bukharan military, Wolfgang Holzwarth identifies a number of ways that weapons technology changed the Bukharan political landscape over the roughly two centuries stretching from 1670 into the Russian colonial era.[121] Holzwarth's study represents the first systematic analysis of Bukharan military history during this period, which includes the elevation of gunpowder weaponry from a minor sup-

---

117. Ostrowski, "Replacement of the Composite Reflex Bow," 526–27.
118. Davies, *Warfare, State and Society*, 71.
119. Ostrowski, "Replacement of the Composite Reflex Bow," 530–31.
120. V. D. Puzanov, *Voennye factory russkoi kolonizatsii zapadnoi Sibiri, konets XVI–XVII vv.* (St. Petersburg: Aleteia, 2010). For a similar argument regarding the Ottoman Empire, see Gábor Ágoston, *Guns for the Sultan: Military Power and the Weapons Industry in the Ottoman Empire* (Cambridge: Cambridge University Press, 2005), 43. For further discussion, see Levi, "Asia in the Gunpowder Revolution."
121. Holzwarth, "Bukharan Armies," 273–354.

porting role under the Toqay-Timurids to a central feature of the Manghit military.[122]

Several factors make the Central Asian case unique. Agrarian empires such as the Ottomans, Mughals, Muscovy, and the Qing could rely on substantial income from agricultural taxes to finance artillery production, and they had access to large populations from which to draw infantry troops for their expanding armies. Conversely, the Bukharan Khanate was restricted to a semiarid zone, it was comparatively sparsely populated, and it had a much smaller agrarian tax base from which to draw revenue, with nearly half of its population living as nomads.[123] Again, with horses abundant and available, the Uzbek forces found little motivation, even less than the Safavids, to stray from traditional cavalry-based military strategies. As was often the case, the prestige of the mounted archer also played a role. And so it remained even to the mid-eighteenth century.

Throughout the Toqay-Timurid era, the strength of the Bukharan military rested on the ability of the Bukharan khan to marshal the support of the nomadic tribes who occupied the open pastures interspersed among the region's urban centers and agricultural zones. While the Toqay-Timurids exercised executive authority, military authority was largely in the hands of the tribal leadership, the most important element of which was the Uzbek amirs, who together represented many hundreds of thousands of people widely dispersed across the region. These were the people whose ancestors had migrated into the region at the turn of the sixteenth century under the leadership of Muhammad Shibani Khan, and who at the turn of the seventeenth century had engineered the elevation of the Toqay-Timurid dynastic line in place of the Shibanids.[124] As a group, they wielded considerable political authority.

Under both the Shibanid and Toqay-Timurid dynasties, the Bukharan state functioned as a collaborative venture involving the Chinggisid dynastic leadership and the tribal amirs. McChesney explains that, "as a working

---

122. Holzwarth incorporates the work of a number of scholars who have engaged themes and subjects within this larger framework. In order to avoid unnecessary repetition, I will identify below those whose work is relevant to our present interests. For his brief historiographical survey, see Holzwarth, "Bukharan Armies," 274–75.
123. Holzwarth's sources suggest that the population of pastoral nomads in the Bukharan Amirate around 1820 was roughly 1 million, among a total population of some 2.5 million. Holzwarth, "Bukharan Armies," 279.
124. See Welsford, *Four Types of Loyalty*. As noted above, Muhammad Shibani Khan is said to have led between two hundred thousand and four hundred thousand Uzbeks into the region. Welsford, *Four Types of Loyalty*, 273; Bregel, "Turko-Mongol Influences," 74 and note.

definition, one can say that the amīrid class was composed of individuals whose positions of power were derived from status within Turco-Mongol tribal organizations, whose main talents lay in military and administrative affairs, and whose political horizons were limited by the Chingīzid dispensation, that is that ultimate political authority was restricted to agnatic descendants of Chingīz Khān."[125] Thus, for an individual to be elevated as khan, that individual must, by definition, be a male descendent of Chinggis Khan with an ancestry traced exclusively through the Chinggisid male line.

The amirs were required to recognize their subordinate status as part of their enforcement of the *yasa*, the Chinggisid legal code. But at the same time, they were also able to exercise considerable power and leverage. Indeed, while the khan may have found individual amirs to be disposable, as a group the Uzbek amirs represented the dominant political force in the region.[126] Authority to elevate the khan rested with the amirs, as did his ability to wage war, and his dynastic legitimacy. When khans were perceived as having overstepped their authority, they upset the delicate balance of their collaborative venture, and the amirs could, and did, remove them from power.[127]

In his study of the Uzbeks' elevation of the Toqay-Timurids over Shibanid claimants at the turn of the seventeenth century, Welsford demonstrates that the amirs gauged what was in their best interest in a very deliberate and calculating manner, firmly grounded in the cultural context and specific circumstances of their time. In the final lines of his study, Welsford notes that "the circumstances of the Tūqāy-Tīmūrid takeover reflected the ways in which it suited members of the wider populace to influence the course of events. Like all social phenomena, the Tūqāy-Tīmūrid takeover was above all a by-product of people's everyday lives."[128]

This logic of loyalty informed the actions of the Uzbek amirs during the Toqay-Timurid rise at the beginning of the seventeenth century, and it continued to do so during the period of their collapse in the eighteenth century. The efforts of the Bukharan khans to integrate artillery into the Bukharan military elicited a hostile response from Uzbek amirs, who saw their traditional positions threatened and who subsequently became even more alienated from their khan. Their decision to withdraw their support was a prod-

---

125. For the seventeenth century, see McChesney, "Amīrs of Muslim Central Asia," 34–35.
126. McChesney, "Amīrs of Muslim Central Asia," 38.
127. McChesney references the case of 'Abd al-Mu'min, the Shibanid son of 'Abdallah Khan who was assassinated in 1598. McChesney, "Amīrs of Muslim Central Asia," 36. See the more recent discussion in McChesney, "Chinggisid Restoration," 279.
128. Welsford, *Four Types of Loyalty*, 303.

uct of their desire to protect that which they valued in their everyday lives, and in the realm of Central Asian politics that was autonomy and control over resources that they believed to be their own. Holzwarth identifies the sustained efforts of the Bukharan khans to assert greater centralized control over the Uzbek tribes as a defining feature of the two centuries stretching from the 1670s into the Russian colonial era.[129] Despite those efforts, the actual trajectory was one of progressive decentralization, with the Uzbek amirs first strengthening their autonomy at the expense of the center, then gradually asserting greater control over the center.[130]

This Central Asian case presents an interesting counterpoint to the European experience. In early modern European history, there is a substantial body of scholarship analyzing various aspects of the "royalization of warfare." This references the process by which early modern European rulers were able to monopolize gunpowder weapons technologies and use them to assert increased centralized control over localized nobles and, some have argued, give rise to the modern centralized state.[131] In the Middle Eastern arena, scholars have emphasized the role that the widespread use of handheld weaponry beyond the state monopoly played in decentralizing power.[132]

In Central Asia, one might be inclined to advance a similar argument for the declining authority of the Toqay-Timurids, but the evidence does not support it: prior to the mid-eighteenth century, gunpowder weaponry simply was not sufficiently widespread to pose a threat to the state. Holzwarth finds that, even toward the end of their tenure as khans, the Toqay-Timurid Bukharans "hardly ever commanded more than 500 slave guards equipped with firearms," as opposed to the Uzbek amirs, who had at their disposal tens of thousands of mounted archers. These troops were enlisted when needed, either by their tribal leadership or by appointed governors,

---

129. Holzwarth, "Bukharan Armies," 277.
130. Wolfgang Holzwarth, "The Uzbek State as Reflected in Eighteenth Century Bukharan Sources," *Asiatische Studien* 60, no. 2 (2006): 333–41. This both affirms and elaborates upon McChesney's earlier conclusions as presented in McChesney, "Amīrs of Muslim Central Asia."
131. See Anthony Grafton and Eugene F. Rice Jr., *The Foundations of Early Modern Europe, 1460–1559*, 2nd ed. (New York: W. W. Norton, 1994). This follows the 1988 publication of the classic study on the Military Revolution by Geoffrey Parker, *The Military Revolution: Military Innovation and the Rise of the West, 1500–1800*, 2nd ed. (Cambridge: Cambridge University Press, 1996). For further discussion of the Military Revolution literature and its implications for Central Asian history, see Levi, "Asia in the Gunpowder Revolution."
132. For the classic study, see Halil Inalcik, "The Socio-Political Effects of the Diffusion of Fire-Arms in the Middle East," in *War, Technology, and Society in the Middle East*, ed. V. J. Parry and M. E. Yapp (London: Oxford University Press, 1975), 211.

and like their Kazakh neighbors to the north they were also predisposed to approach gunpowder weapons with skepticism and disdain.[133] In 1670–1671, the Muscovite envoy to Bukhara, Boris Pazukhin, estimated that at that time the Bukharan army numbered some 150,000 soldiers, with an additional 75,000 in Balkh and 30,000 in Khwarezm. He concluded that while this could potentially represent a formidable force, the troops lacked formal training, neither Bukhara nor Balkh had any infantry, and other than light cannons fired from the backs of camels known as the *zambūrak* ("hornet" or "wasp," also *zanbūrak* or *shutarnāl*), the Bukharan army included no artillery to speak of.[134]

Over the course of the seventeenth century, as the region suffered recurrent famines and the Uzbek amirs resisted Toqay-Timurid centralization efforts, the Chinggisid khans began to perceive the Uzbek nobility as fickle, unreliable partners and a potential threat. Holzwarth rightly observes that the Uzbek amirs "claimed a share of power and agricultural wealth" from the Bukharan khans, as they were "the original mainstay of their power."[135] But in desperation, the Bukharan leadership began to rely more heavily on non-Uzbeks for supportive manpower, including especially Kazakhs and Karakalpaks, while appointing Persian and Russian slaves and other non-Uzbeks to high government posts and leadership positions in the military. But those relationships proved to be fraught as well, as the Kazakhs, for example, were more concerned with protecting their own settlements than completing their service to Bukhara. Tensions between Bukhara and the Uzbek nobles became more pronounced in the latter half of the seventeenth century, during the reigns of ʿAbd al-ʿAziz Khan and his successor, Subhan Quli Khan.[136]

During this same period, economic factors further chipped away at Chinggisid authority.[137] In an effort to increase the reliability of the mili-

---

133. Holzwarth, "Bukharan Armies," 277–79.
134. Burton, *The Bukharans*, 292, 297; Holzwarth, "Bukharan Armies," 283. For more on Pazukhin and other Russian missions to the region in the seventeenth century, see Ron Sela, "Prescribing the Boundaries of Knowledge: Seventeenth-Century Russian Diplomatic Missions to Central Asia," in *Writing Travel in Central Asian History*, ed. Nile Green (Bloomington: Indiana University Press, 2014), 69–88.
135. Holzwarth, "Bukharan Armies," 339.
136. Holzwarth attributes this development to the success of Uzbek "*alaman*," or "raiders," during the aborted Mughal occupation of Balkh. Holzwarth, "Bukharan Armies," 282–83.
137. For additional details on the many crises that unfolded in the region during this period, see the three essays by Holzwarth cited in the bibliography and the final chapter of Sela's volume, *Legendary Biographies*, discussed in chapter one.

Figure 4.4. Zambūrak or Shutarnāl. This lithograph was drawn by Polish artist Aleksander Orłowski ca. 1820, and it is in the public domain: https://commons.wikimedia.org/wiki/File:Camel_artillery_iran.JPG.

tary in the face of a deepening fiscal crisis in the late seventeenth century, Holzwarth finds that the silver-starved Bukharan khans began to pay their military leadership through the issuance of "cheques" (*barāt*), which essentially functioned as a promissory note that permitted recipients to be paid directly from a specific revenue source. Bukharan khans are recorded as having issued such promissory notes against uncertain future tax revenue to support military campaigns. The results were often counterproductive and even devastating to the long-term economic viability of particular regions. Holzwarth notes, for example, that "when in 1692 peasants fled the province of Qarshī, leading to a decline in agriculture there, this was partly due to excesses in issuing such cheques, which overburdened the peasantry."[138]

Our discussions above illuminate the causal factors that drove such crises and rebellions. As farmers in the region suffered from a shortened growing season and smaller, or even failed, harvests, their ability to generate tax

---

138. Holzwarth, "Bukharan Armies," 285.
139. Holzwarth, "Uzbek State," 328.

income decreased. This weakened the state, which diminished the stature of the Bukharan khan in the eyes of the Uzbek tribal amirs, who looked to this central figure of authority primarily to provide security and protect their own interests from other, predatory amirs. Such instances were early indications of still worse things to come.

Indeed, matters deteriorated quickly during the reign of Subhan Quli Khan's son and successor, 'Ubaydullah Khan, whose administration aimed to enact fiscal reforms that included hindering the ability of the Uzbek troops to collect on the various *barāt* that had previously been issued to them. Holzwarth notes, "as the bureaucrats deliberately obstructed the established pattern of redistribution, the soldiers were left with 'uncovered cheques' in their hands. In order to defend and safeguard their vested rights and interests, they directed their military power against the supreme ruler. They killed and replaced him shortly afterwards, in 1711."[139]

Friction continued to grow between the Uzbek tribes and palace forces during the long reign of the final Toqay-Timurid to rule in Bukhara, Abu'l Fayz Khan (r. 1711–1747). As silver flowed eastward into Qing markets, and the Mughal and then Safavid empires collapsed, Abu'l Fayz Khan endeavored to devise some method to consolidate his authority. He pushed rebellious Uzbeks to the margins of power and in their place elevated slaves—especially Russians and Qalmaqs, but also Persians, eunuchs, and others—whom he perceived to be more loyal.[140] It is at this point that the Bukharan military at last began to integrate muskets and other gunpowder weapons into its arsenal, albeit in limited numbers and for the exclusive use of palace forces, not the Uzbek amirs.[141] The strategy was ineffective. Abu'l Fayz Khan found himself facing an Uzbek cavalry of some ninety thousand mounted archers with a much smaller and poorly equipped artillery corps stationed in fortresses dispersed across the khanate. The palace forces were armed with outdated matchlock muskets, they were poorly trained in military strategies, and they were largely incapable of using their new weaponry for anything other than defensive purposes.[142]

Even as late as the 1740s, the overwhelming majority of the Bukharan military force was comprised of mounted archers. While the Persian and Uzbek militaries both emphasized fast-moving cavalry, the Persian forces

---

140. Semenov emphasizes the reliance on Russian and Qalmaq slaves in his notes to Abdurrakhman-i Tali', *Istoriia Abulfaiz-khana*, trans. A. A. Semenov (Tashkent: Akademiia nauk Uzbekskoi SSR, 1959), 145, note 51.
141. Holzwarth, "Bukharan Armies," 286.
142. Holzwarth, "Bukharan Armies," 289.

were much more familiar with the advantages of gunpowder weaponry. The Bukharans suffered a devastating loss to the Afsharid Persian army at Qarshi in 1737, primarily because the Uzbek amirs were overwhelmed by the Persian army's adept use of large cannons, smaller camel-mounted cannons (zambūraks), and muskets.[143] Muhammad Kazim Marvi, the contemporary Afsharid chronicler and minister (*vazir*) of Merv, the Khurasani city near the Persian frontier with Bukhara, describes the victory as follows:

> After the soldiers had arranged themselves in rows, the fearsome clamor of the tools of war from the pitched battle rose to the heavens. Following the orders of The Lord of the Auspicious Conjunction, the master of artillery commanded the heavenly and imperial servants to fire the *tūphā-i ṣa'bān āṣār* (serpentine cannons), *zambūrak* (camel-mounted cannons) and *bādlīj* (large field cannons, capable of firing cannon-balls probably in excess of 60 pounds) and the line of artillery was allowed to fire at will until the battlefield resembled the Plains of Hashar and a great tumult set in.
>
> The Uzbek army, which had never before heard nor seen cannons and mortars, broke ranks until it scattered like the stars of the *banāt al-na'sh*.[144] The brave hawks among them clustered together like the stars of Pleiades. They led successive attacks, when upon the command of the World Conquering *khāqān*, the (Afsharid) *ghāzīs* and brave champions pushed forward and the chaos of fighting and war grew even greater.
>
> The fearsome soldiers followed their orders. The Commander of the Stars did not foresee a losing battle in the quadrant of Tarim, and indeed there was no loss on the battlefield. The instruments of war were twisted everywhere, and blood streamed from everywhere, and in those streams lay the dead and wounded as if they were submerged in water. The bloodthirsty arrows pierced the breasts and livers of the warriors from above, and the serpentine spears, mercilessly thrown as high as the star Suha, were flung into the dust as every eye was afflicted with despair. The sword-bearers [stayed] on the battlefield until the moon rose above the horizon..., and

---

143. See the account of Nadir Shah's use of artillery to his great advantage in Central Asia in Laurence Lockhart, *Nadir Shah: A Critical Study Based Mainly upon Contemporary Sources* (London: Luzac and Co., 1938), 187–90. A detailed survey of Nadir Shah's campaigns into Central Asia and their impact on the region is found in Wilde, *What is Beyond the River*, 1:322–48.
144. The Daughters of the Bier, also referred to as the Mourning Maidens in Arabic astronomical terminology. These are the three stars that constitute the handle of the Big Dipper (U.S.) or the Plough (U.K.), within the constellation Ursa Major, the Great Bear.

then, from the shock of the muskets and their music of death, the men collapsed upon each other like a thousand bloody livers.[145]

When Nadir Shah returned in 1740, the Bukharans simply submitted. It had at last become clear to the Uzbek amirs that if they were to retain any form of autonomy they could no longer cling so tightly to tradition. Even in Central Asia, technological advances had definitively shifted the military advantage in favor of artillery over the traditional mounted archer.[146]

In subsequent years three key developments unfolded in Bukhara. First, when Nadir Shah was assassinated in 1747, the Uzbek Manghit nobility killed Abu'l Fayz Khan and effectively brought an end to the Chinggisid line in that region.[147] Second, regional economic dynamics changed dramatically in the wake of Nadir Shah's sack of Delhi in 1739, as the Persian forces departed India with hundreds of millions of rupees' worth of gold, silver, and jewels from the Mughal treasury.[148] As noted above, although Nadir Shah squandered it rather than use it to build his infrastructure, the wealth was rapidly put into circulation.[149] Third, from his ascension to the throne, Muhammad Rahim, the first Manghit ruler, reformed the Bukharan military, and he quite deliberately modeled it after Nadir Shah's Persian forces. Key features of this reorganization included a new emphasis on equipping soldiers with muskets and other gunpowder weaponry, and the appointment of Uzbek amirs alongside significant numbers of non-Uzbek commanders who were granted military posts, including Afghans, Ottoman Turks, Georgians, and many who had served under Nadir Shah himself. Holzwarth notes that the introduction of a broader and more diverse ethnic composition followed

---

145. Muhammad Kāzim Marvi, *'Ālam ārā-yi Nādirī*, vol. 2 (Tehran: Kitābfurūshī-i Zavvār, 1985), 791. Ernest Tucker finds this source to "offer one of the most detailed contemporary accounts of Nadir's career." I am grateful to James Pickett for bringing this reference to my attention, and to Gibran Siddiqui for providing technical assistance in preparing the translation. Ernest Tucker, "Explaining Nadir Shah: Kingship and Royal Legitimacy in Muhammad Kazim Marvi's *Tārīkh-i 'ālam-ārā-yi Nādirī*," *Iranian Studies* 26, nos. 1–2 (1993): 95. See also the illustration "Battle of Qarshī (1150–1737)" in Holzwarth, "Bukharan Armies," fig. 3, 301. For detailed discussion of Persian firearms technologies as they developed from the fifteenth century, see Matthee's essay in the *Encyclopaedia Iranica*, s.v. "Firearms i. History."
146. Holzwarth, "Bukharan Armies," 281. This is in harmony with the conclusions advanced in Geoffrey Parker and Sanjay Subrahmanyam, "Arms and the Asian: Revisiting European Firearms and Their Place in Early Modern Asia," *Revista de Cultura* (Macau) 26 (2008): 38.
147. Again, the Manghit amirs retained Chinggisid puppets until 1785.
148. As noted above, contemporary sources estimate that the Afsharid troops returned to Iran with wealth valued at some seven hundred million Indian rupees.
149. Cf. Gommans, *Rise of the Indo-Afghan Empire*, 29; Levi, *Indian Diaspora*, 48, 240 and notes.

the Persian military tradition and represents a decisive break from the early Chinggisid structure, which included an Uzbek military estate on the one hand and the ruler's slave guard on the other.[150] This also reflected the local population's desire for a different model of governing power, one that was rooted in local tradition and able to provide sound leadership while balancing the needs of multiple constituencies.

Throughout this period, Bukharan efforts to finance military reform through taxation had provoked rebellions and undermined agricultural tax income in a number of regions. At the same time, efforts to assert greater control over the Uzbek tribes ultimately achieved the opposite effect of repelling those same interests. Chinggisid authority slipped away and political power in Central Asia became further decentralized, shifting from the capital into the hands of the widely dispersed Uzbek tribal nobility. While the Manghit effectively usurped power in Bukhara, other Uzbek tribes elsewhere in the region struggled to assert their authority and devise alternative models for stable governance. Such is the case for the Uzbek Qongrats in the Khivan Khanate, the Uzbek Ming who would give rise to the Khanate of Khoqand in the Ferghana Valley, the Keneges in Shahrisabz, and other groups as well.

The end of the Chinggisid dispensation in Central Asia and the rise of the Uzbek tribal dynasties in its place represent a major political shift in the region, one that had a serious and widespread cultural impact. As noted at the outset of our discussion, Ron Sela identifies one important way that this played out in his analysis of the *Tīmūr-nāma*, a genre of heroic apocrypha that elevates the historical figure of Timur to mythical, even miraculous heights.[151] Sela argues that this literary genre originated in Central Asia and from the early eighteenth century enjoyed considerable popularity across the region. His study identifies a number of common literary themes that indicate the audience for this literature had a heightened awareness of the tumultuous and fraught political culture of their time. And he argues that the Tīmūr-nāma genre rose to popularity as Central Asians looked into their past and struggled to understand who they were in an era of decline. Ultimately, he argues, "this looking inward was not so much a conscious effort to pontificate philosophically about the causes of the predicament, but rather began as an intuitive reaction that envisioned a glorious past, and through that past imagined a better present and future."[152]

---

150. Holzwarth, "Bukharan Armies," 297.
151. Sela, *Legendary Biographies of Tamerlane*.
152. Sela, *Legendary Biographies of Tamerlane*, 6.

The Tīmūr-nāma genre portrays Timur as a wise and gifted ruler with remarkable foresight and an innate gift at acknowledging, respecting, and balancing the needs of his various constituencies. In a historical context, when the Chinggisid mystique had failed, when gunpowder weapons had eclipsed the nomadic advantage, and when Abu'l Fayz Khan was struggling to use slaves and palace forces to subjugate the Uzbek amirs, the stories of the Tīmūr-nāma presented a different and preferable model of governance. Rather than rely on Chinggisids, the Uzbek amirs turned to the traditions of Timur and his Timurid heirs, who, like themselves, were Turks with deep ancestral roots in the region.[153]

THE BUKHARAN CRISIS REVISITED

In 1997, Sanjay Subrahmanyam issued a cautionary note to those whose work aims to transcend the limits of area studies in order to engage in integrative, or "connected," histories. He states, "We tend to focus on such phenomena as world bullion flows and their impact, firearms and the so-called 'Military Revolution,' or the circulation of renegades and mercenaries. But ideas and mental constructs, too, flowed across political boundaries in that world, and—even if they found specific local expression—enable us to see that what we are dealing with are not separate and comparable, but connected histories."[154]

It is important to emphasize that the networks that linked Central Asians with their neighbors on the Eurasian periphery were more than just routes of commercial and material exchange. They were also the avenues through which knowledge of the outside world reached Central Asia, and they were extraordinarily resilient. Gagan Sood's recent study focuses on the ways that the circulation of people and the exchange of ideas shaped everyday lives and worldviews in eighteenth-century South Asia and the Middle East, and his method can be applied to Central Asia as well.[155] Throughout

---

153. Holzwarth also suggests that, in the wake of the highly disruptive campaigns of both the Kazakhs and the Jungars, especially during the 1720s, the Uzbek amirs would have grown considerably more comfortable with the prospect of moving beyond long-held allegiances to the Chinggisids and other aspects of their steppe heritage. Holzwarth, "Relations between Uzbek Central Asia," 207–10. For the use of the Timurid legacy for legitimacy among the Uzbek Ming in the Khanate of Khoqand, see Levi, *Rise and Fall of Khoqand*, 98–119.
154. Subrahmanyam, "Connected Histories," 747–48.
155. Gagan D. S. Sood, *India and the Islamic Heartlands: An Eighteenth-Century World of Circulation and Exchange* (Cambridge: Cambridge University Press, 2016). Several Central Asian case studies can be found among the contributions to Niccolò Pianciola and Paolo Sartori, eds., *Islam, Society and States across the Qazaq Steppe (18th–Early 20th Centuries)* (Wien: Österreichischen Akademie der Wissenschaften, 2016).

the early modern era, Central Asian rulers remained intently interested in the acquisition of knowledge from abroad. In the seventeenth century, Bukharans were involved in the production of that knowledge, and even with his power in steep decline and his attention focused on establishing armed enclaves across the region, Abu'l Fayz Khan also worked to acquire scientific knowledge from abroad.[156] The same Bukharans who stretched their commercial interests into Siberia in the seventeenth and eighteenth centuries were involved in the movement of cultural and intellectual currents as well.[157] While further discussion of this theme rests beyond the parameters of the present study, it would represent a fruitful topic for new research.[158]

This discussion has endeavored to advance an improved understanding of how integrative structures shaped the trajectory of early modern Central Asian history more generally, and it has focused particularly on identifying the factors that caused the Bukharan crisis of the first half of the eighteenth century. I have argued that there was no single causal factor at play. Rather, already during the seventeenth century, multiple historical processes began to converge, and these ultimately placed the Bukharan Khanate on a path toward crisis and decentralization from which it would not recover. These processes include a pattern of climatic cooling that shortened the growing season, decimated livestock in the steppe, killed crops in the fields, and adversely affected the region's agricultural production and tax revenues. This provides a backdrop to understand the increasing friction between the Bukharan state and the Uzbek amirs, especially as the climate crisis grew more severe from the 1640s to the turn of the eighteenth century. This trend was exacerbated by several other contemporary events, all of which were beyond the power of the Bukharan khans to resolve. These include the spike in silver value in Qing territories, which led to the depletion of silver reserves within Central Asia and the debasement of Bukharan coinage. And that occurred alongside the temporary (and partial) dislocation of southward commercial arteries linking Central Asia with the Indian Ocean economy during the early decades of the eighteenth century.

The final factor considered here is the increase in the effectiveness and availability of gunpowder weaponry in the late seventeenth and eighteenth

---

156. As noted in the introduction, see DeWeese, "Muslim Medical Culture," 7.
157. Again, see Frank, *Bukhara and the Muslims of Russia*.
158. For an excellent recent study in this general theme, see Pickett, "Persianate Sphere." See also the essay by Subrahmanyam, "Early Modern Circulation between Central Asia and India and the Question of 'Patriotism,'" in Green, ed., *Writing Travel*, 43–68.

centuries. This process had several results, all of which were detrimental to the well-being of the Bukharan state. First, it left Central Asia's traditional militaries at a disadvantage vis-à-vis their neighbors. Second, it disrupted local power structures and added political stresses as Toqay-Timurid rulers were hard at work trying to centralize their authority over the Uzbek tribal nobility, who represented a powerful political force that vehemently resisted these efforts. Efforts to overcome the Uzbek tribal opposition by enlisting auxiliary forces brought small-scale successes but were ultimately unsuccessful and counterproductive. Opportunities for financial gain through expansion into neighboring regions were also no longer available. Abu'l Fayz Khan lacked the resources to impose the sweeping military reforms that would have been required to restore his centralized authority and protect his realm, and efforts to retrieve those resources by increasing tax revenue in specific regions sparked rebellions. Ultimately, he relied on a specialized slave guard, poorly trained but armed with artillery and placed at key locations. In 1740, as Nadir Shah prepared to march across the Amu Darya, small cadres of several hundred troops armed with outdated matchlock muskets and an insufficient supply of artillery were all that was left of the khan's waning authority beyond the walls of Bukhara.

From the vantage point of the great Ark in Bukhara, during the first half of the eighteenth century, the situation had indeed grown very grim. But standing elsewhere in the region, these same developments presented a number of very attractive opportunities for Uzbek tribes to centralize power in their own hands and pursue their own visions for a new and better future.

CONCLUSION

In a widely circulated public lecture, the Nigerian novelist Chimamanda Adichie argues that it is wholly impossible to define a state, a society, or even an individual with "a single story." Whether one's aim is to characterize an entire civilization or a single person, she observes, to focus only on one type of story is to flatten its existence, to shun nuance in favor of stereotype. She continues, "The problem with stereotypes is not that they are untrue, but that they are incomplete. They make one story become the only story."[1] Adichie eloquently critiques oversimplified, shallow stereotypes of Africa as impoverished at the expense of all else. Yes, there is crushing poverty in Africa, and there is ignorance and violence, but there is also beauty, opulence, kindness, and much, much more.

Adichie's passionate and humorous lesson is in harmony with the central thesis of this book. Words such as *isolation* and *decline* have been used too often and too easily to define early modern Central Asia, and efforts to achieve an improved understanding of the region's history have suffered as a result. There is abundant evidence demonstrating that in the eighteenth century the Bukharan Khanate suffered a severe crisis that was character-

---

1. Chimamanda Adichie, "The Danger of a Single Story," at TEDGlobal, July 2009, http://www.ted.com/talks/chimamanda_adichie_the_danger_of_a_single_story.html.

ized by a decline in its military strength vis-à-vis its neighbors, a decline in the wealth in its treasury, a decline in its ability to control key elements of its administration, and a decline in its legitimacy in the eyes of its people. But the Bukharan experience as viewed from the capital and those dependent upon it does not define the entire region. Even in the first half of the eighteenth century, Central Asian society as a whole cannot accurately be defined as having been "in decline," and long-standing notions of isolation have done little more than obscure how integrative structures shaped the often tumultuous trajectory of early modern Central Asian history.

At the same time, one must not fall into the trap of assuming that if one position is flawed, then the opposite is true. Words such as *vitality* and *renaissance* can be no less misleading when not used with precision. And we have also seen that integrative structures such as those I have drawn attention to throughout this book can provide desirable opportunities for some and unleash harsh realities on others. My objective here is not to replace one overly simplistic historical vision with another. Rather, I argue that directing attention to patterns of historical integration can produce a more nuanced and accurate portrait of early modern Central Asia. For Central Asia specialists, such an approach has the potential to guide us to important new research questions and broadcast our conclusions to a broader scholarly audience, drawing desirable attention to a somewhat marginalized field and adding a critical counterpoint to the narratives of Qing and Russian imperial expansion into the region.

This book has examined multiple ways that Central Asia was connected to the early modern globalizing world, illustrating how Central Asians themselves were sensitive to a number of distinctively early modern processes and also how larger historical trends, even those invisible to people living through them, converged to shape the motivations, objectives, and worldviews of local actors. Again, I do not suggest that a global perspective can take the place of deep "vertical" research in historical sources, and my aim here is not to "demonize philology."[2] The philological skills that enable researchers to extract knowledge from difficult-to-access sources are often at the core of solid historical research. The discussions here have aimed to demonstrate that a connected histories methodology and a global perspec-

---

2. Paolo Sartori, "¡Viva La Filología! Or, the Freedom of Critical Thinking," *Ab Imperio* 3 (2018): 427–35. Literally a "love of knowledge," philology is in practice a critical methodology applied to extract knowledge, or "textualized meaning," from historical texts. For an insightful essay on the value of philological methods, see Sheldon Pollock, "Future Philology? The Fate of a Soft Science in a Hard World," *Critical Inquiry* 35 (2009): 931–61.

tive can place that knowledge in a more complete historical context and add valuable insights that make that knowledge more meaningful.

This book began with a discussion of early modernity that identified a number of historical processes that had a profound and lasting impact on societies across the globe. These include (but are not limited to): a general increase in the long-distance mobility of people; the expansion of Iberian colonial powers in the Americas, the sustained extraction of thousands of tons of gold and silver from those Iberian colonies, and the circulation of that specie across the globe; the transatlantic movement of crops, animals, peoples, and diseases, which revolutionized agricultural production, health and nutrition, and regional demographics; population growth and urbanization; the expansion of plantation-style farming for raw material production; technological and scientific innovations that revolutionized economic, military, and political models; and widespread commercialization, spurred by the circulation of specie and a dramatic increase in maritime mobility. To cite Joseph Fletcher once more: "To find the interconnections and horizontal continuities of early modern history, one must look underneath the surface of political and institutional history and examine developments in the economics, societies, and cultures of the early modern world."[3]

The example one finds in popular understandings of the Silk Road is a case in point. Following a survey of the Bukharan crisis, this book aimed to demonstrate how poorly informed, overly malleable, and often Sinocentric understandings of the so-called Silk Road trade—notions that are grounded in Orientalist literature of a century ago—collapse under the weight of more recent evidence-based analyses. The study of Central Asian history has long suffered from the assumption that, however imagined, at one point or another the Silk Road trade collapsed and sent the region into isolation on "the margins of world history."

Far from signaling an end to Central Asia's role in the mediation of overland Eurasian trade, recent studies support the conclusion that, in economic terms, early modern Central Asians experienced more continuity than change. Trade in silks and some other merchandise diminished, but demand for cotton, tea, and other commodities increased, and they flowed into, and through, regional markets. Foreign demand for horses and other livestock bred in the steppe increased and remained substantial even into the twentieth century. Meanwhile, Indian, Chinese, Russian, and other merchant groups extended their commercial interests deep into the region. And even during the first half of the eighteenth century, Central Asians themselves

---

3. Fletcher, "Integrative History," 38.

were anything but passive. Chapter three identifies two distinct Central Asian merchant networks—the Bukharans and Andijanis—both of which involved thousands of merchants orchestrating an extensive transit-trade in a wide variety of commodities that passed through the region. Recalling the Sogdian merchants of antiquity, the Bukharan and Andijani networks linked Central Asian markets with the larger economies of the sedentary civilizations on the Eurasian periphery. In the field of Indian Ocean history, new work points to a multiplicity of ways that merchant groups linked the maritime world with the hinterland. For Central Asians, too, the evidence suggests that the overall trajectory was one of growth and further integration into the early modern globalizing economy.

This is an important point, but it does not change the fact that, in the first half of the eighteenth century, the Bukharan Khanate plunged into a severe crisis that culminated in revolution and the collapse of Chinggisid authority in the region. Recent scholarship on this period of Central Asian history has made considerable headway in describing this crisis. The discussion in chapter four aims to identify a number of factors that actually caused it, explain why they converged when they did, and illustrate how events in the middle of the century enabled local powers to emerge from the crisis and enter a new era.

This discussion has endeavored to explain, for example, why Central Asian armies resisted the widespread implementation of gunpowder weaponry even as those weapons gradually eroded the nomadic military advantage. Whereas the Ottoman and Mughal militaries invested heavily in incorporating this technology in ways that suited their own particular environments, the Safavid and Uzbek militaries favored their faster and more flexible cavalry over more expensive, slower, and burdensome infantry-based artillery forces. The reasons for their resistance may in part have stemmed from a deep-seated cultural preference for the prestige associated with nomadic warfare and a disdain for the lack of skill required to operate the comparatively slow, imprecise, unreliable, and expensive early muskets. But considered in practical terms, the ecological realities of Central Asia emerge as the most important factor in understanding why, even into the eighteenth century, Central Asians favored cavalry over infantry: Central Asian states had a comparatively small agrarian tax base from which to finance military reform; they had a smaller population from which to build an infantry force to use this unreliable and expensive weaponry; they had access to large numbers of horses; their cavalry soldiers were exceptionally well trained and effective in their use of their superior traditional weaponry; and they had long been able to exploit those skills to great effect against their sedentary neighbors. But as gunpowder weapons technologies improved, especially following the widespread implementation of the flintlock musket from the late seventeenth century, the military advantage permanently shifted in favor of the much larger (if less well-trained) infantry armies. Bukharan efforts to reform its military met with resistance from the Uzbek amirs, and that contributed to the ongoing process of decentralization. In the first half of the eighteenth century, the Bukharan military was at a severe disadvantage vis-à-vis its neighbors, including the newly reformed armies of Nadir Shah in Iran.

Environmental factors add another dimension of understanding to these events. In recent decades, environmental historians have made great progress in exploring how the global climate crisis of the seventeenth-century Little Ice Age affected various types of societies across the globe. As less solar radiation reached the Earth, the planet cooled and weather patterns became erratic. This resulted in a shorter growing season, periods of unseasonably cold weather in much of the Northern Hemisphere that brought late frosts in the spring and early frosts in the fall, failed monsoons and widespread drought in some places, and severe flooding in others. Especially in the middle of the century, the environmental crisis was exacerbated by a high rate of volcanic eruptions spewing millions of tons of toxic ash into the atmosphere, where it veiled the planet from much-needed solar radiation.

Whether the fields were flooded, parched, or killed by frost, the end result was the same: failed harvests, famine, warfare, and revolution. The more densely populated agrarian states on the Eurasian periphery suffered the most, but nomadic and sedentary populations in Central Asia were not immune. The leadership of both the Shibanid and Toqay-Timurid dynastic families had long governed their state through the fundamentally decentralized appanage system. Over the course of the seventeenth century, this environmental crisis helped to drive the Bukharan Khanate deeper into a decentralizing trend. Climatic patterns at last returned to normal in the early decades of the eighteenth century, but that brought no reprieve to the Bukharans. Rather than recovery, the Bukharan crisis deepened, then became critical.

Exploring this from an economic perspective, one finds evidence that Central Asian merchant groups were eager to exploit newly emerging opportunities throughout this period, but that economic integration also carried serious risks. China suffered severely during the seventeenth-century climate crisis. But as Qing markets recovered they exhibited an insatiable thirst for silver, and while Chinese monetary historians have emphasized the absorption of American silver into Chinese markets, there appears to have been an effluence from Central Asian markets as well. Whether Central Asian silver went to China or elsewhere in this period, there was clearly a dearth of it. Numismatic evidence from the early decades of the eighteenth century indicates that Bukharan mints debased the currency until it included barely any silver at all. This fiscal crisis was felt most severely by those dependent upon the Bukharan treasury, including the Uzbek amirs, the core element of the Bukharan military.

The Uzbek amirs, the same group of tribal leaders who had set aside the Shibanids at the end of the sixteenth century and elevated the Toqay-Timurids in their place, had grown progressively more disaffected over the course of the seventeenth century. By the end of that century, the amirs' loyalty to their Chinggisid leadership was supplanted by a new effort to claim permanently the territories that their rulers had earlier assigned to them. Moving into the eighteenth century, as the Bukharan fiscal crisis deepened, the amirs' weakening allegiance to their khan transformed into animosity. 'Ubaydullah Khan and his brother Abu'l Fayz Khan, the last two Toqay-Timurids to rule the Bukharan Khanate, were faced with a severe crisis of legitimacy. But their efforts to use military reform in order to achieve greater control only provoked further resistance. Matters worsened as the Jungar invasions of Kazakh territories propelled the Kazakh Barefooted Flight into Bukharan territory in 1723 and Persian armies invaded in 1737 and again in 1740.

A sudden and dramatic increase in the circulation of erstwhile Mughal silver in Central Asian markets began to ease the fiscal crisis soon after Nadir Shah's second invasion, but the economic recovery was too late to be of any benefit to Abu'l Fayz Khan. After more than half a century spent struggling against the Uzbek tribal leadership, the Bukharan khans had long since lost any legitimacy that they could claim from their Chinggisid bloodline. When news of Nadir Shah's death reached Bukhara in 1747, the Manghit tribal leadership resolved to bring an end to the facade of Toqay-Timurid rule. Abu'l Fayz Khan was executed, his line was terminated, and executive authority shifted to the Manghit tribal leader Muhammad Rahim Bey, the son of Abu'l Fayz Khan's former ataliq, Muhammad Hakim Bey. Although the Manghit retained puppet Chinggisids until 1785, the transition of 1747 effectively marked the end of the Bukharan Khanate and the beginning of the Bukharan Amirate.

The Bukharan crisis was severe, exceptionally so in some places and at certain times. But one must also question both its uniformity and its extent. For eighteenth-century Central Asia, the crisis is not the only story. Even as the Bukharan Khanate teetered, Bukharan merchants continued to run caravans to Siberia, expanding their networks in the Russian Empire and even making their way to Kiakhta. And within the region, Bukharan control over the Ferghana Valley had come to an end already in the late seventeenth century. During the first half of the eighteenth century, the population of the valley was largely unaffected by the crisis. Free from Bukharan control, the Uzbek Ming emerged as a dominant power in the central and western portions of the valley, they managed to repel the Jungars, and, as the Bukharan Khanate collapsed, they assembled the foundations for what would eventually become the Khanate of Khoqand: a new Central Asian polity that would emerge, flourish, and then collapse on the frontier of imperial powers expanding into the region.

BIBLIOGRAPHY

PRIMARY SOURCES

Abdurrakhman-i Tali'. *Istoriia Abulfaiz-khana*. Translated by A. A. Semenov. Tashkent: Akademiia nauk Uzbekskoi SSR, 1959.

Abul Fazl Allami. *The Ain-i Akbari*. 3 vols. Translated by H. Blochmann. 2nd ed. Delhi, 1997.

Antonova, K. A., and N. M. Gol'dberg, eds. *Russko-indiiskie otnosheniia v XVIII v., sbornik dokumentov*. Moscow: Nauka, 1965.

Antonova, K. A., N. M. Gol'dberg, and T. D. Lavrentsova, eds. *Russko-indiiskie otnosheniia v XVII v., sbornik dokumentov*. Moscow: Nauka, 1958.

Beneveni, Florio. *Poslannik Petra i na Vostoke. Posol'stvo Florio Beneveni v Persiyu i Bukharu v 1718–1725 godakh*. Edited by N. A. Khalfin. Moscow: Nauka, 1986.

Bernier, Francois. *Travels in the Mogul Empire, AD 1656–1668*. Translated by Irving Brock and edited by Archibald Constable. Westminster: Constable and Co., 1891.

Chekhovich, O. D., and A. K. Arends. *Dokumenty k istorii agrarnykh otnoshenii v bukharskom khansve XVII–XIX vv*. Tashkent: Fan, 1954.

Coote, Charles Henry, and Edward Delmar Morgan. *Early Voyages and Travels to Russia and Persia by Anthony Jenkinson and other Englishmen, with Some Account of the First Intercourse of the English with Russia and Central Asia by Way of the Caspian Sea*. 2 vols., 1st ser., nos. 72–73. London: Hakluyt Society, 1886.

de Thévenot, Jean. *The Travels of Monsieur de Thevenot, the Third Part, Containing the Relations of Indostan, the New Moguls, and of Other People and Countries of the Indies*. Translated by Archibald Lovell. London: H. Faithorne, 1687.

du Mans, Raphaël. *Estat de la Perse en 1660*. Paris: Ernest Leroux, 1890.

Georgi, Johann Gottlieb. *Russia: Or, a Compleat Historical Account of All the Nations Which Compose That Empire*. 4 vols. London: J. Nichols, 1780.

Ibn Battuta. *The Travels of Ibn Battuta, A.D. 1325–1354*. 3 vols. Translated by H. A. R. Gibb. New Delhi: Munshiram Manoharlal, 1993 (1929).

Islam, Riazul. *A Calendar of Documents on Indo-Persian Relations (1500–1750)*. 2 vols. Tehran: Iranian Culture Foundation, 1982.

Ivanov, P. P. *Iz arkhiva sheikhov dzhuibari: Materialy po zemel'nym i torgovym otnosheniiam Srednei Azii XVI veka*. Moscow: Nauka, 1938–1954.

Mansura Haidar, ed. *Mukātabāt-i-'Allāmī (Inshā'i Abu'l Fazl), Daftar 1*. New Delhi: Munshiram Manoharlal, 1998.

Manucci, Niccolao. *Storia do Mogor, or Mogul India 1653–1708.* 4 vols. Translated by W. Irvine. London: J. Murray, 1907–1908.
Mirakshah Munshi, Mullah Zahid Munshi, and Muhammad Tahir Wahid, comps. *Maktubat munsha'at manshurat.* Institut Vostokovedeniia Akademii Nauk, Uzbekistan, Ms. No. 289.
Muḥammad Kāẓim Marvi. *'Ālam ārā-yi Nādirī.* Vol. 2. Tehran: Kitābfurūshī-i Zavvār, 1985.
Muḥammad Yusuf Munshi bin Khwaja Baqa. *Tadhkira-i Muqīm Khānī.* Institut Vostokovedeniia Akademii Nauk, Uzbekistan, Ms. No. 609/II. Published in Russian as *Mukimkhanskaia istoriia.* Translated by A. A. Semenov. Tashkent: Nauka, 1956.
Munis, Shir Muhammad Mirab, and Muhammad Riza Mirab Agahi. *Firdaws al-Iqbāl*: History of Khorezm. Translated and annotated by Yuri Bregel. Leiden: E. J. Brill, 1988.
Tasmagambetov, I. N., ed. *Istoriia Kazakhstana v Russkikh Istochnikakh XVI–XX vv.* Vol. 2. Almaty: Dayk-Press, 2005.
Tavernier, Jean Baptiste. *Les six voyages de Jean Baptiste Tavernier, Ecuyer Baron d'Aubonne, en Turquie, en Perse, et aux Indes: Pendant l'espace de quarante ans, & par toutes les routes que l'on peut tenir, accompagnez d'observations particulieres sur la qualité, la religion, le gouvernement, les coûtumes & le commerce de chaque païs; avec les figures, le poids, & la valeur des monnoyes qui y ont cours.* 2 vols. Utrecht: Guillaume and Jacob Poolsum, 1712.
Tavernier, Jean Baptiste. *Travels in India.* 2nd ed. 2 vols. Edited by William Crooke and translated by V. Ball. 1676. Reprint. New Delhi: Munshiram Manoharlal, 1995.
Teissier, Beatrice, ed. *Into the Kazakh Steppe: John Castle's Mission to Khan Abulkhayir (1736).* Oxford: Signal Books, 2011.
Witsen, N. *Noord en Oost Tartarye, ofte bondig ontwerp van eenige dier landen en volken, welke voormaels bekent zijn geweest: Beneffens verscheide tot noch toe onbekende, en meest nooit voorheen beschreve Tartersche en naaburige gewesten, landstreeken, steden, rivieren, en plaetzen, in de Noorder.* 2nd edition. Amsterdam: François Halma, 1705. Reprinted in 1785.
Zahir al-Din Muhammad Babur. *The Bábar-náma: Being the Autobiography of the Emperor Bábar, the Founder of the Moghul Dynasty in India.* Facsimile of the Hyderabad manuscript. Edited by Annette S. Beveridge. E. J. W. Gibb Memorial Series, 1. London: Luzac and Co., 1905. Reissue, 1971.
Zahir al-Din Muhammad Babur. *Baburnama: Memoirs of Babur.* Edited and translated by Annette Beveridge. London: Luzac and Co., 1921.
Zahir al-Din Muhammad Babur. *The Baburnama: Memoirs of Babur, Prince and Emperor.* Translated by Wheeler M. Thackston. New York: Modern Library, 2002.

SECONDARY SOURCES

Abazov, Rafis. *The Palgrave Concise Historical Atlas of Central Asia.* New York: Palgrave Macmillan, 2008.

Abu Lughod, Janet. *Before European Hegemony: The World System A.D. 1250–1350*. New York: Oxford University Press, 1991.

Adichie, Chimamanda. "The Danger of a Single Story." TEDGlobal, July 2009, http://www.ted.com/talks/chimamanda_adichie_the_danger_of_a_single_story.html.

Adshead, S. A. M. *Central Asia in World History*. London: Macmillan, 1993.

Ágoston, Gábor. *Guns for the Sultan: Military Power and the Weapons Industry in the Ottoman Empire*. Cambridge: Cambridge University Press, 2005.

Akhmedov, B. A. *Iz istorii Srednei azii i vostochnogo Turkestana, XV–XIX vv*. Tashkent: Fan, 1987.

Aksenov, A. I., et al. *Ekonomicheskaia istoriia Rossii*. Vol. 1. Moscow: Rosspen, 2009.

Alam, Muzaffar. *The Crisis of Empire in Mughal North India, 1707–1748*. Oxford: Oxford University Press, 1986.

Alam, Muzaffar. "Trade, State Policy and Regional Change: Aspects of Mughal-Uzbek Commercial Relations, c. 1550–1750." *Journal of the Economic and Social History of the Orient* 37, no. 3 (August 1994): 202–27.

Alam, Muzaffar, and Sanjay Subrahmanyam. *Indo-Persian Travels in the Age of Discoveries, 1400–1800*. Cambridge: Cambridge University Press, 2007.

Alimova, D. A., ed. *Istoriia Uzbekistana (XVI–pervaia polovina XIX v.)*. Tashkent: Fan, 2012.

Allsen, Thomas T. *Commodity and Exchange in the Mongol Empire: A Cultural History of Islamic Textiles*. Cambridge: Cambridge University Press, 2002.

Amanat, Abbas. *Iran: A New History*. New Haven: Yale University Press, 2017.

Amitai, Reuven, and Michal Biran, eds. *Nomads as Agents of Cultural Change: The Mongols and Their Eurasian Predecessors*. Honolulu: University of Hawai'i Press, 2015.

Anthony, David W. *The Horse, the Wheel, and Language: How Bronze-Age Riders from the Eurasian Steppes Shaped the Modern World*. Princeton: Princeton University Press, 2007.

Askarov, A. A., ed. *Istoriia Uzbekistana*. Vol. 3, *XVI–pervaia polovina XIX veka*. Tashkent: Fan, 1993.

Aslanian, Sebouh David. "From Autonomous to Interactive Histories: World History's Challenge to Armenian Studies." In *An Armenian Mediterranean: Worlds and Worlds in Motion*, edited by Kathryn Babayan and Michael Pifer, 83–132. London: Palgrave, 2018.

Aslanian, Sebouh David. *From the Indian Ocean to the Mediterranean: The Global Trade Networks of Armenian Merchants from New Julfa*. Berkeley: University of California Press, 2011.

Aslanian, Sebouh David. "Une vie sur plusieurs continents: Microhistoire globale d'un agent arménien de la Compagnie des Indes orientales (1666–1688)." *Annales: Histoire, Science Sociales* 73 no. 1 (2018/2019): 19–56.

Atwell, William S. "Another Look at Silver Imports into China, c. 1635–1644." *Journal of World History* 16, no. 4 (2006): 467–89.

Atwell, William S. "A Seventeenth-Century 'General Crisis' in East Asian History?" *Modern Asian Studies* 24, no. 4 (1990): 661–82.

Atwell, William S. "Some Observations on the 'Seventeenth-Century Crisis' in China and Japan." *Journal of Asian Studies* 45, no. 2 (1986): 223–44.

Axworthy, Michael. *The Sword of Persia: Nader Shah, from Tribal Warrior to Conquering Tyrant*. London: I. B. Tauris, 2006.

Azadaev, F. *Tashkent vo vtoroi polovinie XIX veka*. Tashkent: Nauk, 1959.

Balabanlilar, Lisa. *Imperial Identity in the Mughal Empire: Memory and Dynastic Politics in Early Modern South and Central Asia*. London: I. B. Taurus, 2012.

Balabanlilar, Lisa. "Lords of the Auspicious Conjunction: Turco-Mongol Imperial Identity on the Subcontinent." *Journal of World History* 18, no. 1 (2007): 1–39.

Barfield, Thomas. *The Nomadic Alternative*. Englewood Cliffs, NJ: Prentice-Hall, 1993.

Barisitz, Stephan. *Central Asia and the Silk Road: Economic Rise and Decline over Several Millennia*. Vienna: Springer, 2017.

Barnett, Richard. *North India between Empires*. Berkeley: University of California Press, 1980.

Bartold, V. V. *Four Studies on the History of Central Asia*. Vol. 1, *A Short History of Turkestan*. Translated by V. and T. Minorsky. Leiden: E. J. Brill, 1956.

Bartold, V. V. "K istorii orosheniia Turkestana." In V. V. Bartold, *Sochineniia*, vol. 3, 97–233. Moscow: Nauka, 1965.

Bayly, C. A. "'Archaic' and 'Modern' Globalization in the Eurasian-African Arena." In *Globalization in World History*, edited by A. G. Hopkins, 47–93. London: Pimlico Press, 2009.

Bayly, C. A. *Rulers, Townsmen and Bazaars: North Indian Society in the Age of British Expansion, 1770–1870*. Cambridge: Cambridge University Press, 1983.

Becker, Seymour. *Russia's Protectorates in Central Asia: Bukhara and Khiva, 1865–1924*. Cambridge, MA: Harvard University Press, 1968.

Beckert, Sven. *Empire of Cotton: A Global History*. New York: Vintage Books, 2014.

Beckwith, Christopher I. *Empires of the Silk Road: A History of Central Eurasia from the Bronze Age to the Present*. Princeton: Princeton University Press, 2009.

Beisembiev, Timur K. *Kokandskaiia istoriografiia: Issledovaniie po istochnikovedeniiu Srednei Azii XVIII–XIX vekov*. Almaty: TOO Print-S, 2009.

Beisembiev, Timur K. "Migration in the Qöqand Khanate in Eighteenth and Nineteenth Centuries." In *Migration in Central Asia: Its History and Current Problems*, edited by Hisao Komatsu, Chika Obiya, and John S. Schoeberlein, 35–40. Osaka: Japan Center for Asian Studies, 2000.

Beisembiev, Timur K., and Scott C. Levi. "Kokand Khanate." *Encyclopaedia Iranica*, forthcoming.

Blanchard, Ian. *Russia's 'Age of Silver': Precious-Metal Production and Economic Growth in the Eighteenth Century*. London: Routledge, 1989.

Boomer, Ian, Bernd Wünnemann, Anson W. Mackay, Phillip A. Austin, Philippe Sorrel, Christian Reinhardt, Dietmar Keyser, François Guichard, and Michel Fontugne. "Advances in Understanding the Late Holocene History of the Aral Sea Region." *Quaternary International* 194 (2009): 79–90.

Bosworth, Clifford Edmund. *The New Islamic Dynasties: A Chronological and Genealogical Manual*. New York: Columbia University Press, 1996.

Boulnois, Luce. *Silk Road: Monks, Warriors and Merchants on the Silk Road*. Translated by Helen Loveday. Hong Kong: Odyssey, 2005.

Bregel, Yuri. "Barthold and Modern Oriental Studies." *International Journal of Middle East Studies* 12, no. 3 (1980): 385–403.

Bregel, Yuri. "Central Asia in the 12th–13th/18th–19th Centuries." *Encyclopaedia Iranica* V/2, 1992, 193–205, http://www.iranicaonline.org/articles/central-asia-vii.

Bregel, Yuri. *An Historical Atlas of Central Asia.* Leiden: E. J. Brill, 2003.

Bregel, Yuri. "The New Uzbek States: Bukhara Khiva and Khoqand: c. 1750–1886." In *The Cambridge History of Inner Asia: The Chinggisid Age,* edited by Nicola di Cosmo, Allen J. Frank, and Peter B. Golden, 392–411. Cambridge: Cambridge University Press, 2009.

Bregel, Yuri. "Tribal Tradition and Dynastic History: The Early Rulers of the Qongrats According to Munis." *Asian and African Studies* 16, no. 3 (1982): 357–98.

Bregel, Yuri. "Turko-Mongol Influences in Central Asia." In *Turko-Persia in Historical Perspective,* edited by Robert L. Canfield, 53–77. Cambridge: Cambridge University Press, 1991.

Breyfogle, Nicholas, ed. *Eurasian Environments: Nature and Ecology in Russian and Soviet History.* Pittsburgh: University of Pittsburgh Press, 2018.

Brook, Timothy. *The Troubled Empire: China in the Yuan and Ming Dynasties.* Cambridge, MA: Belknap Press, 2010.

Brooke, John L. *Climate Change and the Course of Global History: A Rough Journey.* Cambridge: Cambridge University Press, 2014.

Brooke, John L., and Henry Misa. "Earth, Water, Air, and Fire: Toward an Ecological History of Premodern Inner Eurasia." *Oxford Research Encyclopedia of Asian History,* forthcoming.

Brower, Daniel. *Turkestan and the Fate of the Russian Empire.* London: RoutledgeCurzon, 2003.

Brown, Kendall W. *A History of Mining in Latin America: From the Colonial Era to the Present.* Albuquerque: University of New Mexico Press, 2012.

Burton, Audrey. "Bukharan Trade, 1558–1718." Papers on Inner Asia, no. 23. Bloomington: Indiana University Research Institute for Inner Asian Studies, 1993.

Burton, Audrey. *The Bukharans: A Dynastic, Diplomatic and Commercial History, 1550–1702.* New York: St. Martin's Press, 1997.

Cahun, David-Léon. *Introduction à l'histoire de l'Asie: Turcs et Mongols, des origins à 1405.* Paris: A. Colin, 1896.

Cameron, Sarah. *The Hungry Steppe: Famine, Violence, and the Making of Soviet Kazakhstan.* Ithaca: Cornell University Press, 2018.

Campbell, Ian W. *Knowledge and the Ends of Empire: Kazakh Intermediaries and Russian Rule on the Steppe, 1731–1917.* Ithaca: Cornell University Press, 2017.

Campbell, Ian W. "The Scourge of Stock Raising: Zhŭt, Limiting Environments, and the Economic Transformation of the Kazakh Steppe." In *Eurasian Environments: Nature and Ecology in Russian and Soviet History,* edited by Nicholas Breyfogle, 60–74. Pittsburgh: University of Pittsburgh Press, 2018.

Chase, Kenneth. *Firearms: A Global History to 1700.* Cambridge: Cambridge University Press, 2003.

Chaudhury, Sushil, and Michel Morineau, eds. *Merchants, Companies and Trade: Europe and Asia in the Early Modern Era.* Cambridge: Cambridge University Press, 1999.

Chekhovich, Ol'ga. "O nekotorykh voprosakh istorii Srednei Azii XVIII–XIX vekov." *Voprosy istorii* 3 (1956): 84–95.

Chen, Fa-Hu, Jianhui Chen, Jonathan A. Holmes, Ian Boomer, Patrick Austin, John Boatner Gates, Ning-lian Wang, Stephen J. Brooks, and Jiawu Zhang. "Moisture Changes over the Last Millennium in Arid Central Asia: A Review, Synthesis and Comparison with Monsoon Region." *Quaternary Science Reviews* 29 (2010): 1055–68.

Chin, Tamara. "The Invention of the Silk Road, 1877." *Critical Inquiry* 40, no. 1 (2013): 194–219.

Christian, David. "Silk Roads or Steppe Roads? The Silk Roads in World History." *Journal of World History* 11, no. 1 (2000): 1–26.

Ciocîltan, Virgil. *The Mongols and the Black Sea Trade in the Thirteenth and Fourteenth Centuries*. Translated by Samuel Willcocks. Leiden: E. J. Brill, 2012.

Crews, Robert D. *Afghan Modern: The History of a Global Nation*. Cambridge, MA: Harvard University Press, 2015.

Cronon, William. *Nature's Metropolis: Chicago and the Great West*. New York: W. W. Norton, 1991.

Cushman, Gregory. Review of *Global Crisis: War, Climate Change and Catastrophe in the Seventeenth Century*, by Geoffrey Parker. *American Historical Review* 120, no. 4 (2015): 1429–31.

Dale, Stephen F. *Babur: Timurid Prince and Mughal Emperor, 1483–1530*. Cambridge: Cambridge University Press, 2018.

Dale, Stephen F. *Indian Merchants and Eurasian Trade, 1600–1750*. Cambridge: Cambridge University Press, 1994.

Dale, Stephen F. "The Legacy of the Timurids." *Journal of the Royal Asiatic Society*, 3rd ser., 8, no. 1 (1998): 43–58.

Dale, Stephen F. *The Muslim Empires of the Ottomans, Safavids, and Mughals*. Cambridge: Cambridge University Press, 2010.

David-Fox, Michael, Peter Holquist, and Alexander Martin, eds. *Orientalism and Empire in Russia*. Bloomington, IN: Slavica, 2006.

Davidovich, E. A. *Istoriia monetnogo dela Srednei Azii XVII–XVIII vv. (zolotiie i serebranie moneti Dzhanidov)*. Dushanbe: Akademiia Nauk Tadzhikskoi SSR, 1964.

Davies, Brian L. *Warfare, State and Society on the Black Sea Steppe, 1500–1700*. London: Routledge, 2007.

Davis, Donald R. "Three Principles for an Asian Humanities: Care First . . . Learn from . . . Connect Histories." *Journal of Asian Studies* 74, no. 1 (2015): 43–67.

de la Vaissière, Étienne. *Histoire des marchands Sogdiens*. Paris: Collège France, Institute des Hautes Études Chinois, 2004. See also the English translation, *Sogdian Traders: A History*. Translated by James Ward. Leiden: E. J. Brill, 2005.

de la Vaissière, Étienne. "Trans-Asian Trade, or the Silk Road Deconstructed (Antiquity, Middle Ages)." In *The Cambridge History of Capitalism*, edited by Larry Neal and Jeffrey G. Williamson, 101–24. Cambridge: Cambridge University Press, 2014.

De Vries, Jan. "The Limits of Globalization in the Early Modern World." *Economic History Review* 63, no. 3 (2010): 710–33.

DeWeese, Devin. *Islamization and Native Religion in the Golden Horde: Baba Tükles and Conversion to Islam in Historical and Epic Tradition*. University Park: Penn State University Press, 1994.

DeWeese, Devin. "Muslim Medical Culture in Modern Central Asia: A Brief Note on Manuscript Sources from the Sixteenth to Twentieth Centuries." *Central Asian Survey* 32, no. 1 (2013): 3–18.

DeWeese, Devin. Review of *Lost Enlightenment: Central Asia's Golden Age from the Arab Conquest to Tamerlane*, by Frederick Starr. *Journal of Interdisciplinary History* 45, no. 4 (2015): 611–13.

Di Cosmo, Nicola. "State Formation and Periodization in Inner Asian History." *Journal of World History* 10 (1999): 1–40.

Di Cosmo, Nicola, ed. *Warfare in Inner Asian History (500–1800)*. Leiden: E. J. Brill, 2001.

Di Cosmo, Nicola. "Why Qara Qorum? Climate and Geography in the Early Mongol Empire." *Archivum Eurasiae Medii Aevi* 21 (2014–2015): 67–78.

Di Cosmo, Nicola, Allen J. Frank, and Peter B. Golden, eds. *The Cambridge History of Inner Asia: The Chinggisid Age*. Cambridge: Cambridge University Press, 2009.

Dunning, Chester S. L. *Russia's First Civil War: The Time of Troubles and the Founding of the Romanov Dynasty*. University Park: Penn State University Press, 2001.

Eaton, Richard M., and Philip B. Wagoner. *Power, Memory, Architecture: Contested Sites on India's Deccan Plateau, 1300–1600*. Oxford: Oxford University Press, 2014.

Eaton, Richard M., and Philip B. Wagoner. "Warfare on the Deccan Plateau, 1450–1600: A Military Revolution in Early Modern India?" *Journal of World History* 25, no. 1 (2014): 5–50.

Eaton, Richard M., and Ramya Sreenivasan, eds. *The Oxford Handbook of the Mughal World*. Oxford: Oxford University Press, forthcoming.

Eden, Jeff. "Beyond the Bazaars: Geographies of the Slave Trade in Central Asia." *Modern Asian Studies* 51, no. 4 (2017): 919–55.

Eden, Jeff. *Slavery and Empire in Central Asia*. Cambridge: Cambridge University Press, 2018.

Esper, Jan, Fritz H. Schweingruber, and Matthias Winiger. "1300 Years of Climatic History for Western Central Asia Inferred from Tree-Rings." *Holocene* 12, no. 3 (2002): 267–77.

Fagan, Brian. *The Little Ice Age: How Climate Made History, 1300–1850*. New York: Basic Books, 2000.

Faroqhi, Suraiya. "Crisis and Change, 1590–1699." In *An Economic and Social History of the Ottoman Empire*, edited by Halil Inalcik and Donald Quataert, vol. 1, 411–636. New York: Cambridge University Press, 1994.

Findlen, Paula, ed. *Early Modern Things: Objects and their Histories, 1500–1800*. London: Routledge, 2013.

Findley, Carter. *The Turks in World History*. Cambridge: Cambridge University Press, 2006.

Fleischer, Cornell. *Bureaucrat and Intellectual in the Ottoman Empire: The Historian Mustafa Ali (1541–1600)*. Princeton: Princeton University Press, 1986.

Fletcher, Joseph. "China and Central Asia 1368–1884." In *The Chinese World Order*, edited by John King Fairbank, 206–24, 337–68. Cambridge, MA: Harvard University Press, 1968.

Fletcher, Joseph. "Integrative History: Parallels and Interconnections in the Early Modern Period, 1500–1800." *Journal of Turkish Studies* 9 (1985): 37–57.

Fletcher, Joseph. "The Mongols: Ecological and Social Perspectives." *Harvard Journal of Asiatic Studies* 46, no. 1 (1986): 11–50.

Floor, Willem. *The Economy of Safavid Persia*. Wiesbaden: Dr. Ludwig Reichert, 2001.

Floor, Willem, and Edmund Herzig, eds. *Iran and the World in the Safavid Age*. London: I. B. Tauris, 2012.

Flynn, Dennis O., and Arturo Giráldez. "Born with a 'Silver Spoon': The Origins of World Trade in 1571." *Journal of World History* 6, no. 2 (1995): 201–21.

Flynn, Dennis O., and Arturo Giráldez. "Cycles of Silver: Global Economic Unity through the Mid-Eighteenth Century." *Journal of World History* 13, no. 2 (2000): 391–428.

Flynn, Dennis O., Arturo Giráldez, and Richard von Glahn, eds. *Global Connections and Monetary History, 1470–1800*. Aldershot: Ashgate, 2003.

Fohlmeister, Jens, Birgit Plessen, Alexey Sergeevich Dudashvili, Rik Tjallingii, Christian Wolff, Abror Gafurov, and Hai Cheng. "Winter Precipitation Changes during the Medieval Climate Anomaly and the Little Ice Age in Arid Central Asia." *Quaternary Science Reviews* 178 (2017): 24–36.

Foltz, Richard. "The Mughal Occupation of Balkh, 1646–1647." *Journal of Islamic Studies* 7, no. 1 (1996): 49–61.

Foltz, Richard C. *Religions of the Silk Road: Overland Trade and Cultural Exchange from Antiquity to the Fifteenth Century*. New York: St. Martin's Press, 1999.

Frank, Allen J. *Bukhara and the Muslims of Russia: Sufism, Education, and the Paradox of Islamic Prestige*. Leiden: E. J. Brill, 2012.

Frank, Andre Gunder. *ReOrient: Global Economy in the Asian Age*. Berkeley: University of California Press, 1998.

Frankopan, Peter. *The Silk Roads: A New History of the World*. New York: Alfred A. Knopf, 2016.

Gaborieau, Marc, Alexandre Popovic, and Thierry Zarcone, eds. *Naqshbandis: Cheminements et situation actuelle d'un ordre mystique musulman*. Istanbul/Paris: IFEA et Editiones ISIS, 1990.

Gilani, Arifshah C. Sayyid. *Ghalib: His Life and Persian Poetry*. Karachi: Azam Books, 1962.

Golden, Peter B. *Central Asia in World History*. Oxford: Oxford University Press, 2011.

Goldstone, Jack. "New Patterns in Global History." *Cliodynamics: The Journal of Theoretical and Mathematical History* 1, no. 1 (2010): 92–102.

Goldstone, Jack. "The Problem of the 'Early Modern' World." *Journal of the Economic and Social History of the Orient* 41, no. 3 (1998): 249–84.

Goldstone, Jack. *Revolution and Rebellion in the Early Modern World*. Berkeley: University of California Press, 1991.

Gommans, Jos. "Mughal India and Central Asia in the Eighteenth Century: An Introduction to a Wider Perspective." *Itinerario* 15, no. 1 (1991): 51–70.

Gommans, Jos. *Mughal Warfare: Indian Frontiers and Highroads to Empire, 1500–1700*. London: Routledge, 2002.

Gommans, Jos. *The Rise of the Indo-Afghan Empire, c. 1710–1780*. Leiden: E. J. Brill, 1995.

Gommans, Jos, and Dirk H. A. Kolff, eds. *Warfare and Weaponry in South Asia, 1000–1800*. New Delhi: Oxford University Press, 2001.

Grafton, Anthony, and Eugene F. Rice Jr. *The Foundations of Early Modern Europe, 1460–1559*. 2nd ed. New York: W. W. Norton, 1994.

Green, Nile, ed. *Writing Travel in Central Asian History*. Bloomington: Indiana University Press, 2014.

Gregorian, Vartan. *The Emergence of Modern Afghanistan*. Stanford: Stanford University Press, 196.

Grewell, J. S. *The Sikhs in the Punjab*. Cambridge: Cambridge University Press, 1990.

Gross, Jo-Ann, and Asom Urunbaev. *The Letters of Khwajah 'Ubayd Allah Ahrar and His Associates*. Leiden: E. J. Brill, 2002.

Grousset, René. *L'Empire des steppes: Atilla, Gengis-Khan, Tamerlan*. Paris: Payot, 1939.

Guha, Sumit. "Rethinking the Economy of Mughal India: Lateral Perspectives." *Journal of the Economic and Social History of the Orient* 58, no. 4 (2015): 532–75.

Guilmartin, John Francis. *Gunpowder and Galleys: Changing Technology and Mediterranean Warfare at Sea in the Sixteenth Century*. 2nd rev. ed. Annapolis, MD: Conway Maritime Press, 2003.

Gurevich, B. P. *Mezhdunarodnye otnosheniia v Tsentral'noi Azii v XVII–pervoi polovine XIX v*. Moscow: Nauka, 1979.

Hancock-Parmer, Michael. "Running until Our Feet Turn White: The Barefooted Flight and Kazakh National Identity." PhD diss., Indiana University, Bloomington, 2017.

Hancock-Parmer, Michael. "The Soviet Study of the Barefooted Flight of the Kazakhs." *Central Asian Survey* 34, no. 3 (2015): 281–95.

Hansen, Valerie. *The Silk Road: A New History*. Oxford: Oxford University Press, 2012.

Hathaway, Jane. "Rewriting Eighteenth-Century Ottoman History." *Mediterranean Historical Review* 19, no. 1 (2004): 29–53.

Hedin, Sven Anders. *Die Siedenstrasse*. Leipzig: F. A. Brockhaus, 1936.

Hildinger, Erik. *Warriors of the Steppe: A Military History of Central Asia, 500 B.C. to 1700 A.D.* Cambridge, MA: Da Capo, 1997.

Hodgson, Marshall G. S. *The Venture of Islam: Conscience and History in a World Civilization*. 3 vols. Chicago: University of Chicago Press, 1974.

Holzwarth, Wolfgang. "Bukharan Armies and Uzbek Military Power, 1670–1870: Coping with the Legacy of a Nomadic Conquest." In *Nomad Military Power in Iran and Adjacent Areas in the Islamic Period*, edited by Kurt Franz and Wolfgang Holzwarth, 273–354. Wiesbaden: Dr. Ludwig Reichert Verlag, 2015.

Holzwarth, Wolfgang. "Relations between Uzbek Central Asia, the Great Steppe and Iran, 1700–1750." In *Shifts and Drifts in Nomad-Sedentary Relations*, edited by Stefan Leder and Bernhard Streck, 179–216. Wiesbaden: Dr. Ludwig Reichert Verlag, 2015.

Holzwarth, Wolfgang. "The Uzbek State as Reflected in Eighteenth Century Bukharan Sources." *Asiatische Studien* 60, no. 2 (2006): 321–53.

Hopkirk, Peter. *Foreign Devils on the Silk Road: The Search for the Lost Treasures of Central Asia*. London: John Murray, 1980.

Howard, Douglas A. "Ottoman Historiography and the Literature of 'Decline' of the Sixteenth and Seventeenth Centuries." *Journal of Asian History* 22, no. 1 (1988): 52–77.

Huang, Xiangtong, Hedi Oberhänsli, Hans von Suchodoletz, and Philippe Sorrel. "Dust Deposition in the Aral Sea: Implications for Changes in Atmospheric Circulation in Central Asia during the Past 2000 Years." *Quaternary Science Reviews* 30 (2011): 3661–74.

Inalcik, Halil. "The Socio-Political Effects of the Diffusion of Fire-Arms in the Middle East." In *War, Technology, and Society in the Middle East*, edited by V. J. Parry and M. E. Yapp, 195–217. London: Oxford University Press, 1975.

Inayat, S., and A. Zaidi. "Cavalry Horses in Mughal Army." *Proceedings of the Indian History Congress* 42 (1981): 268–74.

Ismailova, J. Kh., and L. G. Levteieva. *U'zbekiston Harbii San'ati Tarikhi*. Toshkent: U'zbekiston, 2012.

Ivanov, P. P. *Khoziaistvo dzhuibarskikh sheikhov: K istorii feodal'nogo zemlevladeniia v. Srednei Azii v XVI–XVII vv.* Moscow: Nauka, 1954.

Juliano, Annette L., and Judith A. Lerner, eds. *Nomads, Traders and Holy Men Along China's Silk Road*. Turnhout, Belgium: Brepols, 2002.

Kafadar, Cemal. "The Myth of the Golden Age: Ottoman Historical Consciousness in the Post-Süleymânic Era." In *Süleymân the Second and His Time*, edited by Halil Inalcik and Cemal Kafadar, 45–57. Istanbul: Isis Press, 1993.

Kathayat, Gayatri, Hai Cheng, Ashish Sinha, Liang Yi, Xianglei Li, Haiwei Zhang, Hangying Li, Youfeng Ning, and R. Lawrence Edwards. "The Indian Monsoon Variability and Civilization Changes in the Indian Subcontinent." *Science Advances* 3, no. 12 (2017): e1701296.

Kelekna, Pita. *The Horse in Human History*. Cambridge: Cambridge University Press, 2009.

Kelly, P. *The Universal Cambist and Commercial Instructor: Being a Full and Accurate Treatise on the Exchanges, Monies, Weights, and Measures, of all Trading Nations and Their Colonies; an Account of Their Banks, Public Funds, and Paper Currencies*. 2nd ed. Vol. 1. London: Lackington and Co., 1821.

Khazanov, Anatoly M. *Nomads and the Outside World*. Cambridge: Cambridge University Press, 1984.

Khazanov, Anatoly M., and André Wink. *Nomads in the Sedentary World*. Richmond, Surrey: Curzon, 2001.

Khodarkovsky, Michael. *Russia's Steppe Frontier: The Making of a Colonial Empire, 1500–1800*. Bloomington: Indiana University Press, 2002.

Khodarkovsky, Michael. *Where Two Worlds Met: The Russian State and the Kalmyk Nomads, 1600–1771*. Ithaca: Cornell University Press, 1992.

Khoury, Dina Rizk. "The Ottoman Centre versus Provincial Power-Holders: An Analysis of the Historiography. In *Cambridge History of Turkey*, vol. 3, *The Later Ottoman Empire, 1603–1839*, edited by Suraiya N. Faroqhi, 135–56. Cambridge: Cambridge University Press, 2006.

Kim, Kwangmin. *Borderland Capitalism: Turkestan Produce, Qing Silver, and the Birth of an Eastern Market*. Stanford: Stanford University Press, 2016.

Kim, Kwangmin. "Profit and Protection: Emin Khwaja and the Qing Conquest of Central Asia, 1759–1777." *Journal of Asian Studies* 71, no. 3 (2012): 603–26.

Kipling, Rudyard. *Kim.* London: Macmillan, 1901.

Klingaman, William K., and Nicholas P. Klingaman. *The Year without Summer: 1816 and the Volcano That Darkened the World and Changed History.* New York: St. Martin's Press, 2013.

Kočnev, Boris D. "The Last Period of Muslim Coin Minting in Central Asia (18th–Early 20th Century)." In *Muslim Culture in Russia and Central Asia from the 18th to the Early 20th Centuries*, edited by Michael Kemper, Anke von Kügelgen, and Dmitriy Yermakov, vol. 1, 431–44. Berlin: Klaus Schwarz Verlag, 1996.

Kügelgen, Anke von. *Die Legitimierung der mittelasiatischen Mangitendynastie in den Werken ihrer Historiker.* Istanbul: Orient-Institut, 2002.

Lane, Kris. *Potosí: The Silver City That Changed the World.* Berkeley: University of California Press, 2019.

LeDonne, John. "Building an Infrastructure of Empire in Russia's Eastern Theater, 1650s–1840s." *Cahiers du monde russe* 47, no. 3 (2006): 581–608.

Lee, Joo-Yup. Qazaqlïq, *or Ambitious Brigandage, and the Formation of the Qazaqs: State and Identity in Post-Mongol Central Eurasia.* Leiden: E. J. Brill, 2016.

Lee, Wayne E. *Waging War: Conflict, Culture, and Innovation in World History.* Oxford: Oxford University Press, 2016.

Levi, Scott C. "Asia in the Gunpowder Revolution." *Oxford Research Encyclopedia of Asian History*, April 2018, http://asianhistory.oxfordre.com/view/10.1093/acrefore/9780190277727.001.0001/acrefore-9780190277727-e-186.

Levi, Scott C. *Caravans: Indian Merchants on the Silk Road.* Gurgaon: Penguin, 2015.

Levi, Scott C. "Commercial Structures." In *The New Cambridge History of Islam*, vol. 3, *The Eastern Islamic World, 11th–18th Centuries*, edited by D. Morgan and A. Reid, 561–81. Cambridge: Cambridge University Press, 2010.

Levi, Scott C. "Early Modern Central Asia in World History." *History Compass* 10, no. 11 (2012): 866–78.

Levi, Scott C. "The Ferghana Valley at the Crossroads of World History: The Rise of Khoqand, 1709–1822." *Journal of Global History* 2, no. 2 (2007): 213–32.

Levi, Scott C. "Hindus beyond the Hindu Kush: Indians in the Central Asian Slave Trade." *Journal of the Royal Asiatic Society*, 3rd ser., 12, no. 3 (2002): 277–88.

Levi, Scott C., ed. *India and Central Asia: Commerce and Culture, 1500–1800.* Delhi: Oxford University Press, 2005.

Levi, Scott C. "India, Russia and the Eighteenth-Century Transformation of the Central Asian Caravan Trade." *Journal of the Economic and Social History of the Orient* 42, no. 4 (1999): 519–48.

Levi, Scott C. *The Indian Diaspora in Central Asia and Its Trade, 1550–1900.* Leiden: E. J. Brill, 2002.

Levi, Scott C. "Objects in Motion." In *A Companion to World History*, edited by Douglas Northrop, 322–26. Chichester, West Sussex: Wiley-Blackwell, 2012.

Levi, Scott C. *The Rise and Fall of Khoqand, 1709–1876: Central Asia in the Global Age.* Pittsburgh: University of Pittsburgh Press, 2017.

Levi, Scott C., and Ron Sela, eds. *Islamic Central Asia: An Anthology of Historical Sources.* Bloomington: Indiana University Press, 2010.

Li, Narangoa, and Robert Cribb. *Historical Atlas of Northeast Asia, 1590–2010:*

Korea, Manchuria, Mongolia, Eastern Siberia. New York: Columbia University Press, 2014.

Lieberman, Victor. *Strange Parallels*, vol. 1, *Integration on the Mainland*. Cambridge: Cambridge University Press, 2003; vol. 2, *Mainland Mirrors: Europe, Japan, China, South Asia, and the Islands: Southeast Asia in Global Context, c. 800–1830*. Cambridge: Cambridge University Press, 2009.

Lipman, Jonathon, and Beatrice Forbes Manz, eds. *Joseph Fletcher: Studies on Chinese and Islamic Central Asia*. Aldershot: Variorum, 1995.

Liu, Xinru. *The Silk Road in World History*. Oxford: Oxford University Press, 2010.

Liu, Xinru, and Lynda Norene Shaffer. *Connections across Eurasia: Transportation, Communication, and Cultural Exchange on the Silk Roads*. New York: McGraw-Hill, 2007.

Liusternik, E. Ia. *Russko-indiiskie ekonomicheskie sviazi v XIX v*. Moscow: Nauka, 1958.

Lockhart, Laurence. *Nadir Shah: A Critical Study Based Mainly upon Contemporary Sources*. London: Luzac and Co., 1938.

Makeev, D. A. *Rossiisko-vostochnie torgovie sviazi na rubeje Srednevekov'ia i Novogo vremeni (XVI–pervaia chetvert' XVIII veka)*. Vladimir: VIT-print, 2013.

Markovits, Claude. *The Global World of Indian Merchants, 1750–1947: Traders of Sind from Bukhara to Panama*. Cambridge: Cambridge University Press, 2000.

Matthee, Rudi. "Firearms i. History." *Encyclopaedia Iranica* IX/6, 1999, 619–28, http://www.iranicaonline.org/articles/firearms-i-history (accessed April 24, 2018).

Matthee, Rudi. "Mint Consolidation and the Worsening of the Late Safavid Coinage: The Mint of Huwayza." *Journal of the Economic and Social History of the Orient* 44, no. 4 (2001): 505–39.

Matthee, Rudi. *Persia in Crisis: Safavid Decline and the Fall of Isfahan*. London: I. B. Tauris, 2012.

Matthee, Rudi. "Unwalled Cities and Restless Nomads." In *Safavid Persia: The History and Politics of an Islamic Society*, edited by Charles Melville, 389–416. London: I. B. Tauris, 1996.

May, Timothy. *The Mongol Art of War*. Yardley, PA: Westholme, 2007.

May, Timothy. *The Mongol Conquests in World History*. London: Reaktion Books, 2012.

McChesney, Robert D. "The Amīrs of Muslim Central Asia in the XVIIth Century. *Journal of the Economic and Social History of the Orient* 26 (1983): 33–70.

McChesney, Robert D. "'Barrier to Heterodoxy'?: Rethinking the Ties between Iran and Central Asia in the 17th Century." In *Safavid Persia: The History and Politics of an Islamic Society*, edited by Charles Melville, 231–67. London: I. B. Tauris, 1996.

McChesney, Robert D. *Central Asia: Foundations of Change*. Princeton, NJ: Darwin Press, 1996.

McChesney, Robert D. "Central Asia in the 10th–12th/16th–18th Centuries." *Encyclopaedia Iranica* V/2, 1992, 176–93, http://www.iranicaonline.org/articles/central-asia-vi. (accessed April 24, 2018).

McChesney, Robert D. "The Chinggisid Restoration in Central Asia: 1500–1785." In *The Cambridge History of Inner Asia: The Chinggisid Age*, edited by Nicola

di Cosmo, Allen J. Frank, and Peter B. Golden, 277–302. Cambridge: Cambridge University Press, 2009.
McChesney, Robert D. "The Conquest of Herat 995-6/1587-8: Sources for the Study of Ṣafavid/Qizilbāsh- Shībanid/Ūzbak Relations." In Études Safavides, edited by Jean Calmard, 69–107. Paris: Institut Français de Recherche en Iran, 1993.
McChesney, Robert D. "Zamzam Water on a White Felt Carpet: Adapting Mongol Ways in Muslim Central Asia." In *Religion, Customary Law, and Nomadic Technology*, edited by Michael Gervers and Wayne Schlepp, 63–83. Toronto: Joint Centre for Asia Pacific Studies, 2000.
McDow, Thomas F. *Buying Time: Debt and Mobility in the Western Indian Ocean*. Athens: Ohio University Press, 2018.
Millward, James A. *Beyond the Pass: Economy, Ethnicity, and Empire in Qing Central Asia, 1759–1864*. Stanford: Stanford University Press, 1998.
Millward, James A. *Eurasian Crossroads: A History of Xinjiang*. New York: Columbia University Press, 2007.
Millward, James A. "Qing Silk-Horse Trade with the Qazaqs in Yili and Tarbaghatai, 1758–1853." *Central and Inner Asian Studies* 7 (1992): 1–42.
Millward, James A. *The Silk Road: A Very Short Introduction*. Oxford: Oxford University Press, 2013.
Mikhaleva, G. A. *Torgovie i posol'skie sviazi Rossii so Sredneaziatskimi Khanstvami cherez Orenburg (vtoraia polovina XVIII–pervaia polovina XIX v.)*. Tashkent: Fan, 1982.
Monahan, Erika. "Locating Rhubarb: Early Modernity's Relevant Obscurity." In *Early Modern Things: Objects and Their Histories, 1500–1800*, edited by Paula Findlen, 227–51. London: Routledge, 2012.
Monahan, Erika. *The Merchants of Siberia: Trade in Early Modern Eurasia*. Ithaca: Cornell University Press, 2016.
Morgan, David. *The Mongols*. 2nd ed. Oxford: Blackwell, 2007.
Morrison, Alexander. "'Applied Orientalism' in British India and Tsarist Turkestan." *Comparative Studies in History and Society* 51, no. 3 (2009): 619–47.
Newby, Laura J. *The Empire and the Khanate: A Political History of Qing Relations with Khoqand c. 1760–1860*. Leiden: E. J. Brill, 2005.
Noda, Jin. *The Kazakh Khanates between the Russian and Qing Empires*. Leiden: E. J. Brill, 2016.
Oberhänsli, Hedi, Nikolaus Boroffka, Philippe Sorrel, and Sergey Krivonogov. "Climate Variability during the Past 2,000 Years and Past Economic and Irrigation Activities in the Aral Sea Basin." *Irrigation and Drainage Systems* 21 (2007): 167–83.
Ostrowski, Donald. "The Replacement of the Composite Reflex Bow by Firearms in the Muscovite Cavalry." *Kritika: Explorations in Russian and Eurasian History* 11, no. 3 (2010): 513–34.
Papas, Alexandre. *Soufisme et politique entre Chine, Tibet et Turkestan: Étude sur les Khwajas Naqshbandis du Turkestan orientale*. Paris: Jean Maisonneuve, 2005.
Papas, Alexandre, Thomas Welsford, and Thierry Zarcone, eds. *Central Asian Pilgrims: Hajj Routes and Pious Visits between Central Asia and the Hijaz*. Berlin: Klaus Schwarz Verlag, 2012.

Parker, Charles H., and Jerry H. Bentley, eds. *Between the Middle Ages and Modernity: Individual and Community in the Early Modern World*. Lanham, MD: Rowman and Littlefield, 2007.

Parker, Geoffrey. *Global Crisis: War, Climate Change and Catastrophe in the Seventeenth Century*. New Haven: Yale University Press, 2013.

Parker, Geoffrey. *The Military Revolution: Military Innovation and the Rise of the West, 1500–1800*. 2nd ed. Cambridge: Cambridge University Press, 1996.

Parker, Geoffrey, and Lesley M. Smith, eds. *The General Crisis of the Seventeenth Century*, 2nd ed. London: Routledge, 1997.

Parker, Geoffrey, and Sanjay Subrahmanyam. "Arms and the Asian: Revisiting European Firearms and Their Place in Early Modern Asia." *Revista de Cultura* (Macau) 26 (2008): 12–42.

Paul, Jürgen. "Nomads and Bukhara: A Study in Nomad Migrations, Pasture, and Climate Change (11th Century CE)." *Der Islam* 93, no. 2 (2016): 495–531.

Pei, Qing, David D. Zhang, Guodong Li, Philippe Forêt, and Harry F. Lee. "Temperature and Precipitation Effects on Agrarian Economy in Late Imperial China." *Environmental Research Letters* 11, no. 6 (2016): 1–9.

Perdue, Peter. "Boundaries and Trade in the Early Modern World: Negotiations at Nerchinsk and Beijing." *Eighteenth-Century Studies* 43, no. 3 (2010): 341–56.

Perdue, Peter. *China Marches West: The Qing Conquest of Central Eurasia*. Cambridge, MA: Harvard University Press, 2005.

Peterson, Maya. *Pipe Dreams: Water, Technology, and the Remaking of Central Asia in the Russian Empire and Soviet Union, 1848–1948*. Cambridge: Cambridge University Press, 2019.

Pianciola, Niccolò, and Paolo Sartori, eds. *Islam, Society and States across the Qazaq Steppe (18th–Early 20th Centuries)*. Wien: Österreichischen Akademie der Wissenschaften, 2016.

Pickett, James Robert. "The Persianate Sphere during the Age of Empires: Islamic Scholars and Networks of Exchange in Central Asia, 1747–1917." PhD diss., Princeton University, 2015.

Pickett, James Robert. *Polymaths of Islam: Power and Networks of Knowledge in Central Asia*. Ithaca: Cornell University Press, forthcoming.

Pickett, James Robert. "Written into Submission: Reassessing Sovereignty through a Forgotten Eurasian Dynasty." *American Historical Review* 123, no. 3 (2018): 817–45.

Pierce, Richard A. *Russian Central Asia, 1867–1817*. Berkeley: University of California Press, 1960.

Pollock, Sheldon. "Future Philology? The Fate of a Soft Science in a Hard World." *Critical Inquiry* 35 (2009): 931–61.

Prakash, Om. *Bullion for Goods: European and Indian Merchants in the Indian Ocean Trade, 1500–1800*. New Delhi: Manohar, 2004.

Prakash, Om. *The Dutch East India Company and the Economy of Bengal, 1630–1720*. Princeton: Princeton University Press, 1985.

Preiser-Kapeller, Johannes. *Jenseits von Rom und Karl dem Grossen: Aspekte der globalen Verflechtung in der langen Spätantike, 300–800 n. Chr*. Vienna: Mandelbaum Verlag, 2018.

Puzanov, V. D. *Voennye factory russkoi kolonizatsii zapadnoi Sibiri, konets XVI–XVII vv.* St. Petersburg: Aleteia, 2010.

Quataert, Donald. "Ottoman History Writing and the Notion of 'Decline.'" *History Compass* 1 (2003): 1–9.

Rezakhani, Khodadad. "The Road That Never Was: The Silk Road and Trans-Eurasian Exchange." *Comparative Studies of South Asia, Africa and the Middle East* 30, no. 3 (2010): 420–33.

Richards, John F. "Early Modern India and World History." *Journal of World History* 3, no. 2 (1997): 197–209.

Richards, John F. *The Mughal Empire.* Cambridge: Cambridge University Press, 1993.

Richards, John F. *Unending Frontier: An Environmental History of the Early Modern World.* Berkeley: University of California Press, 2003.

Richthofen, Ferdinand von. *China: Ergebnisse eigener reisen und darauf gegründeter studien.* Vol. 1. Berlin: D. Reimer, 1877.

Rohling, E. J., P. A. Mayewski, R. H. Abu-Zied, J. S. L. Casford, and A. Hayes. "Holocene Atmosphere-Ocean Interactions: Records from Greenland and the Aegean Sea." *Climate Dynamics* 18 (2002): 587–93.

Romaniello, Matthew P. "Transregional Trade in Early Modern Eurasia." *Oxford Research Encyclopedia of Asian History*, October 2017, http://oxfordre.com/asianhistory/view/10.1093/acrefore/9780190277727.001.0001/acrefore-9780190277727-e-296.

Romaniello, Matthew P. "True Rhubarb? Trading Eurasian Botanical and Medical Knowledge in the Eighteenth Century." *Journal of Global History* 11, no. 1 (2016): 3–23.

Rossabi, Morris. "The 'Decline' of the Central Asian Caravan Trade." In *The Rise of Merchant Empires*, edited by J. Tracy, 351–70. Cambridge: Cambridge University Press, 1990.

Roy, Tirthankar. *The East India Company: The World's Most Powerful Corporation.* New Delhi: Penguin, 2012.

Russell, Ralph, and Khurshidul Islam. *Ghalib, Life and Letters.* London: George Allen and Unwin, 2010 (1969).

Saguchi, Tôru. "The Eastern Trade of the Khoqand Khanate." *Memoirs of the Research Department of the Toyo Bunko (The Oriental Library)* 24 (1965): 47–114.

Sartori, Paolo. "Introduction: On Khvārazmian Connectivity: Two or Three Things That I Know about It." *Journal of Persianate Studies* 9 (2016): 133–57.

Sartori, Paolo. "¡Viva La Filología! Or, the Freedom of Critical Thinking." *Ab Imperio* 3 (2018): 427–35.

Savory, Roger. *Iran under the Safavids.* Cambridge: Cambridge University Press, 1980.

Schafer, Edward H. *The Golden Peaches of Samarkand: A Study of T'ang Exotics.* Berkeley: University of California Press, 1963.

Schimmelpenninck van der Oye, David. *Russian Orientalism: Asia in the Russian Mind from Peter the Great to the Emigration.* New Haven: Yale University Press, 2010.

Schwarz, Florian. "Bukhara and Its Hinterland: The Oasis of Bukhara in the Sixteenth Century in Light of the Juybari Codex." In *Bukhara: The Myth and the Architecture*, edited by Attilio Petruccioli, 79–92. Cambridge, MA: Aga Khan Program for Islamic Architecture, 1999.

Sela, Ron. *The Legendary Biographies of Tamerlane: Islam and Heroic Apocrypha in Central Asia*. Cambridge: Cambridge University Press, 2011.

Shkunov, V. N. "Russko-indiiskaia torgovlia na Sredneaziatskikh rinkakh v kontse XVIII–nachale XIX v. (po materialam Rossiyskikh arkhivov)." *Vostok, Afro-aziatskie obshchestva: Istoriya I sovremennost'* 3 (1997): 94–101.

Sinha, Ashish, Lowell Stott, Max Berkelhammer, Hai Cheng, R. Lawrence Edwards, Brendan Buckley, Mark Aldenderfer, and Manfred Mudelsee. "A Global Context for Megadroughts in Monsoon Asia during the Past Millennium." *Quaternary Science Reviews* 30 (2011): 47–62.

Skaff, Jonathan. "The Sogdian Trade Diaspora in East Turkestan during the Seventh and Eighth Centuries." *Journal of the Economic and Social History of the Orient* 46, no. 4 (2003): 475–524.

Skaff, Jonathan. *Sui-Tang China and Its Turko-Mongol Neighbors: Culture, Power and Connections, 580–800*. Oxford: Oxford University Press, 2012.

Slavin, Philip. "Death by the Lake: Mortality Crisis in Early Fourteenth-Century Central Asia." *Journal of Interdisciplinary History* 50 (2019): 59–90.

Sneath, David. *The Headless State: Aristocratic Orders, Kinship Society, and Misrepresentations of Nomadic Inner Asia*. New York: Columbia University Press, 2007.

Sood, Gagan D. S. *India and the Islamic Heartlands: An Eighteenth-Century World of Circulation and Exchange*. Cambridge: Cambridge University Press, 2016.

Sorrel, Philippe. "The Aral Sea: A Paleoclimate Archive." PhD diss., Universität Potsdam, 2006.

Sorrel, Philippe, Hedi Oberhänsli, Nikolaus Boroffka, Danis Nourgaliev, Peter Dulski, and Ursula Röhl. "Control of Wind Strength in the Aral Sea Basin during the Holocene." *Quaternary Research* 67 (2007): 371–82.

Sorrel, Philippe, Speranta-Maria Popescu, Stefan Klotz, Jean-Pierre Suc, and Hedi Oberhänsli. "Climate Variability in the Aral Sea Basin (Central Asia) during the Late Holocene Based on Vegetation Changes." *Quaternary Research* 67 (2007): 357–70.

Spuler, Bertold. "Central Asia from the Sixteenth Century to the Russian Conquests." In *The Cambridge History of Islam*, vol. 1, *The Central Islamic Lands*, edited by P. M. Holt, Ann K. S. Lambton, and Bernard Lewis, 468–94. Cambridge: Cambridge University Press, 1970.

Starr, S. Frederick. *Lost Enlightenment: Central Asia's Golden Age from the Arab Conquest to Tamerlane*. Princeton: Princeton University Press, 2013.

Steensgaard, Niels. *The Asian Trade Revolution of the Seventeenth Century: The East India Companies and the Decline of the Caravan Trade*. Chicago: University of Chicago Press, 1974.

Subrahmanyam, Sanjay. "Connected Histories: Notes Towards a Reconfiguration of Early Modern Eurasia." *Modern Asian Studies* 31, no. 3 (1997): 735–62.

Subrahmanyam, Sanjay. *Mughals and Franks: Explorations in Connected History*. Delhi: Oxford University Press, 2012.

Subrahmanyam, Sanjay. *From the Tagus to the Ganges: Explorations in Connected History*. Delhi: Oxford University Press, 2012.

Sultonova, Gulchekhra. "Torgoviie otnosheniia mezhdu Bukharskim i Yarkendskim khanstvami v XVI–nachale XVII veka." *Bulletin of IICAS* 11 (2010): 40–48.

Sultonova, Gulchekhra, and Scott C. Levi. "Indo-Bukharan Diplomatic Relations, 1572–1598: The Role of the Actors." In *Insights and Commentaries: South and Central Asia*, edited by Anita Sengupta and Mirzohid Rakhimov, 95–107. Kolkata: Maulana Abul Kalam Azad Institute of Asian Studies; Tashkent: Institute of History, Academy of Sciences, 2015.

Takahiro, Onuma. "The Development of the Junghars and the Role of Bukharan Merchants." *Journal of Central Eurasian Studies* 2 (2011): 83–100.

Takahiro, Onuma. "Political Power and Caravan Merchants at the Oasis Towns in Central Asia: The Case of Altishahr in the 17th and 18th Centuries." In *Xinjiang in the Context of Central Eurasian Transformations*, edited by Onuma Takahiro, David Brophy, and Shinmen Yasushi, 33–58. Tokyo: The Toyo Bunko, 2018.

TePaske, John J. *A New World of Gold and Silver*. Edited by Kendall W. Brown. Leiden: E. J. Brill, 2010.

Thum, Rian. *The Sacred Routes of Uyghur History*. Cambridge, MA: Harvard University Press, 2014.

Togan, Isenbike. "Inner Asian Muslim Merchants at the Closure of the Silk Routes in the Seventeenth Century." In *The Silk Roads: Highways of Culture and Commerce*, edited by Vadime Elisseeff, 247–63. New York: Bergahn Books, 2000.

Tolz, Vera. *Russia's Own Orient: The Politics of Identity and Oriental Studies in the Late Imperial and Early Soviet Periods*. Oxford: Oxford University Press, 2011.

Trivellato, Francesca. "Is There a Future for Italian Microhistory in the Age of Global History?" *California Italian Studies* 2, no. 1 (2011), https://escholarship.org/uc/item/0z94n9hq.

Tucker, Ernest. "Explaining Nadir Shah: Kingship and Royal Legitimacy in Muhammad Kazim Marvi's *Tārīkh-i ʿālam-ārā-yi Nādirī*." *Iranian Studies* 26, nos. 1–2 (1993): 95–117.

Tulibayeva, Zhuldyz. "The Qazaqs and the Central Asian Principalities in the 18th and the First Half of the 19th Centuries." *Oriente Moderno* 96, no. 1 (2016): 25–45.

Volkov, Denis V. *Russia's Turn to Persia: Orientalism in Diplomacy and Intelligence*. Cambridge: Cambridge University Press, 2018.

Von Glahn, Richard. *The Economic History of China: From Antiquity to the Nineteenth Century*. Cambridge: Cambridge University Press, 2016.

Von Glahn, Richard. *Fountain of Fortune: Money and Monetary Policy in China, 1000–1700*. Berkeley: University of California Press, 1996.

Von Glahn, Richard. "Money Use in China and Changing Patterns of Global Trade in Monetary Metals, 1500–1800." In *Global Connections and Monetary History, 1470–1800*, edited by Dennis O. Flynn, Arturo Giráldez, and Richard von Glahn. Aldershot: Ashgate, 2003.

Wang, Luman. "Money and Trade, Hinterland and Coast, Empire and Nation-State: An Unusual History of Shanxi Piaohao, 1820–1930." PhD diss. University of Southern California, 2014.

Warde, Paul. "Global Crisis or Global Coincidence." Review of *Global Crisis: War, Climate Change and Catastrophe in the Seventeenth Century*, by Geoffrey Parker. *Past and Present* 228 (2015): 287–301.

Waugh, Daniel. "Richthofen's 'Silk Roads': Toward the Archeology of a Concept." *Silk Road* 5, no. 1 (2007): 1–10.

Weinerman, Eli. "The Polemics between Moscow and Central Asians on the Decline of Central Asia and Tsarist Russia's Role in the History of the Region." *Slavonic and East European Review* 71, no. 3 (July 1993): 428–81.

Welsford, Thomas. *Four Types of Loyalty in Early Modern Central Asia: The Tūqāy-Tīmūrid Takeover of Greater Mā warā al-Nahr, 1598–1605*. Leiden: E. J. Brill, 2013.

Wheeler, Geoffrey. *The Modern History of Central Asia*. New York: Frederick A. Praeger, 1964.

White, Sam. *The Climate of Rebellion in the Early Modern Ottoman Empire*. Cambridge: Cambridge University Press, 2013.

Whitfield, Susan. *Life Along the Silk Road*. Berkeley: University of California Press, 2001.

Wilde, Andreas. "The Emirate of Bukhara." *Oxford Research Encyclopedia of Asian History*, October 2017, http://asianhistory.oxfordre.com/view/10.1093/acrefore/9780190277727.001.0001/acrefore-9780190277727-e-14.

Wilde, Andreas. *What is Beyond the River? Power, Authority and Social Order in Transoxania, 18th and 19th Centuries*. 3 vols. Wien: Österreichischen Akademie der Wissenshchaften, 2016.

Wink, André. *Akbar*. Oxford: Oneworld, 2009.

Wink, André. *Al-Hind: The Making of the Indo-Islamic World*. Vol. 2, *The Slave Kings and the Islamic Conquest, 11th–13th Centuries*. Leiden: E. J. Brill, 1997.

Wink, André. *Land and Sovereignty in India: Agrarian Society and Politics under the Eighteenth-Century Maratha Svarājya*. Cambridge: Cambridge University Press, 1986.

Wolff, Christian, Birgit Plessen, Alexey S. Dudashvili, Sebastian F. M. Breitenbach, Hai Cheng, Lawrence R. Edwards, and Manfred R. Strecker. "Precipitation Evolution of Central Asia during the Last 5000 Years." *Holocene* 27, no. 1 (2017): 142–154.

Wood, Frances. *The Silk Road: Two Thousand Years in the Heart of Asia*. Berkeley: University of California Press, 2004.

Wood, Gillen D'Arcy. *Tambora: The Eruption That Changed the World*. Princeton: Princeton University Press, 2014.

Woodworth, Cherie. "How Many Horses? 14th–16th c. Russia in the Economic System of the Steppe's 'Great Churn.'" Unpublished paper presented at the Davis Center for Russian and Eurasian Studies, Harvard University, February 11, 2011.

Yang, Bao, Jinsong Wang, Achim Bräuning, Zhibao Dong, and Jan Esper. "Late Holocene Climate and Environmental Changes in Arid Central Asia." *Quaternary International* 194 (2009): 68–78.

Yukht, A. I. *Torgovlia c vostochnimi stranami i vnutrenniy rinok Rossii (20–60-e godi XVIII veka)*. Moskva: Nauk, 1994.

Zhang, Ling. *The River, the Plain, the State: An Environmental Drama in Northern Song China, 1048–1128*. Cambridge: Cambridge University Press, 2016.

Zhao, Gang. *The Qing Opening to the Ocean: Chinese Maritime Policies, 1684–1757*. Honolulu: University of Hawai'i Press, 2013.

Ziyaev, Hamid. *Ekonomicheskie sviiazi Srednei Azii s Sibiriu v XVI–XIX vv*. Tashkent: Fan, 1983.

Ziyaeva, D. Kh. *U'zbekistonda harbii ish tarikhidan (Qadimgi davrdan hozirgacha)*. Tashkent: Sharq, 2012.

INDEX

Note: Page numbers in *italics* refer to figures.

Abbas, Shah I, 77n14, 80, 136
'Abbasid Caliphate, 56, 58–59
'Abd al-'Aziz Khan, 22, 35–36, 131, 147, 164
'Abd al-'Aziz Khan Madrasa, 22, 81
'Abd al-Karim, 123–25, 127
'Abdallah Khan, 19–20, 154
'Abdallah Khan II, 19, 78–81
'Abd al-Munim, 19–20, 162n127
Abu'l Fayz Khan, 24–26, 123, 132; efforts to maintain authority, 166, 170–72, 178; execution of, 27, 168, 178; rebellions against, 24–25
Abu'l Khayr Khan, 13
Adichie, Chimamanda, 173–74
Afghanistan, 14, 70, 72, 81, 93, 116, 133
Afghans, 26, 82, 135–36, 139, 168
Afsharid dynasty, 26
agriculture, 115; contribution to economy, 49, 165; decline in, 136–37, 140; effects of climate crisis on, 141–42, 149–52, 177; food crops *vs.* cash crops, 95, 118; increasing, 96–98; land used for, 7, 21, 88; loans by Indians for, 83, 97; plantation-style, 73–74
Akbar, Emperor, 78–81
Alam, Muzaffar, 31, 135
Altishahr, 37, 91, 91n59, 91n61, 93, 95–97, 119
Amanat, Abbas, x, 136, 146
Americas, silver from, 74–76, 118–19, 176

Andijanis, trade networks of, 92–95, *94*, 118–19, 176
An Lushan rebellion, 59
Anusha Muhammad Khan, 22
appanage system, 16, 18–19, 35, 122–23, 177
Astrakhan, 20, 103–4, 110–11, 111n118
Astrakhan Khanate, 19, 92, 98
Atwell, William, 144
Aurangzeb, 75, 81, 85, 134–35, 146–47

Babur, Zahir al-Din Muhammad, 12, 17, 72–73, 78, 85, 96n71
Balkh, 16, 20, 22–24, 35, 81, 147, 149, 164
Baraev, Marwari, 110
The Barefooted Flight, 25, 127, 129, 178
Bartold, Vasilii Vladimirovich, 49–53, 55, 68
Bayezid II, Sultan, 17
Beauplan, Guillaume de, 99
Beckert, Sven, 77
Beckwith, Christopher, 32–33, 54–57, 60–62
Beg, Nadir Quli, 26
Begs, and Qing, 97
Bengal, 114–18. *See also* India
Bentley, Jerry, 7–8
Bey, Muhammad Hakim, 26–27, 178
Bey, Muhammad Rahim, 26–27, 178
Blanchard, Ian, 100
Bregel, Yuri, 24, 28–29, 32–33, 50–52, 122

Britain, textile trade of, 114–15
Brook, Timothy, 143–44
Brooke, John, 142, 149–50
Buddhists. *See* Jungars
Bukhara, 25, 27; as dynastic capital, 16, 18, 20, 34–35
Bukharan Amirate, 9, 178
Bukharan Khanate, *15*, 16, 18, 34, 110; beginning of, 14–16; causes of decline of, 3–5, 32–33; causes of political crises in, 121, 134, 140–41, 153–70, 171; crises in, 19, 152; debasement of coins in, 22, 33, 131–32, *132*, 151, 171, 178; decentralization of, 21–23; defeats of, 20, 22, 166–67; end of, 19, 121, 151, 165, 168, 176, 178; evidence of decline of, 121, 123–24; fiscal crises in, 22, 24, 36, 125, 129, 133–34, 151, 161, 165, 173–74, 178; fiscal reforms under, 165–66; immigrants in, 82–84, 96, 126–27; invasions of, 110–11, 121, 124–25, 127; Jungars and, 25–26; Mughal relations with, 80–81; Muslims and, 59, 112; political crises in, 22–27, 112–13, 119, 120, 121, 173–74; political structure of, 35, 122–23; in production and circulation of knowledge, 170–71; rebellions in, 24–27, 169; relations with Safavids, 79–81; sources on decline, 33–34; territory of, 19, 23; Toqay-Timurids ruling, 16, 20–23; use of *khan* in, 27n31; Uzbek amirs and, 23–25, 162–65, 171; weakening of, 35–36, 123
Bukharans: as merchants, 104, 107–12, 178–79; settling in Russia, 107–9
Burton, Audrey, 23, 24n18, 31, 79, 103, 147n77

Cahun, David-Léon, 43
Cameron, Sarah, 102
caravan trade, 28, 39, 49, 57, 60. *See also* trade routes, overland
Castle, John, 156
Central Asia, 36, 57–59, 134; achievements of, 48, 58–60; agency of, 38, 175–76; commercial activities in, 57, 113; connectedness of, 9–10, 69, 71, 80, 88, 98, 118, 139, 170, 174; decentralization in, 139, 169; decline of, 27–28, 49, 53; early modern period in, 6–8; economy of, 31–32, 36, 125, 139; Eurasia and, 53–55, 54n41; Europe and, 9, 49–51; historiography, 31, 66; horse trade of, 84–88, 98–100, 116–18; India and, 84–87; Indians and, 82–84, 86; integration of, 126, 176; isolation of, 29, 32–33, 34, 49; limited understandings of, 173–74; markets in, 81–82, 98; Mughals and, 146–48; Nadir Shah's campaigns in, 110–11, *138*; overstatement of isolation, 129, 175; poverty of, 124–25; transitions in, 5; transnational linkages, 34–35; weapons of, *156, 158, 159*
Central Eurasia, 54n41, 55, 100–101
centralization, 164
centralization, state, 8. *See also* decentralization
Cerro Rico silver mine, 73, *74*
Chin, Tamara, 40, 42
China, 72, 126, 130; Bukharan trade with, 87–89, 103, 107–8; Central Asians mediating trade with, 37–38, 109; Central Asian trade with, 113, 115–16, 139; cotton industry in, 77–78; effects of climate change in, 143–44; expanding territory, 39, 69; horse trade and, 87–89, 99; relations with Central Asia, 10, 39, 134; silver and, 74–75, 118–19, 130–31, 139, 177–78; trade of, 31–32, 90–93, 103, 175; trade with Russia, 31, 91–92
Chinggisid dynasties, 12, 20–21, 122–23; ancestry of, 10, 162; declining authority of, 27, 164–65, 176; end of rule, 112–13, 121, 168; Kazakhs and, 13, 102; Manghits and, 26–27, 168n147, 178; political crisis of, 22–27; regaining power, 14–16, 25,

35; Uzbek amirs and, 21–22, 35–36, 162–63, 164, 178
Chinggis Khan, 13, 162
Christian, David, 45
Giocîltan, Virgil, 61
class, social, 28, 107
climate crisis, 9, 171, 177; recovery from, 151; seventeenth-century, 136, 141–51; sources on, 142, 146n73, 147–49, 147n77
Clive, Robert, 114
colonization, 53, 69, 72–74
Columbus, Christopher, 72
commerce, 25–26, 57, 64–65, 103–4, 112–13; effects of, 47–49; Eurasian, 45, 48; European, 28, 114; historiography on, 31–32, 48; Indians', 81–83. *See also* trade; trade networks
commercial economy, 4, 16, 19, 21, 28, 32, 36, 56, 57, 70, 72–73, 86, 104, 111, 118, 134
commercial history, 4–5, 32, 47–48, 61, 65, 68–69
cotton, 95. *See also* textiles
Cronon, William, 101–3
cultural exchanges, 37, 40, 47–49, 55–56
currency, debasement of Bukharan coins, 22, 33, 131, 171, 178

Dale, Stephen, 31–32
Davidovich, Elena, 131–34
Davies, Brian, 99, 160
Davis, Donald, 67
decentralization, 35, 137, 169, 177; decline *vs.*, 30, 171; effects of climate crisis on, 151–52; firearms' role, 163–64
Delhi, 12, 73, 124, 128, 133, 168
Dunning, Chester, 144–45
Durrani state, 31, 117, 133, 139
Dutch East India Company (V.O.C.), 76, 113–17

early modern period, 6–9, 27–28, 175
East-West dichotomy, 51–52
economy, 97, 109, 133–34, 138–39, 151–52, 168; of Central Asia, 37, 49, 55, 125, 152; effects of precious metals in, 73–74; effects of silver supplies in, 74–75, 88, 130–33; global, 88, 118; importance of horse exports in, 84–85; Indians' influence on, 49, 83, 96, 125
Eden, Jeff, 65
English East India Company, 113–17
Enlightenment, European, 59–60
environment, changes in, 7. *See also* climate crisis
Eurasia, 71, 153
Europe, 8, 113–14, 163; dominance of Indian Ocean trade, 49–50, 113; Race for Empire in, 52–53; role in Central Asia's decline, 28, 49–50; Russian livestock trade with, 100–102; trade with China, 39, 90; using American silver in trade, 76

famines, 9, 142–43, 151; effects of, 144–45, 146n75, 147
Fazl, Abu'l, 78–79
Ferghana Valley, 23, 90, 93–96, 179; immigrant communities in, 96–97, 126–27; Uzbek Ming in, 30–31, 127
firearms. *See* gunpowder weaponry
Fletcher, Joseph, 8–9, 65–67, 175
Floor, Willem, 79
Flynn, Dennis O., 130–31
Frye, Richard, 48, 60

Galdan Khan, 157
Ghalib, Mirza (Muhammad Asadullah Beg Khan), 128–29
Ghilzai Afghan invasion, 134, *138*
Ghilzai uprisings, 110, 134
Giráldez, Arturo, 130–31
Giray (Kiray or Qaray), 13
Golden, Peter, 152–53
Golden Horde, 13, 20, 85
Goldstone, Jack, 6–8
Gommans, Jos, 31, 85, 116–17
governance, 118, 121, 169; of nomads, 16, 35
Guha, Sumit, 138

INDEX

gunpowder weaponry, 152–60, *156*; advances in, 146, 153–70, 176–77; Bukharans', 155–57, 166; effects of, 163–64, 171–72; limitations of early models, 157–59, *158, 159*; manufacture of, 154, 156, 159

Han dynasty, 38–39, 42
Hansen, Valerie, 61–64
Hathaway, Jane, 29–30
Hedin, Sven, 37, 44, 62
Herrmann, Albert, 43–44
Hindus, 83–84, 135
Hindustan, 72, 124
historiography, 52; on Silk Road, 37, 40, 42, 44–46, 54
Holzwarth, Wolfgang, 26, 126, 160–61, 163–66, 168
horses: trade in, 84–88, 98–100, 116–18; in warfare, 157–59
Howard, Douglas, 29, 140

Ibn Battuta, 84, 86
Ibn Sina (Avicenna), 56
Imam Quli Khan, 131
India, 12–13, 125, 136, 146; Central Asia's horse trade with, 84–87, 116–18; Delhi Sultanate in, 73; European commercial interests in Bengal, 114–15; as largest producer of cotton goods, 77–78; relations with Central Asia and, 84–87; Samarqandis moving to, 127–29; in trade, 75–79, 115–16, 133; trade with Central Asia, 73, 82, 107–8, 175. *See also* Bengal; Mughal Empire
Indian communities: in Central Asia, 82, 86, 96–97, 111n118; as merchants, 96, 111
Indian Ocean, 113, 117–18; Central Asian trade around, 129, 134; European trade around, 49–50, 76, 113; Portuguese in, 60, 73
Indians, as merchants, *83*, 81–86
Inner Asia, 10, 126

investments, by Multani families, 82–83, 96
Iran, 8, 26, 29, 31, 80, 82, 110, 136–37, 139, 154; trade in, 73, 78, 145–46. *See also* Persia; Safavids
Iskander Khan, 19, 78
Islam, 13, 21, 50, 60, 109, 122, 127
Ismail, Shah, 16–17, 154

Jahan, Shah, 81, 137, 146–47
Japan, 87–88, 113–14
Jenkinson, Anthony, 153–54
Jochid dynasty, 13–16, 20
Jochi Khan, 13, 20
Jungars, 101–2, 126, 157; invasions by, 111, 123, 178; Kazakhs *vs.*, 24–26, 151
Juybari Sheikhs, 21

Kabul, Afghanistan, 12, 72–73, 78, 85
Kazakh Khanate, 100, 111–12, 165
Kazakhs, 13, 21, 26; displacement of, 25, 127; Jungars *vs.*, 24–25, 151, 153, 178; Russians *vs.*, 156–58; separate groups of, 101–2; trade and, 103, 126; warfare of, 157, 163–64
Kazakhstan, 13, 101, 105
Kazan Khanate, 88, 98–99
Keneges, Ibrahim, 25
Keneges, the, 31, 125, 169
Khivans, 21–22, 26
Khodarkovsky, Michael, 98
Khoqand Khanate, 31, 90–92, 96, 169, 179; trade and, 93, 95; of Uzbek Ming, 30–31, 127
Khurasan, 16–17, 19, 72
Kiakhta, 88, 90, *91, 92*, 93, 105
Kim (Kipling), 117
knowledge, production and circulation of, 59–61, 170–71
Kočnev, Boris, 132
Kukeldash Madrasa, 19

languages, consolidation of vernacular, 8
Lieberman, Victor, 7–8

"Little Ice Age," 140–51
livestock, 99–103, 118, 149. *See also* horses
Lodi Afghan sultans, 12, 73

Manghit tribal dynasty, 26–27, 36, 122, 134, 168–69, 168n417, 178
Manucci, Niccolao, 75–76, 85
markets, in growth of cities, 103
Marvi, Muhammad Kazim, 167–68
Massudov, Irnazar, 111
Matthee, Rudi, 136–37, 139
McChesney, Robert, 23, 31, 122–23, 161–62
Merv, Battle of, 17–18, 154
Mikhail, Tsar, 160
military, 159, 168; Bukharan, 123, 161–62, 166, 169, 177–78; effects of famines on, 146n75, 147; horses for, 84–89; manpower for, 121, 161; weaponry, 121, 166. *See also* gunpowder weaponry; warfare
Millward, James, 71n1, 97
Ming dynasty, 86–87, 122, 143–44
Ming. *See* Uzbek Ming
Mir-i Arab Madrasa, *17*, 18
Mirza Qoqan Beg Khan, 128–29
Monahan, Erika, 98, 104–10, 126
Mongol Qalmaqs (Oirats), 13, 100
Mongols, 13, 59–61, 139
Mughal Empire, 12, 21; Central Asia and, 81–82, 85, 139; collapse of, 135–36, 135n38, 139–40, 166; promoting and protecting trade, 77, 80, 86–87, 134, 139; territories of, 81, 146–47; wealth of, 135, 137–38, 168
Muhammad, Jani, 20
Muhammad, Wali, 131
Muhammad, Yar, 19–20
Muhammad Muqim Khan, 23–24
Multan, 82–83, 135–36, 138–39
Multanis, 82–83, 96, 139
Munshi, Muhammad Yusuf, 147
Murad, Shah, 27
Muscovite military, 158–60, 164
Muscovy Company, 153–54

Muslims, 25–26, 51, 53, 90, 97–98, 108–9, 112

Nadir Muhammad Khan, 131, 147
Nadir Shah, 26–27, 111n118, 136–39, 172, 178; invasions by, 110–11, 124, 127, *135*; sack of Delhi by, 133, 168
Newby, Laura, 90
Nogai Horde, 98–100
nomadic empires, 10, 54, 101
nomads, 54–55, 54n41, 56, 65, 95, 139, 152; decline, 8–9, 13–14; governance of, 16, 35, 122; incursions by, 13–14; Safavids and, 136–37; trade and, 95, 103; warfare of, 121, 152–54, 157, 161

Orenburg, 110–11, 126, 133
Orientalism, 51–53, 68, 175
Ostrowski, Donald, 158–60
Ottoman Empire, 26, 29–30, 122, 127, 145, 155, 160

Panipat, Battle of, 12, 73
Parker, Geoffrey, 142, 145
Pazukhin, Boris, 164
peasants, rebellions of as an attribute of early modernity, 8–9
Pelliot, Paul, 37
Perdue, Peter, 86, 87–88, 90, 130–31
Persia, 36, 168; Afsharid, 166–67; India's trade with, 115–16, 133. *See also* Iran
Pickett, James, 125–26
plague, 139, 144, 148n83
Poi Kalan Masjid, 18, *18*
Polo, Marco, 39, 72
population: decline, 145; growth, 8–9, 73, 130, 175
Portuguese, 55, 60, 73, 76, 114
positivism, German, 50
Prakash, Om, 114–15
precious metals, 115, 130–33, 135; quantities put into economy, 74–75; shipped to Asia, 74–76; silver *vs.* gold, 74, 75n6; trade in, 73, 133

INDEX 205

Qalmaqs. *See* Mongol Qalmaqs (also Oirats)
Qianlong Emperor, 134
Qing, 118, 130, 143; demand for silver, 177–78; Jungars and, 101, 157–58; military horses for, 86–88; promoting agriculture, 96–98; subjects of, 91–92, 96–98, 134, 158–59; trade and, 92, 95, 130–31

Rahim, Muhammad, 168
Registan public square, 21
religions, 8, 21, 51, 59; difference of not allowed to interfere with trade, 79–81; in struggle for control over Khurasan, 16–17
rhubarb, as trade item, 89–90, 93
Richards, John, 7
Richthofen, Ferdinand von, 39–42, 44, 68
Rosen, Victor, 50–53
Rossabi, Morris, 31, 88–89
ruling families, under appanage system, 16, 18–19, 35, 122–23
Russia, 10, 26, 89, 90, 160; Central Eurasia's relations with, 100, 139; commerce and, 103–5, 107, 109, 115; effects of climate change in, 144–45; expanding empire of, 69, 98–100; immigrant communities in, 82–83, 108–9, 112; livestock trade by, 98–102, 118–19; Siberian fortresses of, *106*, 110, 112–13; trade and, 95, 109, 133; trade with Bukhara, 104, 105–7, 110–12; trade with Central Asia, 28–29, 110–11, 117–18, 139, 175; trade with China, 31, 92, 109, 126
Russians, 156–60

Safavids, 77n14, 110, 136, 146; Bukharans and, 79–81, 104; collapse of, 135–36, 139–40, 166; gunpowder weaponry of, 121, 155–56; as Shi'a, 16–17, 79; trade and, 77–81, 86–87, 134; warfare by, 21, 26, 161, 176. *See also* Iran

Samarqandis, 12, 14, 16, 18–19, 21, 25, 35, 126–29
Sartori, Paolo, 33–34
Seidenstrassen, 39, 40, *41*, *45*. *See also* Silk Road
Seitov, Shaba, 108
Sela, Ron, 33, 169
Shah 'Abbas I, 80–81, 136
Shah, Bahadur, 135
Shah, Ismail, 16–17, 154
Sherdar Madrasa, 21
Shi'a Muslims, 16, 79
Shibanids, 14–16, 78–79, 122, 177; descendants of, 18, 100; Toqay-Timurids replacing, 23, 163, 178; wars and internal conflicts under, 17–19, 21
Shibanid Uzbeks, 13–14, *14*. *See also* Uzbeks
Shibani Khan, Muhammad, 12–14, 16–18, 35, 72, 100, 154
Shiban Khan, 12–13
silk, trade in, 42, 63
Silk Road, 57; cities on, 62, 70; cultural exchanges along, 10, 37, 40, 48, 63–65, 68; definitions of, 54–55, 68–69; historiography of, 36, 54; history of, 38–40, 43–44, 70; importance of, 63–65; misconceptions about, 119, 175; as network of local roads, 62–63; prosperity from, 57, 70; romanticization of, 39–40, 44, 62, 68–69; routes of, 40, *41*, 44–45, *45*, *46*; scholarship as ethnocentric, 37–38, 64; usefulness of concept, 28, 46–47, 68
silver: Chinese demand for, 74–75, 130–31, 139, 177–78; in debasement of Bukharan coins, 131–32, *132*, 171; increasing circulation of, 86, 178; injected into economies, 118–19, 134; shortages of, 88–89, 132–33, 171
slave trade, 65
Sogdian Central Asia, 48, 59
Sogdian letters, 63
Sogdian traders, 42, 57, 71, 176

Sood, Gagan, 170
Soviet Union, 27–28, 31, 66
Spain, 72–74
Spuler, Bertold, 28
Starr, S. Frederick, 54, 56–63
Steensgaard, Niels, 76
Stein, Aurel, 37, 44, 62–63
steppes, 36, 39, 45, 87, 110; firearms on, 156, 158; livestock from, 100, 102–3; nomadic migrations from, 13–14
Subhan Quli Khan, 22–23, 24n18, 131–32, 164, 166
Subrahmanyam, Sanjay, 7, 67, 170
Sultan, Mahmud, 18
Sultan, Rajab, 25
Sunni Muslims, 79

Talas, Battle of, 59
Tarim Basin, 44, 62, *64*
Tashkent, 16, 19, 24–25, 35, 147
Tavernier, Jean Baptiste, 85
taxes, 161, 165, 169, 171–72, 176
tea, as trade item, 89, 93, 95
technology, 10, 55, 73, 76, 168, 176–77.
  See also gunpowder weaponry
textiles: China's cotton industry, 77–78; trade in, 71, 75–77, 82, 84, 103, 114–18
Thévenot, Jean de, 85
Tilakari Madrasa and Masjid, 21
Timur, legends of, 169–70
Timurids, 121, 122–23; Chinggisids replacing, 12, 35; Shah Jahan's campaign against, 146–47; Shibanids' defeat of, 35, 122; Uzbek amirs and, 169–70. *See also* Mughal Empire; Toqay-Timurid dynasty
Tīmūr-nama genre, 33, 169–70
"Tobacco, Chinese," 108
Tolz, Vera, 51–53
Toqay-Timurids, 150–51, 177; dynasty of, 18, 20–21; end of, 27, 121; Jochid dynasty and, 14–16; military authority in, 160–61; ruling Bukharan Khanate, 16, 20; Shibanids *vs.*, 23, 162; Uzbek amirs and, 123, 171, 178

trade, 47; as basis of prosperity, 37, 49, 57–59; Bukharan, 104, 109–12, 115, 126, 133, 134; Central Asians as intermediaries in, 37–38, 109–10; Central Asia's, 84, 115–16; Central Asia's role in, 4, 28, 48, 54, 60, 109–10; Central Asia's with China, 86–89, 113, 115; Central Asia's with India, 73, 78–79, 82, 84–87; Central Asia's with Iran, 73, 137; Central Asia's with Russia, 28–29, 95, 109–12, 126; continuity of, 76, 79–81, 175, 178–79; decline in, 36, 146; increases in, 73–74; India's, 75–79; intra-Asia, 114; legal *vs.* contraband, 95; misconceptions about Central Asia's, 68, 70; Mughals and, 81; participants in, 39, 48–49, 69, 95, 120; in precious metals, 73, 133; Russia and China, 90–92, 126; scholarship on, 27–28, 37–38, 53, 64–65; slave, 65; Sogdian letters on, 63–64; states promoting and protecting, 61–62, 78–79, 81, 86, 95; in textiles, 42, 63, 82–83; types of merchandise in, 42, 57, 62–63, 68, 71, 93, 103, 105–7, 115, 118–19, 175. *See also* commerce
trade networks, 45, 72–75, 96, 120; Bukharan, 104–5, 109, 126, 139, 170, 176, 178–79; of Central Asia, 45–46, 140
trade routes, 31, 37, *43*, 44, 70, 72, 78, *79*, 92, 105, 121; Andijani and Bukharan, *94*, 93–94; Central Asia, *41*; dislocations of, 80, 110, 129, 134; maritime, 49, 71, 130–31; northern, *91*; overland, 39, 49, 61, 68, 72–73, *77*; overland and maritime, 32, *47*, *58*, 76, 113, 175; overland *vs.* maritime, 36, 93, 95, 121; on Silk Road, 46. *See also* Silk Road
Transoxania, 13–14, *14*, 16, 26, 35
transregional interactions, 8–9, 19, 28
Treaty of Kiakhta, 90–92, 126
Treaty of Nerchinsk, 90–92, 126
tribal dynasties, 9–10, 122
Turco-Afghan Delhi Sultanate, 84–85

INDEX 207

Turkestan, 24–25, 48, 53
Turkic dynasties, 59

'Ubaydullah Khan, 16, 18, 23–24, 24n18, 122–23, 131–32, 166, 178
Ulugh Beg Madrasa, 21
urbanization, 9, 73–74
Uzbek amirs, 21, 168; authority of, 122, 161–63; Bukharan khans and, 165, 178; Chinggisids and, 35–36, 122, 164, 178; efforts to control, 123, 163, 171; letting go of traditions, 163–64, 170n153; rebellions by, 23, 25, 122–23; Timurids and, 170; Toqay-Timurids and, 23, 123, 151, 170
Uzbek Manghit, 26, 168
Uzbek Ming, 30–31, 127, 169, 179
Uzbeks, 17, 19, 29, 35, 79, 169; firearms and, 154–56, 163, 176; Mughals trying to recover Central Asia from, 146–47; power of, 14, 164; Qongrat, 169; under Shibani Khan, 12–13; trade and, 77, 86; tribal dynasties of, 9, 122, 169; Turkic-Muslim, 13

Vaissière, Étienne de la, 40, 42
von Glahn, Richard, 130, 144

wars, 146, 150, 151; cavalry *vs.* infantry, 176–77; changes in, 158–59, 163; effects of advances in gunpowder weaponry, 153–70. *See also* gunpowder weaponry
Waugh, Daniel, 40–42
weapons, 163–64, 166–68. *See also* gunpowder weaponry
Welsford, Thomas, 19, 150, 162
Witsen, Nicolaes, 107–8
Woodworth, Cherie, 99

Xinjiang (Altishahr), 37, 39, 62, *64*, 91–93, 95–98, 134

Yamysh, 105–7, 109–10
Yongle, Emperor, 86
Yuan court, 39, 72

Ziyaev, Hamid, 109